BLOOD HARVEST

My Hunt For Jack The Ripper

by

David Andersen

Copyright 2020

INTRODUCTION

Few people will not have heard the name Jack the Ripper. This is not surprising in view of the vast number of books plays and films that have been written around his image. He has been a lodger, a lunatic, a surgeon, a devil worshipper, a barrister, a sailor, a royal prince and, according to Bob Dylan's song 'Tombstone Blues', Jack the Ripper sits 'at the head of the chamber of commerce'.

As a child growing up in London, I had heard of Jack the Ripper. An elderly next door neighbour Old Charlie, who practically lived at his front gate, always claimed that he knew who Jack the Ripper was and, that as a young man, he had even met him. I knew hardly anything about what it was that Jack the Ripper was supposed to have done. It was not until the mid-60s that I read my first full-length account of his exploits. My interest was aroused. I wanted to know more. Before too long I had read everything on the subject that I could lay my hands on. I was struck by the many diverse opinions regarding almost every aspect of the Jack the Ripper mystery. He was this person. He was that person. It was more than one person. It was a woman. It was a man. It was both. He killed fifteen women, he killed seven women, he killed five. Faced with these contradictions I thus resolved to undertake my own investigation to try to settle the matter, at least to my own satisfaction.

No work of this kind can ever be, or is, the work of one person entirely. Over the years, as each 'new' theory has been hailed as a final solution, or, a definitive piece of new evidence, real or otherwise has surfaced, it has provided us with another ingredient to add to the mystery. Yet while some dissertations set out to be as accurate, and as honest as is possible, it is clear that others have sought to quite blatantly deceive. Unfortunatly it is so often the case that it is the most outrageous theories which stick in the collective public perceptions of Jack the Ripper. I have, therefore attempted, where possible, to correct at least some of these misperceptions. I have here examined all of the major theories and, I hope that, in doing so, I have been justly critical where necessary.

I concede, from the start that we may never know for sure who Jack the Ripper really was. There is, however, indisputable evidence that all of the actual evidence against one major contemporary suspect was subsequently and systematically destroyed. As far as we are aware this suspect is the only one against whom the evidence was so carefully destroyed. In dealing with this suspect I have attempted to reconstruct what this evidence may have been. I have, reasonably speculated upon its nature and its source. I have also included new, and previously unpublished, evidence against this suspect, which throws new light upon his state of mind, and his motivation for committing these murders. I have also examined the circumstances, which led to the destruction of the evidence against him. The whole, however, shall always be greater than the sum of its parts. I do not seek to claim the final word - but only to add, perhaps just a little, to those parts.

As I commenced to write these words some years ago I learned of the death of Tom Cullen. It was his book Autumn of Terror, which not only inspired my early interests but led me towards my own investigation. I knew Tom well. I met him many times. In 1971 when he saw my early discoveries he was gracious enough to take down, from his bookshelf, one of his own copies of Autumn of Terror which he inscribed to me as – 'following on with ripper research where I left off '- It is my earnest hope that I have done so.

I dedicate these findings to the memory of Tom Cullen and to the Victims of Jack The Ripper.

Mary Ann Nichols
Annie Chapman
Elizabeth Stride
Catherine Eddowes
Mary Kelly

Acknowledgements

I owe a great debt of gratitude to so many people who have assisted me, in some way or another, in producing this work. In the forty, or so, years since I developed my interest in Jack the Ripper. I have sounded my ideas, and theories, ad nauseum to almost anyone who cared to listen - I am grateful to them all, some for just listening, some for helpful feedback.

In particular though I would like to single out a few of those who, during those years of research have been of particular help. In no particular order they are -

Don Rumbelow, Keith Skinner, Martin Fido, Dan Farson, Francis Camps, Malcolm Cameron, Sam Hardy, Sir David Tuke, Tom Cullen, Donald McCormick, Simon Wood, Richard Whittington-Egan, Paul Begg, Robin O'Dell, Andy Spalleck, Colin Evans, Greg Manning, Tony and Sue Manning, both of my ex-wives, most of my ex-girlfriends, the residents of Whitechapel. Vivian Cox, Alan Smith and The Purvis Society (Cranleigh School), Peter Marsh, Robin Maugham, Gerald Hamilton, Brian Desmond-Hurst, Chris and Veronica Mills, Richard Plumley , Ruth Lawton, Inge Lehnert, Alan Arnold, Marion Carson, Librarians from all over London, The Chiswick History society, The Metropolitan Police, including the Thames Division,The City of London Police, The Town Council and the Residents of Wimborne, The Residents of 'Westfield House' Wimborne, The Wellcome Institute, Blooms Kosher Restaurant, The London Hospital Museum, The Ten Bells, The Golden Hart, The Blade Bone, and The Blind Beggar., my good friend Peggy Bentham, and to Michelle Jackson who assisted me in the preparation of my notes.

Authors Note

While I have made every effort to check primary sources. It has not always been possible. In such cases I have relied upon reliable and checkable secondary sources. However, I fully acknowledge that there may be mistakes of a factual nature. Any, and all, such mistakes are mine alone.

This document is not intended as a reference or source document. There are many worthy books which will fulfill the readers need for the minutest of detail. I have included a source list in the appendices.

David Andersen @Katmaniac
David_Andersen20@msn.com

CHAPTER ONE:

WHITECHAPEL

The Whitechapel area of London's East End is still, in many ways, much the same as it was when, in 1888, Jack the Ripper walked its streets. Although it is those very streets which have changed, it is the ethos itself which has the aura of indestructibility about it.

It is a chaotic hive of a place, abundant with warehouses, clutter, and fast-moving traffic. Amid the chaos, tucked away behind the Commercial Road, is a recently built housing development inhabited, in the main by the Bengali community who have settled here. They are following in the footsteps of the Hugenots and the Jews who settled in this area before them.

This part of London has always fostered a solid and cosmopolitan working-class community, nurtured by the many different industries that sprang up in the area during the 19th Century. The close proximity of the River Thames, and the direction of the prevailing-wind, determined the growth of London's industrial East End.

Both religion and politics grew up here. William Booth called the area 'Darkest England'. In 1867 he founded the Salvation Army here in Whitechapel. Socialist pioneers Tom Mann, Ben Tillet and John Burn, organisers of the famous strike of 1899, operated from here. Closely involved with them were Annie Besant, and Eleonor Marx-Aveling, a daughter of Karl Marx. With such a large population, comprised of many different races and creeds, squeezed into such a small area, it sometimes became inevitable that racial, and religious intolerance would flourish. Tensions sometimes ran very high.

As recently as 1936 the British Fascist Movement, led by Oswald Mosley, attempted to exploit these tensions. Mosleys Blackshirt stormtroopers attempted to incite racial hatred by a series of provocative meetings and marches through the area. They were soundly defeated when the population of East London turned out en masse and united to prevent Mosleys Blackshirts from marching through the area. Diverse as the population of the East End was, their dislike of Mosley's fascists was greater than their dislike of each other. The 'Battle of Cable Street' on the fourth of October 1936 was the definitive street battle between the Fascists and their opponents. The defeat of the fascists effectively ended any influence which they might have held in the area.

Between the World Wars much of the Jewish population of the East End moved out of the area and into the more comfortable suburbs of North London. The once flourishing Chinese community of Limehouse has also now disappeared, giving way to a new, and affluent, breed of warehouse dweller - the 'yuppie'.

During the 1950s and 60s the Kray brothers ran their empire from the backstreet house in Vallance Road, where they had grown up. Their regular pubs The Grave Maurice, opposite the London Hospital, and The Blind Beggar, further along Whitechapel High Street, where George Cornell was shot dead by Ronnie Kray, are still visited by curious sightseers.

There is still considerable poverty, in this area of high unemployment, and many of the buildings have a run-down appearance. But today's poverty is not quite the same as the deep squalor, which characterised Whitechapel during the 19th Century when literally thousands of homeless people had only the streets in which to live and sleep. The lucky ones might have found a bed for the night, in one of the many fourpenny doss-houses, if they could afford it. One way of raising money, for a nightly bed, was by prostitution. It is alleged that in 1888, in this small area of London, there were over 5000 prostitutes on the streets. The popular meeting places for prostitutes, and their clients, was usually one of the many pubs. Clients might have been lucky enough to pick up a prostitute who had a room to which they could go. More often than not the business would be concluded down a dark alley, or beneath a railway arch, or somebody's backyard. Even the landings and stairs of accessible houses and factories were utilised for the purpose

Many of the poorest families lived crammed together in single-room accommodations without any sanitation or proper ventilation. There were also over 200 common lodging houses which provided shelter for some 8000 homeless and destitute people each night.

In the mid 1800's attempts were made to improve the conditions of the poor of the area.. One was the establishment of the first Univerity Settlement Toynbee Hall. The purpose of the settlement was to provide accommodation for University students and graduates, between terms, in order that they may provide education, recreation and entertainments for the local population.. According to the founder, of Toynbee Hall, Joseph Barnett , the role of the students was "to learn as much as to teach; to receive as much to give". Most of the students and fresh graduates who answered the call were from either Oxford or Cambridge Universities.

The area also attracted large numbers of sightseers. Often these were wealthy young men who visited Whitechapel for the purpose of, what became known as 'slumming'.
For a considerable number of Victorian gentlemen and ladies slumming was nothing more than a form of illicit urban tourism. They visited the most deprived streets of the East End in pursuit of the 'guilty pleasures' associated with the immoral slum dwellers. Others went there to preach salvation to the distressed and fallen women of the area.

Today, if one walks along the Commercial Road, some of the pubs, such as the Ten Bells, are still there. The steps of Spitalfields church still invite the passer-by to rest awhile and ponder the many secrets witnessed by the silent stones. Toynbee Hall still flourishes. Only two, of the original murder sites, are still recognisable - Bucks Row, now called Durward Street, and, Mitre Square. The other sites have been redeveloped out of all recognition.

Whitechapel is the very heart of Jack the Ripper's territory. It was here that, between the 31st August and the 9th November 1888, five women were murdered. They were killed in a most brutal and horrible way by one man who has been known ever since by the name - Jack the Ripper. The pseudonym accurately describes the dreadful nature of the injuries suffered by the unfortunate victims.

Popular, yet highly fictionalised, representations of these crimes have tended, over the years, to glamourise these women. Often they have been portrayed as beautiful young ladies, dressed in fine clothes, who by chance alone happened to be in the area at the same time as their killer. They were perhaps more fortunate than the vagrants and imbeciles who shared, with them, the streets, but, unlike their more fortunate celluloid counterparts they were, with one exception, middle-aged prostitutes who plied their trade in the dim gas-lit passages, alleyways, gardens and railway arches of the East End. They were all alcoholics and they sold their wares for a few pennies, the price of a drink and a night's lodging.

Over a period of time, during 1888 and 1889, there were eight murders, in the vicinity of Whitechapel, which have come to be known as The Whitechapel Murders. They were not all committed by the same person.

Jack the Ripper had, in all probability, five victims only. Polly Nichols, Annie Chapman, possibly Elizabeth Stride, Catharine Eddowes and Mary Kelly. These five victims are referred to as the canonical victims. It is, however, worth looking at several incidents all of which took place in the months preceding the Jack the Ripper killings.

At 5.00pm, on Saturday 25th February 1888, 38 years old Annie Millwood was admitted to the Whitechapel Workhouse Infirmary. She was suffering from numerous stab wounds in her legs and lower part of the body. She claimed that she had been approached by an unknown man who had taken a clasp-knife from his pocket and proceeded to stab her. It would appear that there had been no witnesses to the attack. Annie Millwood recovered from her injuries and was discharged, to the South Grove Workhouse. However, on the 21st March. ten days later she collapsed and died. A post-mortem examination established that death was due to natural causes.

We do not know what motive Millwoods attacker had. Prostitute rolling, or mugging as it is called today, was common in the area. Prostitutes were frequently robbed of their meager immoral earnings. We do not know that Annie Millwood was a prostitute, but she was a widow, and may have earned a living on the streets. Her attacker may well have assumed her to be a prostitute given that she was evidently alone when he encountered her.

One month later, at half-past midnight on the 28th March, 39 years-old machinist Ada Wilson was disturbed at her home, 19 Maidman Street, Burdett Road, Mile-End, by a knocking on her door. She opened the door to a stranger who, forced his way into her room and demanded money. The man, described as about 5ft 6 1inches tall, 30 years of age, with a sunburnt face and a fair moustache told Ada that if she did not produce any money she would die. Ada refused. The man produced a clasp-knife, from his pocket, and stabbed her twice in the throat. The man ran off when Ada started screaming. A Doctor Wheeler, who lived close by, attended to her wounds and took her to the London Hospital. Much to the surprise of the doctors, who treated her, she recovered fully and was discharged on the 27th April 1888.

The similarities, between the attacks on Annie Millwood and Ada Wilson, namely the clasp-knife produced from a pocket, strongly suggest that the same assailant may have been responsible. But these attacks were more probably committed by a mugger who preyed on prostitutes or unaccompanied women for their money.

Just five days after the attack, on Ada Wilson, another woman, a known prostitute, was mugged for her money. This time, however, there were three assailants involved. This attack was to have more tragic consequences for the victim.

It was about 5.00am on Easter Monday, the 2nd April 1888, Emma Smith, a 45 years old widow of 18 George Street, Spitalfields arrived back at her lodging house. She was described as being very distressed.
Emma told the lodging keeper, Mary Russell, that she had been set upon in the Whitechapel Road at about 1.30 in the morning. It appeared that she had seen three men walking towards her. Emma had crossed over the road, by St Marys Church, in order to avoid the men. The three men had, however, followed her into Osborn Street where they attacked her, raped her, and stole her money. Emma Smiths face and head was injured. Her right ear was almost severed. A blunt instrument had been inserted into her vagina with such great force that it had ruptured her perineum. Emma had placed her shawl between her thighs to soak up the blood and somehow managed to walk home to her lodgings. Mary Russell took Emma to the London Hospital where she died a little over 24 hours later. Before she died Emma claimed that one of her assailants appeared to be a youth aged about 19.

Once again this was, clearly, a case of prostitute mugging. We are not told whether a knife was used to almost sever Emma Smiths ear or whether it could have been torn in her struggles. It is however, entirely possible that the same person responsible for the earlier muggings, of Annie Millwood and Ada Thompson, an individual known to carry and use, a pocket clasp-knife, may well have been involved, this time with others, in this fatal attack on

Emma Smith. Contemporary police reports certainly indicate that such individuals operated in the area for that very purpose.

It is therefore quite possible that the same assailant, acting either alone, or in concert with others, may have been responsible for the killing of yet another prostitute.

CHAPTER TWO

PRELUDE

It was bank holiday Monday the 6th August 1888. 35 years-old Martha Tabram, (sometimes called Turner) a married woman who worked as a prostitute was out and about enjoying herself in the Whitechapel pubs. That evening she was drinking in the Angel and Crown, a public house close to Whitechapel church. She was seen to leave the pub, at closing time, with a soldier. It was the last time that she was seen alive.

At 3.00am on the following morning Alfred Crow, a cab driver, returned home to his apartment at 35 George-Yard buildings. As he passed the first-floor landing he saw a body on the ground. He later claimed that he often saw bodies lying around there and did not take any particular notice of this one. Crow claimed that he did not know whether the body was alive or dead, He went to bed. He awoke at 9.30am and went downstairs. The body was no longer there. He heard no noise while he was in bed.

Crows neighbour, John Reeves, of 37 George-Yard buildings did find a body on the stairs at 4.45am. It was a woman. She was lying on her back in a pool of blood. The police were notified. Doctor Killeen, of Brick Lane attended the scene and pronounced the woman dead. Killeen found 39 stab wounds on the body, which he claimed had been dead for about three hours. The body was taken to the Whitechapel mortuary.

A few days later the body was identified as that of Martha Tabram. A prostitute friend of the murdered woman, Mary Connelly told the police that she and Martha had been out drinking together on the night that Martha was killed, but, that they had become separated. Connelly claimed that they had been in the company of two soldiers, a private and a corporal in the guards, from 10.00pm until 11.45pm. She claimed that Martha had gone off with the private for business.

Despite identity parades, held at the Tower of London, and the Wellington barracks Connelly was unable to pick out either of the two soldiers they had been with. Several soldiers were, however, interviewed but they were all able to account for their whereabouts at the time of the murder

Martha Tabram had left her husband some thirteen years earlier, and, for the last twelve years she had been living with Henry Turner. Twelve years living with the hard-drinking Martha was evidently all that Henry Turner could take He had ended their relationship just three weeks before Martha met her death. At the subsequent inquest the Coroner recorded a verdict of murder by person or persons unknown.

It is now generally accepted that the murder of Martha Tabram was, in all probability, not the work of Jack the Ripper. Indeed no one had even yet heard of Jack the Ripper. Given the earlier, and similar attacks, upon Annie Millwood, Ada Wilson, and Emma Smith, it is not unreasonable to postulate the possibility that the attack upon Martha Tabram was committed by the same individual or gang. Martha may have scored, possibly with her soldier client, earlier in the evening, and the motive for her murder may well have been, like the others, one of robbery.

In all probability these attacks were not the work of Jack the ripper. Jack the Rippers motive was not robbery or rape, and, he did not stab his prostitute victims. He disembowelled them.

Fortythree years old Polly Ann Nichols was a typical example of the type of prostitute to be found in the area. With five of her front teeth missing she had a history of drunkeness, vagrancy and petty crime. For the last six years she had shuffled between infirmary and workhouse. Usually she ended up sleeping rough in Trafalgar Square.

In June 1888 Polly Nichols made an attempt at gainful employment. She found work as a servant at a large family house in Wandsworth. However, after a few weeks she disappeared from the house wearing a set of new clothes stolen from Mrs Cowdry, her employer. A few days later she was back in the East End living at a doss-house, 18 Thrawl Street. She shared a room with three other women, sharing a bed with one of them.

At 1.20am on Friday 31st of August Polly Nicholls returned, slightly tipsy, to her lodgings. Polly was wearing a brand-new bonnet. She was turned away, from the lodging-house, because she did not have the fourpence for her nightly bed. She asked the deputy lodging-keeper to keep her bed for her. She would soon return with the money. An hour later she was seen in Osborn Street, Whitechapel, in conversation with fellow prostitute, and bedmate, Emily Holland. According to Emily Holland Polly told her that she was going to try her luck along the Whitechapel Road.

A little over two hours later, at about 3.40am, two men, Charles Cross and Robert Paul were making their way along Bucks Row, towards Spitalfields market, when they saw what at first appeared to be an old tarpaulin lying in the roadway. This item was clearly of interest to Charles Cross. He was a carter by trade. They crossed the road in order to examine their find.

As they approached the object they quickly realised that it was not a discarded tarpaulin. It was a woman. Thinking that the helpless woman was drunk they attempted to help her to her feet. It was then that they noticed that her throat had been cut. Both men

hurried to the corner to see if they could summon aid. Within a few minutes several police constables were at the scene awaiting the arrival of the Divisional Police Surgeon, Dr Llewellen. When the doctor arrived he needed no convincing that the woman was dead. After a cursory examination he declared her dead and ordered the removal of the body to the mortuary shed at Old Montague Street Workhouse Infirmary. It was not until Polly Nichols' body was at the mortuary, being prepared for post-mortem examination, that it was noticed that she had been disembowelled.

Police enquiries established that although several men had been working at the time of the murder, in the slaughterhouse a few yards from where the body had been found, no one recalled hearing any cry or sounds of a struggle.

The occupant of 'New Cottage', the house next to the murder scene, said that she had heard no sign of a quarrel or scuffle. She claimed that if the woman had screamed she would have heard her. Furthermore, a patrolling policeman, PC Neil had passed the spot only a few minutes earlier and had noticed nothing unusual.

The following day, Saturday the 1st of September, William Nichols, the estranged husband of Polly Nichols, a printer by trade, attended at the mortuary where he identified the body as that of his wife. He said that his wife had gone off with another man many years before. He had not seen, or heard from her for several months. As he stared at the mutilated remains of his wife he is reported to have said,
"I forgive you for what you did to me now that I see you like this."

Later on that same day the inquest on Polly Nichols was opened at the Working Lad's Institute, in Whitechapel Road, under the direction of the Coroner Mr Wynne-Baxter. After the jurors had been sworn-in they were taken along to the Old Montague Street mortuary, staffed by workhouse inmates, to view the body. When they returned they heard the evidence of PC Neil and the two porters who had found the body. Dr Llewellen told the court that he had examined the body in situ and again at the mortuary where he had conducted a post-mortem examination of the body. After describing the injuries to the body he stated that in his opinion the killer had held his hand across the mouth of the victim while making a left-to-right cut across the throat. He suggested that the killer might have been left-handed. After hearing the medical evidence the coroner adjourned the inquest until the following Monday morning.

It appears to have been at this point that the authorities, and certainly the press, started to speculate at a connection between the murder of Polly Nichols, with the murder of Martha Tabram three weeks earlier, and the murder of Emma Smith five months earlier.

On the 3rd September 'The Times' reported -
THE WHITECHAPEL MURDER

Up to a late hour last evening the police had obtained no clue to the perpetrator of the latest of the three murders which have so recently taken place in Whitechapel, and there is, it must be acknowledged, after their exhaustive investigation of the facts, no ground for blaming the officers in charge should they fail in unravelling the mystery surrounding the crime.
The murder, in the early hours of Friday morning last, of the woman now known as Mary Ann Nicholls, has so many points of similarity with the murder of two other women in the same neighbourhood-one Martha Tabram, as recently as August 7, and the other less than 12 months previously- that the police admit their belief that the three crimes are the work of one individual. All three women were of the class called "unfortunates," each so very poor, that robbery could have formed no motive for the crime, and each was murdered in such a similar fashion, that doubt as to the crime being the work of one and the same villain almost vanishes, particularly when it is remembered that all three murders were committed within a distance of 300 yards from each other.

It is clear, from this report, that by now the police were beginning to suspect that these killings were the work &one and the same villain yet surprisingly the motive of robbery, the clear, and obvious motive in the earlier attacks, are dismissed

On Thursday September 6th, Polly Nichols, the first canonical victim of Jack the Ripper, was buried in Ilford Cemetery.

On Saturday the 22nd of September the inquest on Polly Nicholls eventually resumed. In his summing-up the Coroner was critical as to the lack of proper mortuary facilities and properly trained persons to staff them. Coroner Wynne-Baxter then recorded a verdict of wilful murder.

However, even before the inquest, on Polly Nicholls, had been concluded the killer had already struck again.

On the evening of the day following Polly Nichols' funeral, the 7th September, 47 year old Annie Chapman was looking for the price of a bed. Like Polly Nichols she had been separated from her husband. Until his death, two years before, he had paid her a weekly allowance of ten shillings (50p). Since becoming widowed she had attempted, several times, to form relationships with different men. Recently she had been in the habit of meeting a bricklayers' labourer named Edward Stanley. She had known Stanley for some time but it is not known how frequently they met.

It was Saturday night. If Annie had made any money at all that evening she had evidently drunk it at the Prince Albert public house in Brushfield Street. Timothy Donovan, the warden of her doss-house, Crossinghams at 35 Dorset Street, had allowed to her warm herself and take some refreshment. She evidently ate a baked potato. A fellow-resident, Frederick Stevens drank a pint of beer with her in the kitchen before Donovan finally turned her out, at about 1.00am, due to her not having the price of her bed.

Annie left the doss-house at about 2.00am and wandered along Dorset Street towards its junction with Commercial Street. She turned left at this junction, and walked along Commercial Road for a hundred yards or so, towards the Ten Bells pub, she came to Hanbury Street.

Number 29 Hanbury Street was a lodging house. On that night it contained no less than sixteen occupants. One of these, John Davies, awoke just before 6.00am. He chanced to look out of the window overlooking the dingy rear garden. Close up, against the back door of the house, and resting against the fence separating the rear gardens, was the body of a woman. He raised the alarm. Within minutes a crowd had gathered outside the building.

George Bagster-Phillips, the police divisional surgeon, arrived at the house shortly afterwards. Annie Chapman's body was lying on its back. Her throat had been cut across so deeply that she had almost been decapitated. Her legs had been drawn up while her feet were resting on the ground. Her knees were turned outwards. Her face was bruised and her swollen tongue was protruding between her teeth. The lower half of her body had been savagely mutilated. Like Nichols, Annie Chapman had been disembowelled. Her uterus, and its appendages, had been completely removed. Doctor Phillips declared that the killer must have taken at least half an hour to perform his grisly task.

News of the murder quickly spread around the area and, within hours, printed broadsheets describing the crime in lurid detail, were being hawked along the Whitechapel Road. Crowds of excited onlookers gathered in Hanbury Street. Angry at this latest outrage they soon formed into violent mobs, roaming the area attacking anyone who looked the least bit suspicious. To them it meant anyone who looked even the slightest bit foreign. It was not a weekend to be Jewish-looking in Whitechapel. The East London Observer tells us why:

A PLOT AGAINST THE JEWS

On Saturday in several quarters of East London the crowds who assembled in the streets began to assume a very threatening attitude towards the Hebrew poulation of the district. It was repeatedly asserted that no Englishman could have perpetrated such a horrible crime as that of Hanbury Street, and that it must have been done by a JEW - and forthwith the crowds began to threaten and abuse such unfortunate Hebrews as they found in the streets. Happily the presence of a large number of police prevented a riot actually taking place.

The garden, of 29 Hanbury street had, evidently, given up what were believed to be clues. A piece of torn envelope bearing the initial 'M', Two pills, wrapped in paper, were also found. These items were later identified by Frederick Stevens. He had seen her put the pills into the piece of envelope. He recognised it since it also bore the crest of the Middlesex regiment, together with the initial M. An apron made of leather and saturated with water, was found close to the body. News of this find soon reached the ears of the mob who made their way to 22 Mulberry Street the home of John Pizer. Pizer, a local Jewish bootmaker, was known to wear an apron of this type. Indeed he was known locally by his nickname - 'Leather-Apron'. Pizer had already served a sentence of six months hard labour for stabbing another bootmaker through the hand.

It would seem that Pizer was not very popular. On Monday 10th September Sergeant Thicke accompanied by another officer, made his way to Pizers house and arrested him. A number of leather-working knives were found. Pizer was taken to Leman Street police station where he was detained. This may have been more for his own protection rather than for any other reason. He was however subected to an identification parade. Mrs Fiddymont, the landlady of The Prince Albert, failed to identify him, but another witness, Emmanuel Violenia, did. Violenia was convinced that Pizer was the man he had seen talking angrily with a woman outside 29 Hanbury Street in the early hours of the morning of 8th September. Violenia claimed that he knew Pizer by his nickname of Leather Apron. Pizer was outraged at this identification. HoweverViolenias' identification of Pizer was considered, by the police, as unreliable and Pizer was released after 48 hours.

John Pizer was by no means the only person taken in. On the very day after Annie Chapman's murder no less than fourteen suspects were being held in the Commercial Street police station alone.

Great excitement was caused in the neighbourhood of Commercial Street Police station during the afternoon on account of the arrival from Gravesend of a suspect whose appearance resembled in some respects that of "Leather Apron." This man, whose name is William Henry Pigott, was taken into custody on Sunday night at the Pope's Head public house, Gravesend. Attention was first attracted to Pigott because he had some bloodstains on his clothes. Superintendent Berry, the chief of the local police, was communicated with, and a sergeant was sent to the Pope's Head to investigate the case. On approaching the man, who seemed in a somewhat dazed condition, the sergeant saw that one of his hands bore several recently-made wounds.
Being interrogated as to the cause of this Pigott made a somewhat rambling statement to the effect that while going down Brick Lane, Whitechapel, at half-past 4 on Saturday morning he saw a woman fall in a fit. He stooped to pick her up, and she bit his hand. Exasperated at this he struck her, but seeing two policemen coming up he then ran away. The sergeant, deeming the explanation unsatisfactory, took Pigott to the police-station, where his clothing was carefully examined by Dr. Whitcombe, the divisional surgeon.
The news of Pigott's arrival, which took place at 12 48, at once spread, and in a few seconds the police-station was surrounded by an excited crowd anxious to get a glimpse of the supposed murderer. Finding that no opportunity was likely to occur of seeing the prisoner, the mob after a time melted away, but the police had trouble for some hours in keeping the thoroughfare free for traffic. Pigott arrived at Commercial Street in much the same condition as he was when taken into custody. He wore no vest, had on a battered felt hat, and appeared to be in a state of high nervous excitement.
Mrs. Fiddymont, who is responsible for the statement respecting a man resembling "Leather Apron" being at the Prince Albert public house on Saturday, was sent for, as were also other

witnesses likely to be able to identify the prisoner; but after a very brief scrutiny it was the unanimous opinion that Pigott was not "Leather Apron." Nevertheless, looking to his condition of mind and body, it was decided to detain him until he could give a somewhat more satisfactory explanation of himself and his movements. After an interval of a couple of hours, the man's manner becoming more strange and his speech more incoherent, the divisional surgeon was called in, and he gave it as his opinion that the prisoner's mind was unhinged. A medical certificate to this effect was made out, and Pigott will, for the present, remain in custody.

On 10th September, the same day that Pizer and Pigott were arrested, the inquest on Annie Chapman opened. Once again the venue was the Working Lads' Institute with Mr Wynne-Baxter as the Coroner. This time the police were more than just interested. They had sent along no less than five of their top officers to witness the proceedings. Detective Inspector Abberline had been called in from Scotland Yards Criminal Investigation Division due to his intimate knowledge of the locality. Abberline was accompanied by Detective Inspectors Helson and Chandler. Together with Detective Sergeants Thicke and Leach they monitored the inquest. The mood of the mob, which had congregated outside of the Working Lads Institute however, was such that Mr Wynne-Baxter ruled that the crowd should not be admitted to the proceedings.

This inquest lasted for an incredible five sessions, over the next fifteen days.
One witness, Mrs Richardson, the landlady of 29 Hanbury Street, told the court that couples often used the through entrance to the rear garden. She added that she would not have allowed it if she had known that they used the garden for immoral purposes. Her son John Richardson also gave evidence. When asked if he had ever seen any strangers in the garden he replied - Yes, plenty, at all hours - both men and women. I have often turned them out. We have had them on the first floor as well, on the landing.
Wynne-Baxter: -Do you mean to say that they go there for an immoral purpose?
Witness: - Yes they do.

Doctor Phillips, who had examined the body in situ, gave evidence that the murdered woman had been dead for about two hours, making the time of death at around 4.30am. He then gave a summary of the injuries stating that the work was '...that of an expert, or one, at least, with such a knowledge of anatomical or pathological examinations, as to be enabled to secure the pelvic organs with one sweep of the knife'. He believed the murder weapon to be a long-bladed knife at least six inches long. He suggested that a post-mortem knife might have been the instrument used.

The Coroner gave a summary of the events along with reasons as to why no cries were heard from the victim.

He seized her by the chin. He pressed her throat, and while thus preventing the slightest cry, he at the same time produced insensibility and suffocation. There was no evidence of any struggle. The clothes were not torn. Even in those preliminaries, the wretch seems to have known how to carry out efficiently his nefarious work. The deceased was then lowered to the ground, and laid on her back: and although in doing so she may have fallen slightly against the fence, the movement was probably effected with care. Her throat was then cut in two places with savage determination, and the injuries to the abdomen commenced. All was done with cool impudence and reckless daring; but perhaps nothing was more noticeable than the emptying of her pockets, and the arrangement of their contents with business-like precision in order near her feet. The murder seemed, like the Buck's-Row case, to have been carried out without any cry. None of the occupants of the houses by which the spot was surrounded heard anything suspicious. The brute who committed the offence did not even take the trouble to cover up his ghastly work, but left the body exposed to the view of the first comer. That accorded but little with the trouble taken with the rings, and suggested that, as daylight broke, a sudden fear suggested the danger of detection that he was running. There were two things missing. Her rings had been wrenched from her fingers and had not since been found, and the uterus had been taken from the abdomen. (The Times 20th September 1888)

The inquest was adjourned and reopened again on Wednesday 26th September. Wynne-Baxter, in his summation, suggested that:

'...the desire (of the killer) was to possess the missing abdominal organ... the amount missing would go into a breakfast cup... and, had not the medical examination been of a thorough and searching character it might easily have been left unnoticed that there was any portion of the body which had been taken... The difficulty in believing that the purport of the murderer was the possession of the missing abdominal organ was natural.'

The Coroner then explained that a matter had been drawn to his attention which he thought may be of some relevance. He explained that several months earlier the sub-curator of a pathological museum had been approached by an American. The American had offered to pay £20 for each preserved specimen Uterus which the curator could supply.
He concluded his summing-up by suggesting that there might be a market for such an anatomical specimen. Wynne-Baxter told the jury that:

'...We are confronted by a murder of no ordinary character, committed not from jealousy, revenge, or robbery, but from motives less adequate than the many which still disgrace our civilisation, mar our progress and blot the pages of our Christianity.'

After thanking the Jury he pronounced a verdict of Wilful Murder.

During the adjournment break the Home Secretary, Henry Mathews, sent a memo to his secretary, Evelyn Ruggles-Brise directing him to obtain a progress report on the investigation into the murders. Ruggles-Brise did not receive the memo since he was out of London at the time and so the memo was sent on to Charles Warren the Metropolitan Police Commissioner. Warren responded straight away with a report dated 19th September 1888.:

'No progress has as yet been made in obtaining any definite clue as to the Whitechapel murderers. A great number of clues have been examined and exhausted without finding anything suspicious.
A large staff of men are employed and every point is being examined which seems to offer any prospects of a discovery.
There are at present three cases of suspicion.
1. The lunatic Isensmith a Swiss arrested at Holloway who is now in an asylum at Bow and arrangements are being made to ascertain whether he is the man who was seen on the morning of the murder in a public house by Mrs Fiddymont.
2. A man called Puckeridge was released from an asylum on 4th August. He was educated as a surgeon and has threatened to rip people up with a long knife. He is being looked for but cannot be found as yet.
3. A brothel keeper who will not give her address or name writes to say that a man living in her house was seen with blood on him on morning of murder. She described his appearance and said where he might be seen. When the detectives got near him he bolted, got away and there is no clue to the writer of the letter.
All these three cases are being followed up and no doubt will be exhausted in a few days - the first seems a very suspicious case, but the man is at present a violent lunatic.

Jacob Isenschmid, Warrens' first suspect had been a pork butcher with premises at 59. Elthorne Road. Holloway. The business had failed and Isenschmid began to suffer from fits of depression. During such fits he was said to be very violent threatening to put peoples 'lights out'. He also suffered delusions and described himself as ' the King of Elthorne Road.'

On the 24th September 1887 he had been admitted to Colney Hatch Lunatic asylum. He was, however discharged as cured on the 2nd December. But, during the spring of 1888 his mental ilness returned in the form of religious mania. According to his wife he refused to wash and sat reading the bible for hours on end. His wife seems to have attempted to have Jacob incarcerated again but he left home.

On the 18th September 1888 Inspector Abberline had noted ' Although at present we are unable to procure any evidence to connect him with the murders he appears to be the most likely person that has come under our notice to have committed the crimes'.

There doesn't appear to be any evidence against Isenschmid and it is not known if he was ever identified by Mrs Fiddymont. According to a report in 'The Star' 21st September 1888. Isenshmids' brother gave him an alibi for the morning of the Chapman murder. Furthermore since Isenshmid was confined, in the Grove Hall asylum, when the Whitechapel murderer struck next, on the night of the 30th September, it would tend to exonerate him from further suspicion.

Warrens' second suspect, Oswald Puckridge, had, like Isenshmid, a history of mental illness. He had been admitted to the Hoxton House Lunatic Asylum, in Shoreditch, on the 6th January 1888 and discharged as 'relieved', but not cured, on the 4th August.

Oswald Puckridge was born at Burpham, not far from Arundel in Sussex, in 1838. He married Ellen Puddle, at St. Pauls Church Deptford when he was thirty. His occupation is given, in the parish records as 'Chemist'. Apart from the fact that Puckridge evidently suffered from mental illness there appears to be absolutely no reason whatsoever for him to have been considered as a suspect. Furthermore, since he was born in 1838 he would have been fifty at the time of the Whitechapel murders. His age is quite inconsistent with all known alleged sightings, of Jack the Ripper, which are within the age range of twenty-eight to thirty-five. Puckridge was admitted to the Holborn Workhouse on the 28th May 1900. He died there four days later of Broncho-Pneumonia.

Coroner Wynne-Baxters' comments, that it was the killers desire to possess the missing organs of his victims, had stirred up a hornets nest.
The day after the inquest on Annie Chapman had been closed, a letter was received by the Central News Agency in Fleet Street. Dated the 25th September, 1888. It read:

'

I keep hearing the police have caught me but they wont fix me just yet. I have laughed when they look so clever and talk about being on the right track. That joke about leather apron gave me real fits. I am down on whores and I shant quit ripping them till I do get buckled. Grand work the last job was. I gave the lady no time to squeal. How can they catch me now. I love my work and want to start again. You will soon hear of me with my funny little games. I saved some of the proper red stuff in a ginger beer bottle over the last job to write with but it went thick like glue and I cant use it. Red ink is fit enough I hope ha ha. The next job I do I shall clip the ladys ears off and sent to the police officers just for jolly wouldnt you. Keep this letter back till I do a bit more work then give it out straight. My knife so nice and sharp I want to get to work right away if I get a chance.Good luck!
Yours truly
Jack the Ripper
Dont mind me giving the trade name.'

By this time the police had already received hundreds of bogus confessions and their first reaction was to dismiss this letter as another hoax. But closer investigation of this letter, and indeed several subsequent letters, made reference to details about the murders which had not been made public at the time the letters had been received by the Central News Agency.. The writer of the above letter, signed himself Jack the Ripper. This now became the name by which the killer was, and is still, known by.

The murder of Annie Chapman was reported, in all of its full horror, by the newspapers of the day, particularly in 'The Times', which spared its readers none of the ghastly details. Letters appeared in the press condemning the police for their apparent inability to apprehend the killer. The police responded by hiring two bloodhounds from an animal trainer. It was reported that the hounds were taken to Tooting Common, for practice, and promptly lost themselves. All Metropolitan Police stations were put on full alert to find them. The press had a field day. The police, and the Home Secretary, Henry Mathews were lampooned in the newspapers.

It was now believed that the murder of Martha Tabram had been the work of Jack the Ripper. Her murder, together with the earlier, and similar killing of prostitute Emma Smith, in April 1888, appeared to give Jack the Ripper a greater tally of victims than was actually the case. Some of the good citizens of Londons' East-End decided to take the law into their own hands.

Two days after the murder of Annie Chapman, bodies of citizens formed themselves into vigilance committees to patrol the streets of Whitechapel.

At a meeting of local ratepayers, held in the Crown public House, Mile End Road, on the 10th of September, George Lusk, a recently widowed father of seven children, and self employed builder and renovator of music-halls, was elected President of the, newly-formed, Whitechapel Vigilance Committee. With these men, who all knew the area well, on patrol, and with extra police already in the area, they felt that they could prevent what was beginning to look like a series of murders. They were wrong. Horribly wrong. Just three weeks later Jack the Ripper doubled his real tally by claiming two victims in one single night.

In the early hours of Sunday 30th September, Louis Diemschutz, a hawker of cheap jewellery drove his pony and trap along Berner Street and into Dutfields yard, at the rear of the Workers Educational club, where he worked part time as the steward. As the pony made its way into the yard it shied with alarm. Diemschutz climbed down from the drivers seat to see what appeared to be spooking the animal. He saw a bundle against the wall. The bundle turned out to be the body of a woman. It was that of forty five year old Elizabeth Stride. When Diemschutz looked more closely, at the woman, he could see that blood was still pouring from a gaping wound in her throat.

The police summoned Dr Frederick Blackwell to the scene. He examined the body at 1.15am. He pronounced Elizabeth Stride dead as a result of the throat injury. Apart from the throat wound there were a few nicks in the ear-lobes and slits in the eyelids. It is believed that the arrival of Diemschutz probably disturbed the killer before he was able to perform any further mutilations to the body.

Earlier that evening, Elizabeth Stride had been drinking in a public house in Commercial Street. She was in her lodging house at 32 Flower and Dean Street until about 8.00pm when she left to go out. At 11.00pm she was seen to leave The Bricklayers Arms in Settles Street, with a young Englishman. They walked in the direction of Commercial Road and Berner Street. At 11.45pm she was still in Berner Street with 'an Englishman'. A witness, William Marshall, a resident of Berner Street later gave evidence, to the subsequent inquest, that he had heard the man say to the woman,
"You would say anything but your prayers."

Marshall described the man as 'mild speaking', and said he appeared to be an 'educated man.' The couple moved away towards the direction of Dutfields yard. At 12.30am, Police

Constable William Smith saw Elizabeth Stride standing with a man opposite the open gates of Dutfields Yard. The policeman provided a clear description of the man. He was of medium height, about 28 years of age, clean shaven and of respectable appearance. He wore a dark overcoat, a hard felt deer-stalker hat, and he carried a newspaper parcel some eighteen inches in length.

Fifteen minutes later, Elizabeth Stride evidently managed to get into some kind of scrape with a passer-by, since another passer-by, Israel Schwartz, witnessed Stride being assaulted on the pavement outside Dutfields Yard by a young, intoxicated man whom Schwartz had followed from the Commercial Road end of Berner Street.

Israel Schwartz told the police that at 12.45am on turning into Berner Street from Commercial Road and having got as far as the gateway, to Dutfields yard where the murder was committed, he saw a man stop and speak to a woman, who was standing in the gateway. The man tried to pull the woman into the street, but he turned her round and threw her down on the footway and the woman screamed three times, but not very loudly. On crossing to the other side of the street, he saw a second man standing lighting his pipe. The man who threw the woman down called out, 'Lipski' apparently to the man on the opposite side of the road. At his point Schwartz walked away. But upon realizing he was being followed by the other man he away.

It was during the following fifteen minutes that Stride was murdered.

Schwartz was taken to the mortuary where he identified Stride's body as that of the woman he had seen being attacked. He gave descriptions of both of the men he had seen.
The man who had thrown the woman down was described as; aged about 30, 5' 5" tall, fair complexion, dark hair, small brown moustache, full face, broad shouldered. He was wearing a dark Jacket and trousers, black cap with peak. The man who lit his pipe, and followed Schwartz, is described as; aged about 35, 5' 11" tall, fresh complexion, light brown hair. He was wearing a dark overcoat, an old black hard felt hat with a wide brim.

Ten days later, on 10th October, Schwartz elaborated his story. He evidently told the 'Star'

newspaper that while making his way to new lodgings he had followed the first man, who appeared to be drunk, into Berner Street and had seen him accost Stride. He (Schwartz) had crossed over the road, to avoid becoming involved. Schwartz told the 'Star' that he had not gone too far when he heard the noise of a quarrel. Looking back he had seen the second man coming out of a nearby pub shouting some kind of warning to the man who was with the woman. (It is claimed that the man called out Lipski, the name of a Jew who had lived in the area and who had been executed a year earlier for murder. It is suggested that the expression was intended to be a racist insult. An alternative view is that the man actually called out Strides name (Lizzie). Schwartz also claimed that the second man had rushed toward the couple as if to attack the first man. He also claimed that the second man had a knife in his hand. At this point, however, Schwartz admitted that he had "fled incontinently to his new lodgings

Twelve minutes walk away from Berner Street is Mitre Square. It is just over the boundary of the City of London between Mitre Street and Dukes Place. There were three entrances to Mitre Square.

Whilst Doctor Blackwell was still examining the body of Elizabeth Stride, in Berner Street, Police Constable Edward Watkins of the City Police was making his quarterly-hour check on Mitre Square.

At 1.30am Watkins noticed nothing at all suspicious. Watkins evidently then went into one of the warehouses overlooking the square, to check with the nightwatchman on duty. He returned to the square at approximately 1.44am. There he found the butchered body of a woman in the south-west corner. He ran to Kearley and Tonge's warehouse opposite and told the nightwatchman, George Morris. Morris ran to Aldgate for assistance, while PC Watkins waited by the body until the arrival of help.

Doctor Sequeira was summoned from Jewry Street. He was joined by F. Gordon Brown, a police surgeon, and several police officers. The City of London Police Commissioner, Sir Henry Smith also subsequently arrived at the murder scene. From pawn-tickets discovered upon the body the murdered woman was soon identified as Catharine Eddowes. The body was later removed to the mortuary in Golden Lane.

Catharine Eddowes, the daughter of a tin-plate worker was born in Wolverhampton in 1842 but as a child of two she had moved, with her family, to Bermondsey, and educated at the St. John's charity school in Tooley Street. Her mother died in 1855 and it would appear that Catharine moved back to Wolverhampton to live with an aunt.

Catharine Eddowes had told friends that she had married a pensioner Thomas Conway and lived with him for a while in the Midlands. There is no record of the marriage, but they had three children; Annie born in 1865, George born 1868, and another son born in 1873.

In 1880 the couple had separated. Catharine took custody of Annie, and returned to London. Thomas kept the two sons. Catharine's drinking was said later by her daughter to have been the

cause of the family breakdown. Thomas Conway was also said to have been violent towards Catharine.

By 1881 Catharine Eddowes was living with John Kelly, an Irish porter, in Flower and Dean Street, Whitechapel.

In September 1888, Eddowes and Kelly had gone hop picking in Kent, but evidently did not earn much money. They returned to London on the 28th September. Eddowes went to the Shoe Lane Workhouse to find a bed for the night. The following day the couple met up and decided to pawn Kelly's boots. This they did and with the 2/6 they bought food and alcohol. Sometime during the afternoon Eddowes left Kelly saying that she was going to find Annie, her daughter, to see if she could borrow some money from her.

Like Elizabeth Stride, Catharine Eddowes' last hours are well documented. Six hours before she met her death she had been arrested by PCs Robinson and Simmons in the Aldgate High Street for causing a drunken disturbance. She had been locked safely away in Bishopsgate Police Station until 1.00am when PC George Hutt released her as fit to take care of herself. He had told her that it was now too late for her to buy anymore drink. As she left the Police Station she is alleged to have said, "Goodnight, Old Cock".

During a search of the area, which followed the Mitre Square murder, Police Constable Long, a constable drafted in from A1 (Westminster) division found a piece of bloodstained cloth lying in a passageway at Wentworth Street Dwellings in Goulston Street. The cloth, subsequently proved to be of the same material as the apron worn by the victim Catherine Eddowes. Doctor Brown matched the material to that of the apron worn by the victim. It is not known why the cloth had been torn from Eddowes apron. If it was to wipe the blade of the knife the killer could have easily done that on the apron without having to detach part of it. PC Long claimed that the cloth showed traces of faeces. This may suggest that the killer had been caught short. Alternatively the cloth may have been used to carry a body part. Close by where the cloth was found was a communal sink. PC Long concluded that the killer might have paused here long enough to wash his bloodstained hands. Above the sink, and freshly written in chalk upon the jamb of a doorway were the words:

"THE JEWES ARE THE MEN THAT WILL NOT BE BLAMED FOR NOTHING".

City of London detectives descended on the area of Goulston Street but no further clues were discovered. Detective Daniel Halse was given the job of standing guard over the chalked message while a photographer was sent for. They would have to wait until daylight before it could be properly photographed. In the meantime however, before any photographs could be taken, the Commissioner of the Metropolitan Police, Charles Warren arrived on the scene. Catherine Eddowes had been murdered in Mitre Square, a few streets away within the jurisdiction of the City Police. But Goulston Street was in the Metropolitan area, where the City officers had no jurisdiction. Warren refused to allow the message to remain in case it inflamed racial hatred against the Jews. He ordered it to be washed away.

There can be little doubt but, that by ordering the destruction of what could have been a vital piece of evidence, Warren was guilty of crass stupidity.

Warren attempted to defend his action in a report made to the Home Secretary dated November 6th 1888: -

Confidential
Sir,
In reply to your letter of the 5th instant, I enclose a report of the circumstances of the Mitre Square Murder so far as they have come under the notice of the Metropolitan Police, and I now give an account regarding the erasing of the writing on the wallin Goulston Street which I have already partially explained to Mr. Mathews verbally.
On the 30th September on hearing of the Berner Street murder, after visiting Commercial Street Station I arrived at Leman Street Station shortly before 5 a.m. and ascertained from Superintendent Arnold all that was known there relative to the two murders.
The most pressing question at the moment was some writing on the wall in Goulston Street evidently written with the intention of inflaming the public mind against the Jews, and which, Mr. Arnold with a view to prevent serious disorder proposed to obliterate, and had sent down an inspector with a sponge for that purpose, telling him to await his arrival.
I considered it desirable that I should decide this matter myself, as it was one involving so great a responsibility whether any action was taken or not.
I accordingly went down to Goulston Street at once before going to the scene of the murder: it was just getting light, the public would be on the streets in a few minutes, in a neighbourhood very much crowded on Sunday mornings by Jewish vendors and Christian purchasers from all parts of London.
There were several Police around the spot when I arrived, both Metropolitan and City.
The writing was on the jamb of the open archway or doorway visible to anybody in the street and could not be covered up without danger of the covering being torn off at once.
A discussion took place whether the writing could be left covered up or otherwise or whether any portion of it could be left for an hour until it could be photographed; but after taking into consideration the exited state of the population in London generally at the time, the strong feeling which had been exited against the Jews, and the fact that in a short time there would be a large concourse of the people in the streets, and having before me the Report that if it was left there the house was likely to be wrecked (in which from my own observation I entirely concurred) I considered it desirable to obliterate the writing at once, having taken a copy of which I enclose a duplicate.
After having been to the scene of the murder, I went on to the City Police Office and

informed the Chief Superintendent of the reason why the writing had been obliterated.
I may mention that so great was the feeling with regard to the Jews that on the 13th ulto. the Acting Chief Rabbi wrote to me on the subject of the spelling of the word "Jewes" on account of a newspaper asserting that this was a jewish spelling in the Yiddish dialect. He added "in the present state of exitement it is dangerous to the safety of the poor jews in the East (End) to allow such an assertion to remain uncontradicted. My community keenly appreciates your humane and vigilant action during this critical time."

It may be realised therefore if the safety of the Jews in Whitechapel could be considered to be jeopardised 13 days after the murder by the question of the spelling of the word Jews, what might have happened to the Jews in that quarter had that writing been left intact.

I do not hesitate myself to say that if that writing had been left there would have been an onslaught upon the Jews, property would have been wrecked, and lives would probably have been lost; and I was much gratified with the promptitude with which Superintendent Arnold was prepared to act in the matter if I had not been there.

I have no doubt myself whatever that one of the pricipal objects of the reward offered by Mr. Montagu was to shew to the world that the Jews were desirous of having the Hanbury Street Murder cleared up, and thus to divert from them the very strong feeling which was then growing up.

I am, Sir,
Your most obedient Servant,
(signed) C.Warren

It is interesting to note that this report, made by Warren, in an attempt to justify his actions was written on the 6th November - five weeks after he had taken the actions described. It is made even more interesting to note that it was only three days after Warren penned this note that the Home Secretary accepted Warrens' resignation.

Elizabeth Stride, the Berner Street victim, had been born in Sweden on the 27th November 1843. Her parents, Gustaf and Beata Carlsdotter, were farmers near the town of Torslanda, on the outskirts of Gothenburg. Elizabeth had worked as a domestic help but, by early 1865 she was registered as a prostitute. She had been treated on several occasions for venereal disease. By 1866, aged twenty-three, she was living in London. In March 1869, Elizabeth Carlsdotter maried John Stride, a carpenter. He was twenty three years older than she.

Elizabeth Stride was, by all accounts, something of a 'mythomaniac'. She had invented, for herself, a romantic past in which she herself was cast as the tragic heroine. One such story was that she had borne nine children who were all being cared for at a school run by the Swedish church. However, at her inquest, a witness, Sven Olson, a clerk of the Swedish church, stated that in the seventeen years that he had known the deceased he had never known her to give birth to a child. Furthermore the Swedish church did not run such a school.

Elizabeth's best known story was that she claimed to have been a passenger on the ill-fated 'SS Princess Alice', which had sunk in the River Thames in 1878. Almost seven hundred people had perished in the disaster. According to Elizabeth Stride she had managed to save herself by clinging on to a rope as the vessel sank. She claimed that her husband, and two of her children, had drowned in the disaster. Despite thorough searches through the passenger lists, however, no one by the name of 'Stride' was on board. The only case of a father and his two children drowning in the accident was that of a family named 'Bell'. Elizabeth's husband, John Stride, had in fact, died on the 24th October 1884 of a heart attack whilst an inmate of the Poplar Workhouse.

Two murders in one night. By early next morning word of the latest carnage had started to spread around the area and the mobs again began to gather. Angry scenes of protest took place as soapbox orators competed with each other in the universal cry for the resignations of

Charles Warren, the Commissioner of Police, and Henry Mathews, the Home Secretary.

At some point during this weekend, Sir Robert Anderson, newly appointed to head the CID, returned prematurely to England from his convalescent holiday in Switzerland.

Almost immediately after the discovery of Eddowes body the police had commenced an intense house-to-house search. Their enquiries led them to interview three men, who had all been in the vicinity of Mitre Square at about the time Eddowes was killed.

Joseph Lawende, a commercial traveller, had been drinking with friends at the Imperial Club, in Dukes Place, close to Mitre Square. He told police that he had left the club with two friends, Joseph Levy, a butcher of Aldgate, and Harry Harris, a furniture dealer of Whitechapel. Lawende claimed that they had left the club at about 1.34am. He had seen a man and a woman. He described the man and later identified Eddowes' clothes as those worn by the woman he had seen. His two companions, Levy and Harris, said that they had noticed very little. Levy did, however, attend Eddowes' inquest and, along with Lawende, gave evidence.

The inquest upon Elizabeth Stride was held in the Vestry Hall in Cable Street. The Coroner, once again, was Mr Wynne-Baxter.

Identification evidence was given by a fellow female lodger from the Flower and Dean Street doss-house. Doctor Blackwell, who had examined Stride's body whilst it was still warm, told the court that he thought the murderer had pulled his victim backwards by her scarf. He could not say whether she had been standing up or lying down when her throat was cut. She would have been unable to call out once her wind-pipe had been severed. He went on to say that the victim probably bled to death in less than two minutes. The cause of death was 'haemorrhage, through the partial severance of the left carotid artery'.

Doctor Phillips, who with Blackwell had performed the post-mortem upon Stride, told the court that apart from the throat injury there were no other marks upon the body apart from some partly-healed sores. Phillips believed that bruising on the victim's shoulders indicated that she had been forced to the ground and that her throat had been cut after she was on the ground.

The inquest on Catherine Eddowes opened three days later at the Golden Lane mortuary. The Coroner was Mr S.F. Langham.

A list, of Eddowes clothing, and property is appended to the Coroners papers. It is a motley assortment of rags and petticoats. I have reproduced the list here:

Black straw bonnet trimmed with green and black velvet and black beads black strings.
Black cloth jacket, initation fur edging around the collar, fur round sleeves.
Chintz skirt, three flounces, brown button on waistband.
Brown Linsey dress bodice, black velvet collar, brown metal buttons down front.
Grey stuff petticoat, white waistband.
Very old green Alpaca skirt.
Very old ragged blue skirt.
White calico chemise.
Mans white vest.
No drawers or stays.
Pair of mens lace-up boots.
One piece of red gauze silk
One large white handkerchief

Two unbleached calico pockets (a type of apron)
One blue striped pocket
One cotton pocket handkerchief - red and white border.
One pair of brown-ribbed stockings. Feet mended with white.
Twelve pieces of white rag.
One piece of white coarse linen.
One piece of blue and white shirting.
Two small blue bed ticking bags.
One tin box containing tea.
One tin box containing sugar
One piece of flannel and six pieces of soap.
One small tooth comb.
One white table knife.
One metal tea spoon.
One red leather cigarette case white metal fittings.
One empty tin matchbox.
One piece of red flannel containing pins and needles.
One ball of hemp (string) and one piece of old white apron.
Almost all of the clothing was bloodstained and showed signs of slashing.

Evidence of identification was given by Eliza Gold, a sister of the deceased.
Inspector Collard gave evidence that no money had been found on the body. He also confirmed that the fragment of material, found in Goulston Street, was from the apron which Eddowes had been wearing at the time of her death.

Doctor's Sequira and Brown provided the medical evidence.

Doctor Frederick Brown had conducted the post-mortem. He provided a very detailed report for the Coroner. After undressing the body, and noting that a piece of the deceased's ear had dropped from the clothing, the doctor continued:

'I made a post-mortem examination at half past two on Sunday afternoon. Rigor Mortis was well marked: body not quite cold. Green discolouration over the abdomen.
After washing the left hand carefully, a bruise, the size of a sixpence, recent and red, was discovered on the back of the left hand between the thumb and the first finger. A few small bruises on right shin of older date. The hands and arms were bronzed. No bruises on the scalp, the back of the body, or the elbows.
The face was very much mutilated. There was a cut about a quarter of an inch through the lower left eyelid dividing the structures completely through. The right eyelid was cut through to about half an inch.
There was a deep cut over the bridge of the nose extending from the left border of the nasal bone down near to the angle of the jaw on the right side of the cheek. This cut went into the bone and divided all the structures of the cheek except the mucuous membrane of the mouth.
The tip of the nose was quite detached, from the nose, by an oblique cut from the bottom of the nasal bone to where the wings of the nose join onto the face. A cut, from this, divided the upper lip and extended through the substance of the gum over the right upper lateral incisor tooth. About half an inch from the top of the nose was another oblique cut. There was a cut on the right angle of the mouth as if the cut of a point of a knife. The cut extended an inch and a half parallel with lower lip.
There was, on each side of the cheek, a cut which peeled up the skin, forming a triangular flap about an inch and a half. On the left cheek there were two abrasions of the epithelium under the left ear.
The throat was cut across to the extent of about six or seven inches. A superficial cut

commenced about an inch below, and about two and a half inches below and behind the left ear, and extended across the throat to about three inches below the lobe of the right ear. The big muscle across the throat was divided through on the left side. The large vessels, on the left side of the throat, were severed. The larynx was severed, and, below the vocal chord all the deep structures were severed to the bone, the knife marking intervertabral cartilages. The sheath of the vessels, on the right side, was just opened. The carotid artery had a fine hole opening. The internal jugular vein was opened an inch and a half - not divided. The blood vessels contained clot. All these injuries were performed by a sharp instrument like a knife and pointed.

The cause of death was haemorrhage from the left common carotid artery. The death was immediate and the mutilations were performed after death.

We examined the abdomen. The front walls were open from the breast bone to the pubes. The cut commenced opposite the enciform cartilage. The incision went upwards not penetrating the skin that was over the sternum. It then divided the enciform cartilage. The knife must have cut obliquely at the expense of the front surface of that cartilage.

Behind this, the liver was stabbed as if by the point of a sharp instrument. Below this there was another incision into the liver of about two and a half inches, and, below this the left lobe of the liver was slit through by a vertical cut. Two cuts were shewn by a jagging of the skin on the left side.

The abdominal walls were divided in the middle line to within a quarter of an inch of the navel. The cut then took a horizontal course for two inches and a half, and, made a parallel incision to the former incision, leaving the navel on a tongue of skin. Attached to the navel was two and a half inches of the lower part of the rectus muscle on the left side of the abdomen. The incision then took an oblique direction to the right and was shelving. The incision went down the right side of the vagina and rectum for half an inch behind the rectum.

There was a stab, of about an inch, on the left groin. This was done by a pointed instrument. Below this was a cut of three inches going through the perinium about the same extent.

An inch below the crease of the thigh was a cut extending from the anterior spine of the ilium obliquely down the inner side of the left thigh and seperating the left labium forming a flap of skin up to the groin. The left rectus muscle was not detached.

There was a flap of skin formed from the right thigh, attaching the right labium, and extending up to the spine of the ilium. The muscles on the right side, inserted into the frontal ligaments, were cut through.

The skin was retracted through the whole of the cut in the abdomen but the vessels were not clotted. Nor had there been any appreciable bleeding from the vessels. I draw the conclusion that the cut was made after death, and, there would not be much blood on the murderer. The cut was made by someone on the right side of the body kneeling below the middle of the body.

I removed the content of the stomach and placed it in a jar for further examination. There seemed very little in it, the way of food or fluid, but from the cut end partly digested farinaceous food escaped.

The intestines had been detached to a large extent from the mesentry. About two feet of the colon was cut away. The sygmoid flexure was invaginated into the rectum very tightly.

Right kidney pale and bloodless with slight congestion of the base of the pyramids.

There was a cut from the upper part of the slit on the under surface of the liver to the left side, an, another cut at right angles to this, which were about an inch and a half deep and two and a half inches long. Liver itself was healthy.

The gall bladder contained bile. The pancreas was cut, but not through, on the left side of the spinal column. Three and a half inches of the lower border of the spleen by half an inch was attached only to the peritoneum.

The peritoneal lining was cut through on the left side and the left kidney carefully taken out and removed. The left renal artery was cut through. I should say that someone who knew the position of the kidney must have done it.

The lining membrane over the uterus was cut through. The womb was cut through horizontally leaving a stump of three quarters of an inch. The rest of the womb had been taken away with some of the ligaments. The vagina and cervix of the womb was uninjured.

The bladder was healthy and uninjured and contained three or four ounces of water. There was a tongue like cut through the anterior wall of the abdominal aorta. The other organs were healthy.

There were no indications of connection.

I believe the perpetrator of the act must have had considerable knowledge of the position of the organs in the abdominal cavity and the way of removing them. The parts removed would be of no use for any professional purpose. It required a great deal of knowledge to have removed the kidney and to know where it was placed. Such a knowledge might be possessed by one in the habit of cutting up animals.

I think the perpetrator of this act had sufficient time or he would not have nicked the lower eyelids. It would take at least five minutes.

I cannot assign any reason for the parts being taken away. I feel sure there was no struggle. I believe it was the act of one person.

The throat had been instantly severed so that no noise could have been emitted. I should not expect too much blood to have been found on the person who had inflicted these wounds. The wounds could not have been self inflicted.'

Doctor Brown then dealt with the matter of the fragment of apron found by Police Constable Long.

' My attention was called to the apron. It was the corner of the apron with a string attached. The blood spots were of recent origin. I have seen the portion of an apron produced by Doctor Phillips which, was stated to have been found in Goulston Street. It is impossible to say it is human blood. I fitted the piece of apron which had a new piece of material on it which had evidently been sewn on to the piece I have. The seams of the two actually corresponding. Some blood, and, apparently, faecal matter was found on the portion found in Goulston Street. I believe the wounds on the face to have been done to disfigure the corpse.'

The two other doctors, Sequeira and Saunders who had attended the post-mortem, did not think that the killer had shown any special anatomical knowledge, yet the killer had, somehow, located and severed the left kidney, a difficult organ to find. It is, of course, quite possible that the killer, while hacking his way through the body cavity, had chanced upon the kidney. The murderer took the kidney away with him along with the victim's uterus and womb.'

Joseph Lawende told the court that he had left the Imperial Club shortly after 1.30am. He had walked a little way ahead of the others when they saw a couple standing together at the Duke Street passage which leads into Mitre Square. He described the woman as wearing a black bonnet and Jacket. He had already identified these articles earlier at the police station. When asked by the Coroner to describe the man, Mr Crawford, representing the police at the inquest, asked that no details be given. The Coroner did however, establish that Lawende had given a description to the police. Lawende had added that he doubted that he would be able to identify the man if he saw him again.

Joseph Levy, one of Lawende's drinking companions, confirmed Lawende's story in all of the details, even though he claimed to have seen very little. Harry Harris, the other companion, did not attend the inquest. He later told reporters from the 'Evening News' that he had not paid any attention to the couple and that all that he could see was the man's back. He also stated that it was his opinion that his two friends, Lawende and Levy, did not see any more of the man than he had.

Catherine Eddowes was buried on 8th October. Her body had been placed in a polished elm coffin with oak mountings. The coffin, donated by a local undertaker, was placed in an open glass carriage drawn by horses. The funeral cortege was escorted by a contingent of City and

Metropolitan police officers. It made its way through St Marys, Whitechapel, and along the Mile End Road. Onlookers lined the route five-deep. On through Bow and Stratford and eventually to Ilford Cemetery where over five hundred people attended the graveside service. No mention was made of the manner in which the deceased had met her death.

All of this was in total contrast to the funeral of Elizabeth Stride. Two days before Eddowes extravagant funeral Stride's body had been quietly interred in a paupers' grave at the East London Cemetery, West Ham.

Some theorists have argued that Elizabeth Strides murder could not have been the work of Jack the Ripper. Some claim that it is impossible for the killer to have reached Mitre Square and killed, and disembowelled Catharine Eddowes, in the time available. But Mitre Square is not that far away and it only takes about eleven, or twelve minutes to walk there from Berner Street, at a reasonable pace. However, I would concede that it is possible that Elizabeth Stride may have been another victim of the same person, or gang, which appeared to specialise in prostitute mugging. The knife wounds to Strides throat are reminiscent of the attack on Ada Wilson. Furthermore, according to Doctor Phillips, like Ada Wilson, Elizabeth Stride had been killed with a short round-bladed knife. In my opinion it is unlikely that Jack the ripper would kill one victim with one type of knife and, only 15 minutes later, kill another victim using a different knife. We must accept that Stride may not have been a victim of Jack the Ripper.

It is possible to assume that Stride had completed her business with the young Englishman with whom she had been seen with at 11.45.pm. According to Police Constable Smith she was evidently, with the same man three-quarters of an hour later at 12.30am. It was about fifteen minutes later that Elizabeth Stride was seen to be arguing with the drunk, evidently not the young Englishman, who threw her to the ground. The argument, that Elizabeth Stride may have been killed by a prostitute mugger can be strengthened by the fact that no money was found on Strides person. Though this is not conclusive since it is also quite possible that she had earned no money.

The day after Catharine Eddowes' funeral the 'Evening News' published an article claiming that Joseph Lawende was being looked after by the police, to the extent that all of his expenses were being paid, and that he was being guarded by police officers. The paper contended that Harry Harris had told them that neither Lawende or Levy had seen any more than he... which was nothing. The paper claimed that Levy was '..absolutely obstinate' and refused to give the slightest information. 'He leaves one to infer that he knows something, but is afraid to be called on the inquest. Hence he assumes a knowing air.'

Like Israel Schwartz, who had seen a man tormenting a woman in Berner Street, and had been kept under wraps by the Metropolitan Police, Lawende was now being closely observed.

Clearly, at this point, the police believed that one, or all, of these men might have seen Jack the Ripper.
A rumour, that a strange man had been seen on the streets on the night of the double-murder, carrying a shiny black bag, meant that anyone known to possess one was a suspect and, as such, was likely to be lynched by the mob if caught. Such bags, which were in fact quite common, very soon went out of fashion.

One curious aspect of the killers actions that night was the leaving of possibly the only real clue the killer ever left. The piece of Eddowes apron found in Goulston Street. It is worth giving this clue some consideration. More so perhaps than the graffiti since we dont know who wrote it. But we do know that the apron came from the killers victim. We should consider that, according to PC Alfred long who discovered the apron at 2.55am, it had not been there when he patrolled the area 35 minutes earlier at 2.20am. Given that Eddowes was murdered no later than 1.44am, the time that her body was discovered it follows that the killer was in possession of the apron fragment for at least 34 minutes. Goulston Street is only a few minutes walk from Mitre Square, where Eddowes was murdered, so one may ask - Where was the killer during that 34 minutes.? And what was his purpose in cutting away and removing a piece of the victims apron. We may never know the answer to the first question but there are several possibilities regarding the apron. The killer had eviscerated his victim and removed a kidney. He may have used the material in which to wrap his trophy. This may account for the blood spots found on the cloth, but what about the faeces? It is highly likely that the killer might have punctured the victims bowel while performing his mutilations and that he picked up faeces upon his knife, or upon his trophy. If the cloth was used to clean his knife he may have transferred it that way. Another possibility is that the killer found himself caught short, not suprising if he had just almost been caught in the act in Berner Street. He may have used the cloth to clean himself. This may account for the time between the murder of Eddowes, at 1.44am, and the finding of the cloth just over an hour later.

On the sixteenth of October, four days after the inquest on Eddowes had closed, George Lusk, the chairman of the recently-formed Whitechapel Vigilance Committee was sitting indoors at his home in Alderney Road, Mile End, when a small packet was delivered to him by a man, described by one witness as being, dressed in clerical garb. The packet, wrapped in brown paper, and addressed to Mr Lusk, was said to measure a little over three square inches. Inside was a kidney and a letter which read:-

Mr Lusk Sir,
I send you half the Kidne I took from one Woman praserved it for you
 tother piece I fried and ate it was very nise
 I may send you the bloody knif that took it out if you only wate a whil longer
signed Catch me when you can Mishter Lusk

George Lusk's response to this weird gift was to dismiss it at first as a practical joke. We are told that over the next few days he showed the kidney to his friends. They appeared to show more concern to discover whether the kidney was genuine or not. Eventually Lusk was persuaded to take the kidney to a doctor for examination. They took the kidney to the surgery of Doctor Wiles at 56 Mile End Road. Doctor Wiles' locum, Mr Reed, took the kidney to Doctor Openshaw of the London Hospital. According to Reed, Openshaw told him that the kidney belonged to a female. It was part of a left kidney and the woman must have been a heavy drinker.

On the 19th October, a press association report elaborated upon Doctor Openshaws opinion, by claiming that the kidney had belonged to a woman aged about 45, and, had been removed from her body within the last three weeks. The conclusion, therefore, was that this must be the missing part of Eddowes kidney. However, on the same day Doctor Openshaw gave an interview to The Star newspaper, in which he claimed that it was impossible to say that the kidney was female or to determine how long ago it had been removed.

Lusk, and the other committee members, Harris, Reeves and Lawton, took the kidney and the letter to Leman Street police station where it was handed to Inspector George Abberline. It was then sent on to Major Henry Smith, the acting head of the City of London Police, in whose area the murder of Eddowes had taken place. The, much travelled, kidney was now forwarded on, by Major Smith, to Doctor Gordon Brown. He had performed the post-mortem on the body of Eddowes. His task was to establish whether the kidney, now in his possession, was the one which had been taken from Eddowes' body by the killer. Unfortunately though, the body of Eddowes had been buried eleven days earlier, so any real comparison would have been impossible, unless the doctors performing the post-mortem had removed and preserved the relevant tissues.

Any report, which Doctor Brown may have made, alas, no longer seems to exist. It is therefore impossible to say, with any certainty, that the Lusk kidney was the kidney missing from Eddowes' body.

The writer of a letter sent to Doctor Openshaw, on 29th October, was in no doubt that the kidney once belonged to Eddowes. He wrote;

Old Boss
you was rite it was the left kidny I was going to hopperate agin clos to your ospitle just as I was goin to dror mi nife along of er bloomin throte them cusses of coppers spoilt the game but I guess I wil be on the job soon and I will send you another bit of innerds.
Jack the Ripper

Was the writer of these letters the real killer? If so then the kidney was probably that which was taken from Eddowes. Likewise if the kidney did belong to Eddowes then the letter writer was probably the killer.

In a period of just over four weeks Scotland Yard had received, into their files, over 1,400 letters in relation to the Whitechapel killings. Many were offering advice or making accusations against someone. Some were bogus confessions. About 150 purported to have been written by the murderer.

A recently discovered letter, found still sealed in the Public Records Office bundle and signed Jack the Ripper, is dated 17th September (HO144/221/A49301C) it reads:

17th September 1888

Dear Boss
So now they say that I am a Yid
 when will they lern Dear old Boss?
You an me know the truth Dont we.
Lusk can look forever hell never find me
But I am rite under his nose all the time.
I watch them looking for me and it gives me fits ha ha
I love my work and I shant stop until I do get buckled and
Even then watch out for your old pal Jacky

Catch me if you Can
Jack the Ripper

Ps Sorry about the blood still messy from
 The last one. What a pretty necklace I
 gave her.

The provenance of this letter has not yet been determined. But if it proves to be a contemporary letter from 1888 it will carry the distinction of being the first to use the name of Jack the Ripper.

The best known letter is the 'Dear Boss' letter dated 29th September, 1888. Though the letter was denounced by Sir Robert Anderson as a hoax, it was nevertheless printed and published as both handbills and posters and distributed throughout the capital. The letter informs the reader that;

'....the next job I do I shall clip the ladys ears off...' (See appendix for the letter in full)

At the inquest on Eddowes, Doctor Brown had told the court that the lobe of the right ear had been obliquely cut through, thus suggesting an attempt to remove it.
Indeed a postcard had been sent. Dated the 1st October, and apparently written in the same hand and signed 'Jack the Ripper', it read;

I wasnt codding dear old Boss when I gave you the tip   youll hear about saucy Jackys work tomorrow   double event this time number one squealed a bit couldnt finish straight off   had no time to get ears for police thanks for keeping this letter back till I got to work again
Jack the Ripper

It has been suggested that the writer of these letters, and in particular the postcard, is demonstrating a knowledge of the injuries inflicted upon the victim Elizabeth Stride, which had not yet been made public. But the postcard was, in fact, posted after the murders and after the facts, regarding Strides injuries, were generally known, - and after the 'Dear Boss' letter had been published in the early-morning papers of Monday October 1st.

It is curious, however, that the reference, in what may be the first Dear Boss letter, dated 17th September, to the mutilation of Annie Chapman, and described, by the writer as a pretty necklace. had not been made public in any detail at the time the letter was written. It was known that Chapmans throat had been cut but details of the mutilations (ieThe pretty necklace?) were not disclosed to the inquest until 19th September two days after the letter was written.

Furthermore the 17th September Dear Boss letter and the Dear Boss letter of the 27th September, and the Lusk letter, of the 15th October accompanying the kidney appear, to the untrained eye, to have been penned by the same unknown hand.

At Scotland Yard there was some scepticism as to the authenticy of these communications. But notwithstanding this they were still reproduced, as posters and handbills, and, subsequently plastered across the capital with the request that anyone recognising the handwriting should communicate with the police.

According to Donald McCormick (The Identity of Jack the Ripper - 1959) a certain Doctor Dutton, a close friend of Inspector Abberline, examined the letters and declared that thirty four of them were written in the same hand.

Thirty two year old Doctor Thomas Dutton lived in Uxbridge Road, Shepherds Bush, on the west side of London. McCormick claimed that Dutton had specialised in microscopy and microphotography. It was this 'specialised knowledge' which Dutton was now able to bring to bear on the case in his consideration of the handwriting. Among those letters, which Dutton claimed were written in the same hand, were two from Liverpool and one from Glasgow. The first Liverpool letter made reference to The Minories, a street not far from Mitre Square. The second Liverpool letter gave a Prince William Street address. It taunted the police...

'What fools the police are. I even give them the name of the street where I am living'.

The Glasgow letter told police that in future Jack may be using a...

'... Scotch Dirk... that will tickle up their ovaries.'

McCormick claims to have seen, and thus quoted from, the extensive notes, made by Dutton, on the matter. These would appear to have comprised a part of a volume of hand-written notes and reminiscences written by Dutton and titled 'Chronicles of Crime'.

Thomas Dutton was born in London and educated at the Bayswater Grammar School. In 1876 he attended Aberdeen University and, two years later, Durham University, where he gained some impressive degrees. Apart from his practice, at 25 New Cavendish Street, Harley Street, he was also:
 Honorary surgeon to the Uxbridge Road Maternity and Child Welfare Clinic
 Honorary Surgeon to the Royal Defence Corps (Hammersmith)
 A fellow of the Hunterian Society
 A member of the Infant Welfare Maternity Centre
 Vice-Chairman of the Pure Foods Society
 Medical Officer to the 'SS Elysia', Royal Marine Tongariro, and
 Medical Officer to the 'SS Argonaut'.
 His hobbies were yachting and swimming.
 He was also a member of the Shepherds Bush Cricket Club.

In spite of all of this Dutton still found time to write the following books;-
 'Sea Sickness, Cause, Treatment, and Prevention'.
 'Indigestion Clearly Explained, Treatment and Diet'.
 'Obesity, its Cause and Treatment'.
 'Cult of the Open Air Treatment of Tuberculosis'.
 'Digestion and Diet, and
 'Every Mothers Book and Young Wives Guide'.

It is a great pity that Dutton appears to have been unable to publish anything at all which related to his alleged passion for understanding the criminal mind. His hand-written memoir, 'Chronicles of Crime', allegedly seen, and copied by McCormick, in 1932, has long since vanished, together with any report or memoir which he may have made for Abberline on the authenticity of the letters. When, in 1971, I spoke with Donald McCormick, he claimed that all of his notes, transcribed from Duttons Chronicles of Crime had long since vanished

Sir Robert Anderson, in charge of the CID, claimed, in his memoirs, that the 'Jack the Ripper' letter 'which is preserved in the Police Museum at New Scotland Yard, is the creation of an enterprising London journalist.' Senior policemen were, it would seem, still very sceptical about the authenticity of the letters and did not ascribe any real significance to them. On the 10th October Charles Warren told Geoffrey Lushington 'I think the whole thing a hoax but we are bound to try to ascertain the writer in any case.' Putting a name to the 'enterprising journalist' has become yet another branch of this compelling mystery. It is another tangent where pursuit of the hoaxer becomes almost as compulsive as trying to catch the killer.

A recently discovered letter, written in 1913 by Chief Inspector John Littlechild, claims that the belief at Scotland Yard was that Tom Bulling, of the Central News Agency, together with his Chief, Charles Moore were the originators, if not the actual authors of the Jack the Ripper letters. The implication is that they contrived the letters so as to bolster their own reputations, and those of their agency, as well as the agencies, and their own, income. This suggestion may also explain how it was that some of the letters contained information, about the murders, which had not been made public.

A journalist, named Best, who claimed to have covered the Whitechapel murders as a freelance jounalist, has also been suggested as the author of the Dear Boss letter and postcard. Best, in later life, had confided this information to the unnamed writer of an article which appeared in the August 1966 issue of Crime and Detection. Best had told the writer that he, and a provincial colleague were responsible for all the Ripper letters, to keep the business alive. Best had suggested to the writer that a close reading of The Star, of the time might be informative, and that an experienced graphologist with an open mind would be able to find in the original letters numerous earmarks of an experienced journalist at work.

We may deduce therefore that the first letters which purport to come from the killer may well have been penned by an enterprising journalist hoping to increase newspaper circulation. But, the publicity, which resulted from the widespread publication of these communications, in the form of posters and handbills published by the Metropolitan police, not only created widespread panic among the population in general, but also, undoubtedly, fuelled the imaginations of the many subsequent hoax letter writers. This may help to explain the close similarities in the prose and style of many of the letters. The spelling, the style, and the general content of the first letters were splashed into the public domain as posters and handbills and, therefore, available for any mindless individual to emulate.

A very comprehensive study of all of the letters, currently held on record, at the Public Records Office, has been undertaken by Stewart Evans and Keith Skinner and is published in a lavishly produced book Jack the Ripper Letters from Hell (Sutton Publishing 2001). A brilliantly conceived sourcebook it is a must for any serious student of the case.

Four women were in their graves. Women murdered in a most brutal way. Two of them laid open and disembowelled. Two had their uteruses removed and, in Chapman's case, it had been taken away by the killer.

Victorians asked what kind of madman it was that could do such a thing. What kind of madness was it that could motivate one human being to hunt down and destroy another in such a fashion?

Since Wynne-Baxter's bold assertion, at the inquest upon Catherine Eddowes, that the purpose of the murder 'was to possess the missing organ', Many Londoners, particularly in the East-End, were too terrified to go out at night. During the day the children of the area taunted each other. At night their parents told them to come indoors 'before Jack gets you.'

There was considerable public dissatisfaction and anger with the police. They had failed to apprehend the killer and appeared to be powerless in their attempts to prevent further outrages. There was considerable dissention within the police service as well. Not only within the ranks but also at the highest levels.

The London police were divided then, as they are still, into two separate and distinct forces. In 1888 The Metropolitan police was commanded by General Sir Charles Warren. The much smaller City of London police was commanded by Major Henry Smith with the rank of Acting Police Commissioner. Warren and Smith did not get along with each other. The somewhat blimpish Warren was, in fact, despised by Major Smith.

Since the murder of Catherine Eddowes had taken place within the boundary of the City of London, Major Smith, and his City police force, had now become involved in the case. Major Smith had adopted an investigative approach to the case by sending out scores of plain-clothed police officers to pick up gossip and other tit-bits of information. Warren however, in contrast, forbade his men to enter a public house, even in the line of duty.

Charles Warren's action - ordering the removal of the writing on the Goulston Street wall - had exasperated Major Smith. Smith described the action as an 'unpardonable blunder.' He was later tentatively supported in this view by Sir Robert Anderson who stated that...

'the writing on the wall may have been written, and I think probably was written, to throw the police off the scent, to divert suspicion from the Gentiles and to throw it upon the Jews. It may have been written by the murderer or it may not. To obliterate the words, which might have given us a most valuable clue, most especially after I had sent a man to stand over them until they were photographed, was not only indiscreet, but unwarrantable.'

He added that...

'it was done by the officers of the uniformed force... upon an order given by one of my colleagues.' (Warren)

Sir Robert Anderson had been forced to return to his post from a holiday in Switzerland, where he had been since his appointment as head of the CID following the sudden resignation, on 31st August, of his predecessor James Monro.

Anderson swept into action and gave an order that all available constables should be sent into the area to bolster-up the 546 constables, 44 sergeants, and 29 inspectors already attached to 'H' division - Whitechapel. The effect, of this flood of extra police to the area seems, however, to have achieved very little except to inflame even further the feelings of the local population, who were not known for their love of 'peelers'. Confidence in the police was certainly very low indeed.

General Warren had always believed that the police should be independent of statutory controls. He would have liked to have organised and operated the police in a way very similar to the army. He was opposed in this aim, not only by the Home Secretary, Henry Mathews, but also by many of his own subordinate officers.

One such officer had been James Monro. Monros resignation on the eve of the first murder had been forced by Warren. But, although Monro had resigned his position, in the Police force, he had in fact been moved sideways to the Home Office where he was put in charge of a secret department. (This secret department was later to be known as the Special Branch). Monro's duties were unspecified, but Home Secretary Mathews later explained to the House of Commons that Monro would be an advisor to him in all matters relating to crime. Now, to Warren's chagrin, Monro had become a much more powerful and potent enemy than he had been before.

James Monro was born in Edinburgh in 1840. The son of a solicitor, he was educated in Scotland and Germany before joining the Indian Civil Service in 1858. Five years later, aged 23, he married. In 1877 he was appointed to the position of Inspector General of Police. In 1884 Monro retired from the Indian Civil Service and made the journey back to England where he took up the appointment of Assistant Commissioner of the Metropolitan Police.

Sometime in June 1888 Monro started to lobby Henry Mathews, the Home Secretary, on the behalf of one of his close personal friends, for the newly created position of Assistant Chief Constable. His friend, Sir Melville MacNaghten had known and worked with James Monro in India. At first Warren had grudgingly agreed to allow MacNaghten's name to go forward with his own endorsement. The Home office accepted MacNaghten for the position but, Warren suddenly withdrew his recommendation with the explanation that circumstances had come to his knowledge which made it undesirable that the gentleman in question (MacNaghten) should be appointed.

Warrens stated objections were that MacNaghten, while a planter in India, had provoked some peace-loving natives so much that they had attacked and badly beaten him. Warren claimed that MacNaghten was the one man in India who had been beaten by Hindoos. Warren also pointed out that MacNaghten had no qualifications for the job of Assistant Chief Constable while plenty of well-qualified men were available for the position.

It is probable however that the real reason was the realisation that the appointment of one of Monro's oldest and closest friends may tip the balance of power, in the police hierarchy, in Monro's favour.

Now however, Monro was at the Home Office and he was clearly very closely involved in overseeing the hunt for the Whitechapel killer. He seems also to have retained some considerable influence over his old CID department. On 22nd September, 1888, Henry Mathews, the Home Secretary wrote to his private secretary, Evelyn Ruggles-Brise ...'...stimulate the police about the Whitechapel murders. Monro might be willing to give a hint to the CID people if necessary.' This leaves no doubt but that Monro must have been in possession of information which had not yet been passed to the detective officers of the CID.

By the beginning of November Charles Warren had had enough. He had been lampooned in the press, criticised for ineptness and had his authority undermined, not only by Monro's appointment to the Home Office, but also by his own officers, who increasingly disagreed with Warren's internal administration of the Metropolitan Police. His report justifying his actions in obliterating the writing on the wall, at Goulston Street, however understandable given the circumstances, had clearly not been enough. Warren resigned, as Commissioner, on 8th November.

As if to rub salt into the unhappy Warren's wounded pride, James Monro was now appointed to the freshly vacated position as commissioner. Monro was, however, ordered to continue with his Home Office duties as head of the secret department. Six months later he was successful in his bid to secure an appointment for his old pal Melville MacNaghten.

There can be no doubt that James Monro was the one person who would have known all there was to know about the investigations, and any conclusions reached, in connection with the Whitechapel Murders.

James Monro eventually resigned from the police two years later and returned to India where he set up a religious retreat called DAYABARI - abode of mercy. He returned again to England in 1902 and died, in Chiswick West London, aged 80, in 1920.

Melville MacNaghten, in his memoirs, writes affectionately about Monro...

'I doubt whether any of the gentlemen who filled his position before or after his time ever gained more completely the affection and confidence of their officers.'

Clearly these two men had been very good friends. There can be no doubt that they would have discussed the Whitechapel murders. MacNaghten, though not appointed to the police until June 1889, would, without any doubt, have shared the confidences of the only man in the police heirarchy who knew what both hands were doing as far as the 'Ripper' investigations were concerned.

But before these political machinations could come into play the killer struck again.

Twenty five years old Mary Kelly had not paid her rent for several weeks. It was thus that on the morning of Friday 9th November her landlord, John McCarthy, sent his assistant, Thomas Bowyer, around to collect the arrears.

Mary Kelly lived in a tiny, ground-floor back room which was partitioned off from the rest of the house. Her room had its own front door, numbered 13, which opened up onto a small enclosed courtyard known as Millers Court. Entry, to the courtyard, was through a tunnel-like alleyway which led, directly, onto Dorset Street. Known locally as Dosset Street, no doubt due to the large numbers of casual sleepers, the Dorset Street area was, without doubt, one of the capital's most criminally infested areas. Even up until its eventual demolition, in the 1960s, by which time it had changed its name to Duval Street, it was still unofficially, very much a no-go area for lone policemen.

Mary Kelly, like Elizabeth Stride, had invented a romantic past for herself. She claimed to have French ancestry and often insisted that her real name was Marie Jeanette Kelly. She had, or so it is believed been born in Limerick, and when still young, her father, John Kelly, had taken his family to Carmarthenshire where he became a foreman in an iron-foundry. At sixteen Mary married a collier named Davies. He was killed in a mine explosion a year or two later. By the time the mine owners decided to pay Mary a small widow's pension, she had already started to support herself by prostitution, in and around the Tiger Bay area of Cardiff. She appears to have arrived in London sometime during 1884.

It is said that at first she worked in a high-class London brothel where she met a gentleman who took her to Paris. She soon, however, became disillusioned with life in France and returned to London after a few weeks. All of this may be true, but she appears to have ended up working the area of the notorious Ratcliffe Highway. From there she graduated to Stepney, Bow, and the beats of Bethnal Green. Eventually Mary ended-up living with a Billingsgate fish-porter named Joseph Barnett. She lived with him for almost two years. Just recently though Barnett had moved out after a row with Mary over her wish to give shelter to a prostitute friend. Sometimes though, it would seem Joseph Barnett would visit and stay for the night.But Mary appeared to be alone on the night of Thursday 8th November.

Two people, however, did see Mary Kelly that night. One was a young man, 22 years old George Hutchinson who claimed to have occasionally patronised her. The other was Jack the Ripper. Curiously Hutchinson was not called to give evidence at Kelly's inquest. Instead a statement made by him was admitted to the proceedings. Inspector Abberline had taken the statement from Hutchinson, at the Commercial Street Police Station on the evening of the 12th November and forwarded it to the inquest with a covering note in which he stated that he was of the opinion that the statement was true.

Hutchinson had told the police that he had met Mary Kelly at about 2.00am on the morning of Friday 9th November near Thrawl Street. He was walking alone having no money for a bed. According to Hutchinson he was accosted by Mary Kelly who asked him for sixpence. Hutchinson explained that he had no money. Mary shrugged, wished him 'good morning', and walked off in the direction of Thrawl Street. As she did so Hutchinson saw a man walking from the opposite direction. As they met, the man tapped Mary on the shoulder and said something which made Mary laugh. Hutchinson was intrigued to see what would happen next. The well-dressed man was aged about 34-35, about five feet six inches in height. He had a pale complexion, dark hair and a slight moustache which was curled at the ends. He wore a long dark coat - the collar and cuffs were trimmed with astrakhan. Underneath he wore a dark-coloured Jacket and a light coloured waistcoat holding a very thick gold chain. His trousers were dark, with button boots, and gaiters with white buttons. His white shirt, and black tie, were fastened with a horseshoe pin. According to the highly observant Hutchinson, the man looked respectable and Jewish. The man carried a small parcel, in his left hand, with

34

a strap around it. Hutchinson, who must have been quite close, heard Mary say to the man... 'alright.' The man replied... 'you will be alright for what I have told you.' The man then put his arm around Mary's shoulder and together they walked towards Hutchinson who was, by now, leaning against the lamp-post outside The Queens Head public house. The man kept his dark felt hat pulled down low across his eyes.

Hutchinson claimed that he had followed the couple into Dorset Street and watched for a while as they stood at the entrance to Millers Court. Hutchinson then heard Mary say 'alright my dear, come along, you will be comfortable'. The man then put his hand upon her shoulder and kissed her. The couple then disappeared into the entrance which led to her room. Hutchinson evidently hoped that Mary's client might not be too long about his business, and then she might invite him in for the rest of the night, since he told the police that he had waited for about three-quarters of an hour to see if they came out again. But they did not, and so, he walked off.

The following morning saw the landlords assistant Thomas Bowyer on his mission to collect Marys rent. He walked through the archway at the side of McCarthys shop and into the dingy little courtyard behind. He knocked upon Marys door. There was no reply. Thinking that Mary might have been hiding from him he tried to open the door. It was locked. He looked through the keyhole and noticed that the key was not in the lock. He went to the side of the building and tried to see through her window. The top right-hand pane of glass was broken, so Bower, taking care not to cut himself on the jagged glass, reached inside and pulled aside the flimsy curtain. His eyes took in the scene.

The mattress, on the bed, was soaked in blood. Upon it lay a raw mass of flesh. Mary Kelly's throat had been cut from ear to ear. Her ears, and her nose, had been cut off. She had been partially skinned and her entire abdomen had been laid open. She had been entirely disembowelled. Her liver had been cut away and placed upon her thigh. Pieces of intestine and flesh had been left lying around the body. One of her severed breasts had been placed under her head. The other was by her right foot. The flesh from the front of her body had been placed upon a table next to the bed. Mary Kelly's heart had been cut out. It was never found. Several photographs of the scene were taken.

Sir Charles Warren, whose resignation took effect from that day, had ordered that, in the event of another Jack the Ripper murder, the body was not to be disturbed until the bloodhounds had been called in. The problem was that no one knew where the bloodhounds were. So it was not until almost three hours after Bowyer's discovery that the door was eventually broken down and the room entered.

It was a poorly furnished room, about twelve feet square. Apart from the old bedstead, there were two old tables and one chair. The bedclothes had been turned-down. There was no suggestion that any struggle had taken place, and, although a careful search of the room was made no knife or instrument was found. The scene was photographed.

Surgeon, and ripperologist, Nick Warren has determined, from the photographs, that the splitting of Mary Kellys thighbone was inflicted by an axe or a hatchet. This view appears to be confirmed by a report in The Globe 16th February 1891. The reporter describes his visit to the Convict Office at Scotland Yard where he was shown a hatchet said to have been used by the Whitechapel murderer during his attack on the Dorset Street victim. However, given the statement that no knife or instrument was found in the room the provenance of the convict office hatchet must remain doubtful.

The opinion, of those who saw what remained of the body was that the killer must have taken at least three hours to perform his ghastly work. It was clear, from the contents of the fireplace, that a blazing fire had been going for some time, so much so that the heat from it had melted the handle of a tin kettle which stood nearby. It was believed that it was by the light from this fire that the killer had performed his dissection of the body.

At 3.50 that afternoon a one-horse carriers cart, with an ordinary tarpaulin cover was driven into Dorset Street, and halted outside Millers Court. News soon got around the area that the body was about to be removed and a great crowd of people descended into Dorset Street. A crowd tried to rush the police cordon which had been set up at the Commercial Street end of Dorset Street. 'The Times' of the 10th of November described it thus:

'The crowd, which pressed round the van, was of the humblest class, but the demeanour of the poor people was all that could be described. Ragged caps were doffed and slatternly-looking women shed tears as the shell, covered with a ragged-looking cloth, was placed in the van.'

What remained of Mary Kelly was trundled off, to the Shoreditch mortuary, followed by a ragbag of curious onlookers.

At almost precisely the same time, and just less than two miles away, in complete contrast to this sorry little procession the new Lord Mayor of London was waving to the crowds from the window of his gilded carriage as it made its way to the Mansion House. As the Lord Mayor, and his guests sat down to a sumptuous banquet. Two surgeons commenced the task of reassembling Mary Kellys corpse so that it could be, hopefully, identified.

The police responded, to this latest outrage, with the knee-jerk reaction of rounding-up the usual suspects and searching the common lodging-houses in the area.

Throughout the following day, Sunday 11th November, an intense excitement swept through London's East End. Several thousand sightseers had converged upon Dorset Street, all clamouring for a glimpse of the scene of this latest and most awful murder. The people of East London were angry. Ugly mobs formed and roamed the area seeking release from the pent-up anger and frustration which they felt at this most awful outrage. They called again for the resignation of Charles Warren, being unaware that Warren had already resigned.

Police rescued one man from a lynch-mob at the corner of Wentworth Street. The man, somewhat naively, had attracted attention to himself by painting his face with blackened cork in such a way as to resemble a skull, and standing on the corner of the street declaring himself to be Jack the Ripper. The Eastenders were in no mood for jokes. The man was later identified as Doctor Holt of Willesden. He explained that he had been in the habit of disguising himself and patrolling the streets of Whitechapel in order to catch Jack the Ripper. He was released from Leman street police station in the early hours of Monday morning, 12th November, after the mob had gone home for the night.

Later that same day the inquest, on Mary Kelly, opened at the Shoreditch Town Hall. The coroner was Roderick MacDonald MP, a surgeon and Coroner for North East Middlesex.

The inquest opened with a row, between a member of the jury and the Coroner, over jurisdiction. The juryman claimed that they, the jury, had been called from the Shoreditch district, when the murder had been committed in the Spitalfields district. The Coroner insisted that jurisdiction lay where the body lay, and not where the murder took place, and that would be the end of the matter. The jury was then sworn-in and they viewed the body in the mortuary adjoining Shoreditch church. They were then taken to view Mary Kelly's room at Millers Court, before returning to the Town Hall.

Joseph Barnett, who had recently lived with Kelly, was questioned. He told the Court that he had seen the body and had identified it by the eyes and the ears. 'I am certain it is the same woman'. He had last seen Mary at about 7.45pm on the day before she had met her death. She had been in her room, at 13 Millers Court, with her prostitute friend Maria Harvey. Barnett was unhappy about Mary's friendship with Maria and so he had separated from her on the 30th October. Barnett claimed that Mary had asked him, on several occasions, to read to her about the murders. He claimed that she had seemed to be afraid of someone though this was no particular individual.

A neighbour of Mary's, the widow Cox, told the Coroner that she had heard a man leaving Millers Court at about 6.15am. Elizabeth Prater, a prostitute who occupied the room above Mary's, testified that she had not been able to find a client that night and so she had gone to bed at about 1.20am. Neither woman had seen a light burning at number 13. Prater claimed that a cat had woken her up at about 3.45am, and, as she turned over to go to sleep again she heard a very faint cry of 'Murder'. Sarah Lewis corroborated this. She had gone to Millers Court to visit a friend. She saw a man standing at the entrance. (This was probably Hutchinson who had claimed to have 'hung around' for three quarters of an hour.)

Sarah Lewis told the Court that she had been visiting her friend Mrs Keyler who lived at no 2 Millers Court. She had dozed in her friend's armchair. She said that she had heard no noise until she heard the Spitalfields church clock strike the half-hour at 3.30am. She did not sleep after that. At almost 4.00am she too heard a woman crying 'Murder'. Like Elizabeth Prater she had only heard the one scream.

The next witness was Caroline Maxwell. Her husband was the lodging-house keeper at 14 Dorset Street opposite the entrance to Millers Court. She did not know Mary very well and had only spoken to her once or twice, but she swore on oath that she had seen Mary Kelly standing at the entrance to Millers Court at 8.00am on the Friday morning. She said that Mary had not looked well. This is not surprising since, by all other accounts, Mary had been dead for some four hours before Maxwell claims to have seen her. Caroline Maxwell's evidence has been used to suggest that the body found in Mary's room might not have been that of Mary Kelly and that it might well have been the body of one of her prostitute friends whom Mary often allowed to use her room. However, the Coroner warned the jury that Caroline Maxwell's testimony was at such variance with the known facts that they should be careful in their consideration of it.

Now it was time for the medical evidence.

The room quietened as Doctor Phillips took the stand. The Coroner had indicated that he would only be taking preliminary evidence at this hearing and that the details could be enquired into when the inquest reconvened. Phillips told the inquest that the cause of death was severance of the right carotid artery. The jury wanted more. But it was all that they were going to get.

The Coroner, much to the surprise, and annoyance, of the jury, press, and those who had managed to gain entry to the proceedings, then announced that... 'there is other evidence which I do not propose to call. For if we make public every fact, brought forward in connection with this terrible murder, the ends of justice might be retarded.'

At that, and with the consent of the bewildered jury, the Coroner formally recorded a verdict of 'wilful murder by person or persons unknown' and closed the inquest.

Not only was this a highly irregular procedure but clearly a failure, on the part of the Coroner, to discharge his common-law duty to enquire into, and establish precisely, the nature of any injuries upon the body of the deceased. Furthermore, and most importantly in a case of this importance, it meant that there was no adequate cross-examination of the witnesses.

This peculiar action of the Coroner, together with the illegal removal of Mary Kelly's body out of the district in which she was murdered, suggests a conspiracy to suppress some evidence which the police were anxious should not be made public.

If Mary Kelly's body had not been removed from the Spitalfields district, the inquest upon her would have been heard by the outspoken Wynne-Baxter. Wynne-Baxter had already caused a sensation with his assertion that Jack the Ripper's motive was to... 'possess the missing organs.'

Although the Coroner's actions have been rightly criticised, it is clear that an even greater panic might have ensued if the public were made aware of what was now becoming only too apparent to the authorities. Wynne-Baxter, at the inquest on Catherine Eddowes, had put his finger on the very point that the authorities were now trying to suppress. They knew now that they were not dealing with an ordinary killer. They knew that they were dealing with a madman whose desire was not just to kill prostitutes, but to reap a bloody harvest of bodily organs. There can be little doubt but that this was the true reason behind the decision to hold the inquest on Mary Kelly, out of the jurisdiction of the flamboyant and critically outspoken Wynne-Baxter.

Thus the evidence was suppressed. There was, naturally, some considerable speculation as to what it might have been. One very strong rumour was that Mary Kelly had been pregnant and that the twelve-week foetus was among the missing bits. The truth of this rumour has been entirely discounted with the discovery, in 1987, of the following report made by Doctor Thomas Bond.

POSITION OF BODY
The body was lying naked in the middle of the bed, the shoulders flat, but the axis of the body inclined to the left side of the bed. The head was turned on the left cheek. The left arm was close to the body with the forearm flexed at a right angle and lying across the abdomen. The right arm was slightly abducted from the body and rested on the mattress, the elbow bent and the forearm supine with fingers clenched. The legs were wide apart, the left thigh at right angles to the trunk and the right forming an obtuse angle with the pubes. The whole of the surface of the abdomen and thighs was removed and the abdominal cavity emptied of its viscera. The breasts were cut off, the arms mutilated by several jagged wounds and the face hacked beyond recognition of the features. The tissues of the neck were severed all around down to the bone. The viscera were found in various places viz: the uterus and Kidneys with one breast were found under the head, the other breast by the right foot, the liver between the feet, the intestines by the right side and the spleen by the left side of the body. The flaps removed from the abdomen and thighs were on a table. The bed clothing at the right corner was saturated with blood, and on the floor beneath was a pool of blood covering about two feet square. The wall by the right side of the bed and in line with the neck was marked by blood which had struck it in a number of separate splashes.

POSTMORTEM EXAMINATION
The face was gashed in all directions the nose, cheeks, eyebrows and ears being partly removed. The lips were blanched and cut by several incisions running obliquely down to the chin. There were also numerous cuts extending irregularly across all the features. The neck was cut through and the skin and other tissues right down to the vertabrae the 5th and 6th being severely notched. The skin cuts in the front of the neck showed distinct ecchymosis. The air passage was cut at the lower part of the larynx through the cricoid cartilage. Both breasts were removed by more or less circular incisions, the muscles down to the ribs being attached to the breasts. The intercostals between the 4th, 5th, and 6th ribs were cut through and the contents of the thorax visible through the openings. The skin and tissues of the

abdomen from the costal arch to the pubes were removed in three large flaps. The right thigh was denuded in front to the bone, the flap of skin, including the external organs of generation and part of the right buttock. The left thigh was stripped of skin, fascia and muscles as far as the knee. The left calf showed a long gash through skin and tissues to the deep muscles and reaching from the knee to five inches above the ankle. Both arms and forearms had extensive and jagged wounds. The right thumb showed a small superficial incision about one inch long, with extravasation of blood in the skin and there were several abrasions on the back of the hand moreover showing the same condition. On opening the thorax it was found that the right lung was minimally adherent by old firm adhesions. The lower part of the lung was broken and torn away. The left lung was intact: it was adherent at the apex and there were a few adhesions over the side. In the substances of the lung were several nodules of consolidation. The pericardium was open below and the Heart absent. In the abdominal cavity was some partly digested food of fish and potatoes and similar food was found in the remains of the stomach attached to the intestines.

THE HEART WAS ABSENT ! !

This then was the evidence which Coroner MacDonald had successfully suppressed. The penny had finally dropped. The victims of Jack the Ripper were not only being murdered and butchered, in the most unspeakable of ways, their bodies were being systematically harvested of their vital organs . This revelation was evidently considered as unsuitable for making public. Given the mood of the general population of London, particularly in the East-End with its ambivilence towards, what it saw, as an inept police force, such a revelation might well have caused a general panic.
The police did however break with precedent.
An official announcement bearing the signature of Charles Warren, the newly resigned Commissioner, was made...

'MURDER - PARDON.
Whereas on 8th or 9th November in Millers Court, Dorset Street, Spitalfields, Mary Jane Kelly was murdered by some person or persons unknown. The Secretary of State will advise the grant of Her Majesty's pardon to any accomplice not being a person who contrived or actually committed the murder who shall give such information and evidence as shall lead to the discovery and conviction of the person or persons who committed the murder.' The offer was never taken up.

Mary Jane Kelly's funeral was even more grandiose than that of Catherine Eddowes.
The funeral expenses were paid for by Henry Wilton. He had been the Clerk of Saint Leonard's Church, in Shoreditch, for fifty years.

By noon, on Sunday 18th November, as the church bell tolled, a crowd, mostly women, had gathered in front of the church. The polished elm coffin, containing the remains of Mary Kelly, was borne by four men. The name plate on the coffin was engraved... 'MARIE JEANETTE KELLY Died 9th November 1888 aged 25.'

The boys at a Leytonstone school had collected money for a large floral cross which rested upon the coffin. Mary's favourite pubs, The Britannia and the Ten Bells, sent bunches of artificial flowers. The wreaths bore cards from 'Friends using certain public houses in common with the murdered woman.'

The huge crowd seemed greatly affected at the sight of the coffin and men and women were seen to weep quite openly. Many surged forward in order to touch the coffin, as if it were a sacred relic, as it was placed on an open hearse. The coffin was followed by the widow Cox and a few friends of Mary. One who was there was Maria Harvey, the girl who Mary had given shelter to. The mourners had all met up in the Ten Bells earlier in order to give themselves some Dutch courage and to fortify themselves for the two-hour journey, in open carriages to Saint Patrick's Cemetery, Leytonstone.

It was 2.00pm when the cortege finally reached the cemetery where it was met by Father Colomban. Henry Wilton had canvassed support to assist in meeting the funeral expenses. He suggested that any surplus could be used to erect a tombstone.

I visited Saint Patrick's Cemetery in the late 1960s with the object of visiting Mary Kelly's grave. I searched among the graves for some considerable time. Where was the grave? It had featured in a television documentary some years earlier.

I searched again through a cluster of graves from the late 1800s but I could find no marker for Kelly's grave. I was soon joined by the Cemetery Superintendent, an interesting and intelligent man. We found the burial entry in the relevant book. The problem appeared to be that some years earlier the row and plot numbers of the graves had been redesignated. I was told that the TV crew, who had filmed the programme which I had seen, had in fact, built a 'prop' grave in the cemetery and filmed it as Mary Kelly's.

All was not lost though. By finding a grave of the same period, and checking on the inscribed designations, we were able to step out the differences, counting the rows and the numbers of the graves using the old numbers. We came to a blank patch. Clearly it was a grave. There was no marker or stone. The elation which one naturally feels at the end of a successful search was strangely tempered by an overwhelming feeling of pity for the poor woman whose torn remains lay beneath our feet.

A marker was subsequently erected and has now been replaced with a marble headstone.

In 2015 a new book claimed to reveal Mary Kellys true identity. The author Dr Wynne Weston-Davies, an eminent surgeon, claimed that the woman known as Mary Kelly was in fact his Great Aunt Elizabeth Weston-Davies who had assumed the name Mary Kelly so as not to be found by her estranged husband Francis Spurzheim Craig who, in 1888 at the time of the murders was a 51 years old newspaper reporter covering the courts in Londons East End.
Crag lived in Mile End Road, a few minutes walk from the first murder scene.

Wynne-Davis Claims that his great Aunt (Kelly) was murdered by Craig and that the other murders were a "cover" for his intention to kill his wife who had returned to prostitution having left her much older husband shortly after their wedding in 1885. The claim is also made that Craig was also the author of the 'Dear Boss' letters.

Apart from the claims made in the book there is no real evidence offered to support the theory that Craig was the killer, or indeed that Mary Kelly was actually Elizabeth Weston-Davies.

Yet the book generated considerable publicity not least because of the authors assertion that he had obtained provisional consent, from the Home Office, to exhume the Kelly grave to obtain DNA samples which would prove or disprove his claim that she was, in fact, his Great Aunt Elizabeth.

On June 29th 2016 a privately commissioned ground survey of the area around the grave was undertaken using ground penetrating radar. The report states that 'The purpose of the investigation is to determine if the location of the nominated gravestone is actually indicating the presence of a grave and if there are other graves around it.

The ground below Kellys gravestone showed a buried feature at 0.7-10m depth assumed to be a grave as the reflection pattern is similar to the other ones observed in the same area. A second reflection pattern has been observed adjacent to it but further from the gravestone. It is not possible to establish conclusively whether they belong to the same feature or they are two different objects although from their reflections they are believed to be two separate features.

The depths reported…for the assumed and possible graves are referred to the reflection believed to be the top of the burial, however it is possible that the reflections caused by the backfill material has been misinterpreted (due to interference with adjacent reflections or similarity in the reflection patterns) leading to depth inaccuracies.'

These findings suggest, at least to me as a layman, that below the Kelly gravestone at a depth of just short of a metre there would appear to be a feature which in all likelihood is the top of what remains of a coffin. A similar feature is close by possibly an indication of another body.

In 2016 The University of Leicester, famed for their discovery of the body of King Richard 111 were contacted by author Patricia Cornwell to examine the feasibility of finding the exact burial location and the likely condition and survival of Kellys remains.

Following a visit to St Patricks Cemetery the team concluded the exact location of the grave is unknown and that any exhumation may well involve disturbing the remains of many other individuals. Franky I do not accept either of these two points.

So what information could be gained from an exhumation of Kellys body assuming that it could be correctly identified as such. Two things. It may yield additional information regarding the injuries she sustained, and it may confirm Wynne Weston-Davies belief that Kelly was indeed his Great Aunt Elizabeth Weston-Davies, which would certainly be of interest to Ripper enthusiasts. Other than that I do not believe that it would bring us any closer to identifying her killer.

Chapter Three

SUSPECTS AND THEORIES

The slaying of Mary Kelly was, in all probability, the last murder committed by Jack the Ripper.

He disappeared from the streets of Whitechapel as surreptitiously as he had appeared. It is the identity of the killer, which today, constitutes the main area of debate between 'Ripperologists'. (A term coined by Colin Wilson)

For a little over one hundred years a plethora of names have been put forward.
The suggestions have ranged from the noblest in the land to the most humble, and, from the ridiculous to the sublime. Names have been suggested by writers, and others, who, in some cases, have claimed to have had access to secret files, death-bed confessions, previously undiscovered diaries, or even psychic powers. One can therefore, easily forgive the great mass of readers who have a confused understanding of the actual events. Speculation and rumour, and fact, fiction, fraud, and forgery, have all assimilated into the story and found a niche in the mystery.

New books, television programmes and films have, with only a few exceptions, claimed the last word.

A television film, called 'Jack the Ripper', and starring Michael Caine, was broadcast during the Autumn of 1988 to mark the centenary of the events. The film, which cost several million pounds to produce, ended with Michael Caine, as Inspector Abberline, capturing no less than the eminent Victorian surgeon Sir William Gull, who, together with a coachman called John Netley, apparently roamed the streets of London in a coach occasionally used by members of the Royal Family.

The story is remarkably similar to a television programme broadcast in 1973.
Entitled 'The Ripper File', the 1973 programme featured the unlikely duo of Gull and Netley under orders from top Government officials and politicians who were concerned that several East London prostitutes, particularly Mary Kelly, had information which could topple no less than the Royal Family. Gull and Netley had been ordered to kill the prostitutes in order to silence them.

'The Ripper File' was followed by a book elaborating upon the same theory. Written by Stephen Knight and entitled 'The Final Solution' (Harrap & Co.1976), this publication caused a sensation suggesting, as it did, that the mystery involved Prince Edward Albert Victor, the eldest son of the then Prince of Wales (later King Edward the Seventh) and the grandson of Queen Victoria, in an illegal marriage, with a Roman Catholic girl, and the subsequent attempts to silence those who knew of these events.

Edward Albert Victor was heir apparent to the English Throne. He is sometimes referred to as the Duke of Clarence but he was not given that title until more than a year after the events described here. He was however often referred to, affectionately, as 'Eddy'.

In order to test this theory, crime writer Simon Wood set out to check Stephen Knight's story.

He discovered that the source of the 'Gull/Netley/Royalty/Masonic' theory seemed to emanate from Joseph Gorman Sickert, a painter and picture restorer who claims to be an illegitimate son of the artist Walter Sickert.

This is how Simon Wood told it in 'Bloodhound' (March 1987)...

'In 1884, when Prince Eddy was about twenty, his mother, Princess Alexandra, concerned about his lack of worldliness and the stifling enviroment of his court upbringing, asked Walter Sickert to introduce him into artistic circles. Prince Eddy was taken to Sickert's rented studio at Cleveland Street where the heir to the throne met Annie Elizabeth Crook, a shop girl who modelled for Sickert. Annie Crook lived in the basement of 6 Cleveland Street and worked in a tobacconists shop a few doors along at number 22. They fell in love, the girl becoming pregnant almost immediately.

The following year, 1885, she gave birth to a daughter at the Marylebone Workhouse. The child, Alice Margaret, underwent two baptisms as Anglican and Catholic. Because of Annie's Catholicism, marriage to Eddy was constitutionally unthinkable, but so deep was their love that they went through a secret Catholic wedding ceremony at a St Saviours' chapel. There were two witnesses to the wedding. One was Walter Sickert. The other was an Irish Catholic girl who had worked with Annie in the Cleveland Street shop and later been paid, by Sickert, to be the child's nanny. Her name was Mary Jane Kelly.

Queen Victoria soon learned of these events and Salisbury, the Prime Minister, took responsibility for clearing up the mess which the Queen's grandson had got himself into.

In 1888, Salisbury staged a raid on Cleveland Street, whisking Eddy back to court from Sickert's studio at number 15, and dragging Annie from the basement of Number 6, to spend the next 156 days incarcerated in Guys' Hospital. Mary Kelly managed to escape and made her way to the East End of London.

That should have been the end of the matter, but Kelly fell in with a group of prostitutes and between them they conceived an ambitious blackmail plan. Thus, according to Sickert, 'Jack the Ripper' was born.

He was not a lone avenger, stalking the streets on a misguided moral crusade, but an unholy trinity of officially sanctioned killers out to silence those who knew of Prince Eddy's marriage to the Catholic girl.

The three men who formed the composite identity of Jack the Ripper were; Walter Sickert himself, a coachman named John Netley and Sir William Gull, physician in ordinary to Queen Victoria. While Netley drove, Sickert and Gull lured the members of the blackmail cartel into the coach where they were fed poisoned grapes. Once dead, their bodies were mutilated by Doctor Gull and dumped in quiet alleyways and backyards.

Mary Kelly was the last to be located and, as she was the only one of the five victims to have her own room, hers was the only murder to be committed indoors.

With the death of Mary Kelly, silence regarding the events in Cleveland Street was assured and Jack the Ripper vanished as mysteriously as he had first appeared on the streets of Whitechapel.

During her time, at Guys' hospital, Annie Elizabeth Crook underwent an operation at the hands of Doctor Gull to erase from her mind the events of Cleveland Street. The operation left her an epileptic. She was now a broken woman, both in body and spirit. Yet the Freemasons, of whom Gull was a member, thought it a wise precaution not to allow her to return to normal life. She spent the rest of her days in prisons, workhouses and infirmaries.

Annie died, hopelessly insane, in 1920.

Alice Margaret Crook, the daughter of Annie and Prince Eddy, was brought up by Walter Sickert. In 1918, she married a man named Gorman, who proved to be impotent. She turned to Walter Sickert, became his mistress and in 1925 bore him a son, Joseph.

Fifty years later Joseph Sickert told his story to Stephen Knight.

Stephen Knight began his investigation of the Sickert story with this paragraph...

'Unlikely as Sickert's story was, it would have been irresponsible to dismiss it merely because it sounded absurd, it cried out to be investigated. To be fair though, even 'absurd' was an understatement. It sounded the most errant, if entertaining, nonsense ever spun about Jack the Ripper, with the possible exception of the suggestion that the murderer was an escaped gorilla.'

Wood continues...

'Having nailed his disbelief to the masthead, Mr Knight set out, quite properly, to see if Annie Crook had actually existed. He had no luck, in this direction, but Karen de Groot, a BBC researcher, made a discovery in the 1888 rate book for Cleveland Street...
Number 6: Elizabeth COOK (Basement)'

Crook - Cook. It was close.
According to Sickert her surname was often given as Cook. So far, so good.
Next, the birth certificate of Alice Crook turned up.

When and where born... 18th April 1885, Marylebone Workhouse
Name, if any... Alice Margaret
Sex... Girl
Name and surname of father... blank
Occupation of father... blank
Name, surname and maiden name of mother... Annie Elizabeth Crook
Occupation of mother... Confectionery assistant from Cleveland Street
Signature ... X the mark of Annie Elizabeth Crook.
Description and residence of informant... Mother, 6 Cleveland Street

From these two pieces of information, Mr Knight had arrived at a confident conclusion...

'The address shows that Elizabeth Cook of the rate book and Annie Elizabeth Crook were one and the same.'

Simon Woods next stop was the Greater London Record Office where Mr Alan Neate, the record keeper, was able to provide a few details of Annie Elizabeth Crook's life in various workhouses and infirmaries. From the time of her daughter's birth, in 1885, to her death in 1920, fifteen entries are listed as the sad sequel to her romance with Prince Eddy.

Stephen Knight had her in his sights - Annie Elizabeth Crook, the woman whose involvement with Prince Eddy was at the centre of the 'Ripper' murders. Here was the key to unlock an almost century-old mystery.
This was the breakthrough 'Ripperologists' had been searching for. The evidence in support of Sickert's story was overwhelming... or was it?
Frankly it wasn't.

In fact, the information contained in the Cleveland Street rate book and documents supplied by the Greater London Record Office rule out any involvement on the part of Annie Elizabeth Crook with events in the context of Stephen Knight's book.

Mr Alan Neate... 'was kind enough to supply me (Simon Wood) with the information he had given to Stephen Knight. When he put this together, with what he had gleaned from the Cleveland Street rate books, the 1885 St Marylebone Electoral register, and the 'Kelly' Street Directories 1883 - 1888, a rather different picture of Annie Elizabeth Crook emerged. It is no less harrowing and drab than Stephen Knight's heavily wrought account of her demise, but it is the truth?'

What follows is an account of what is known about Annie Elizabeth Crook and her family 1838 - 1925, with special reference to the events described in Knight's book. The original documentation is on file at the local history department of the Tower Hamlets Public Library.

ANNIE ELIZABETH CROOK... was born 10th October 1862 at the St Marylebone Infirmary. No birth certificate under this name, date, or place is held at St Catherines House. It is possible that, as she was born a year before her parent's marriage, her birth might have been registered in her mother's maiden name. Records of births in workhouses, held by the GLC, only go back as far as 1866, so it has not been possible to discover her mother's maiden name. On the 19th August 1880, Sarah Ann Crook, Annie's mother, was brought by the police to the St Marylebone workhouse.
She was ill, and a note on her admission form reads... 'to be seen again.'
At this time, she was living with her husband at 44 Berwick Street. They had been living there since September 1879. A statement taken from her husband, William Crook, reads...

'When about 15 years of age, I was apprenticed to a Mr Charles Boddy, a cabinet maker of 55 Eagle Street, off Red Lion Square, under judicature, premium fourteen pounds. Bound for seven years. Served four and a half years'.

Sarah Ann was discharged to her husband.
13th May 1882. Sarah Ann and William Crook were destitute.
The St Pancras Relieving Officer gave them meat and bread to the value of one shilling and fivepence (about 7p).

Sarah Ann was suffering from epilepsy. This suggests that Annie Elizabeth's epilepsy was inherited from her mother and not brought about by surgery at the hands of Doctor Gull. An order was made to admit Sarah to the workhouse but, as someone wrote across the Relieving Officer's report... 'she didn't come.'

The couple had been living at 24 Francis Street for three months. No mention was made of their daughter Annie.

ALICE MARGARET COOK... was born on the 18th April 1885, at the St Marylebone Workhouse. In the workhouse creed register both Alice and Annie's creed is given as Church of England. This documented fact knocks a sizeable hole in Stephen Knight's story. Why should Eddy and Annie go through with a Catholic wedding ceremony when neither of them were of that religion?
Knight had used the birth certificate as proof that Annie worked in the shop at 22 Cleveland Street. The certificate reads... 'Annie Elizabeth Crook - confectionery assistant - from Cleveland Street.'
But, even assuming the former interpretation, it is equally possible that she could have worked in any of the following establishments...

1885 - Cleveland Street
22... James Currier - confectioner
74... Jeremiah Poll - tobacconist
75... Edward Chapman - confectioner
113... Charles Chapman - confectioner
116... Mrs R. Jackson - confectioner

In the events described by Sickert, having Annie working in the shop at number 22 is most desirable. It was only eight doors away from where she lived at number 6 and almost opposite number 15, where Sickert had his studio.
Let us bear these addresses in mind and go on to one of the hard facts we can glean from Alice Margaret Cook's birth certificate.

In 1885, Annie Elizabeth Crook was living at number 6 Cleveland Street.
Next, to the rate books and another hard fact...
In 1888, Elizabeth Cook was living in the basement of number 6 Cleveland Street.
Same address... same person?

If we were glancing at this information, with nothing more than a faint interest, we might be forgiven for believing that these two items refer to the same person. But this is a murder enquiry and we have to be sure of our facts.

We are told that in 1888 Prime Minister Salisbury staged a raid on Cleveland Street.
A fat man and a woman went into the basement of number 6 and dragged Annie Elizabeth off to Guys' Hospital, while two men in brown tweed went into Sickert's studio at number 15 and dragged Prince Eddy back to Court.

From 1885 to 1857 the ratepayer for number 6 Cleveland Street was William Tubb. The address was a ground floor shop run by John Pugh - hairdresser, and the Electoral Roll for 1885, shows James Hinton and Charles Horne also living at this address.
At this time women did not have the vote, so the only record of tenure would have been the landlord's rent book.
It has not been possible to discover where Annie Elizabeth Crook was living from late 1886 to early 1888, but one thing is certain, it wasn't at number 6 Cleveland Street. In between these dates, numbers 4 - 14 were pulled down and the row of shops with their upstairs rooms replaced with Cleveland Residences, the flats which stand there today.
On completion of the flats, Elizabeth Cook moved into the basement of number 6 and, according to the rate book, continued to live there until 1893.
So it wasn't Elizabeth Cook who was dragged to Guys' hospital. So who was it?

To answer this let us turn our attention to the other half of the raiding party - the two men in brown tweed who, allegedly took Prince Eddy from Sickert's studio. They would have had a difficult job on their hands - not to say impossible. In 1887, a year before the raid, number 15 Cleveland Street, which housed Sickert's studio, was pulled down and rebuilt in 1888, as the Middlesex Hospital Trained Nurses Institute. Depending on the exact date of the raid, the raiders would have found either a building site at this address, or a collection of very confused nurses.
Clearly the raid could not have taken place. The incident is a complete fabrication.

22nd January 1889 - further proof that Crook and Cook were not one and the same person can be found on Annie Crook's Admission Form to the Endell Street workhouse by PC453D. She was destitute and had last been living at 9 Pitt Street, Tottenham Court Road.

Two points here. At this time, Elizabeth Cook was living at 6 Cleveland Street. Also, this document does nothing to support Sickert's assertion that his father Walter brought up the child.
Annie's marital status was recorded as 'single'. Her occupation was given as 'charring' and a note on the bottom of the form reads... 'woman left next morning before ARD (Assistant Relieving Officer) arrived'.

By the 29th April 1894, Annie Elizabeth Crook was in prison. Her daughter Alice was living at 42 New Compton Street. On the 23rd of March 1920, Annie Elizabeth Crook died in the lunacy ward of the Fulham Road Workhouse.
Stephen Knight stated... 'The St Georges Club ran a hospital at 367 Fulham Road where Annie Crook died.'

This new evidence indicated how the Freemasons, in charge of the cover-up, could have handled the incarceration of Annie Elizabeth. However, in a letter accompanying the documents recieved from the GLC, Alan Neate wrote:

'Knight's statement that the St Georges Club ran a hospital at 367 Fulham Road in the period under review is quite untrue. At all times material to the present consideration this was an address of the Fulham Road Workhouse maintained by the Statutory Poor Law Authority - The St Georges (Westminster) Board of Guardians up to 1913 and the City of Westminster Board of Guardians thereafter.'

The Crook family were no strangers to the workhouse and there is not one shred of evidence to suggest that Annie Elizabeth Crook's mental and physical decline was due to anything other than natural misfortune.
We know that she was not a Catholic - the very crux of this elaborate 'Ripper' theory - and that her epilepsy was, more than probably, inherited from her mother.
We know that she was not living in Cleveland Street in 1888 and that Sickert's studio, if it ever existed at all at this address, had been demolished a year earlier and that in the light of the foregoing, certain events at the heart of Stephen Knight's book could not have taken place.

Indeed, it was after the publication of Knight's book that Joseph Sickert eventually recanted his story and admitted that it was all an elaborate hoax. He has, however, subsequently, changed his mind again and now insists that the story is not a hoax

Notwithstanding these facts, Knight's book 'The Final Solution', became a best-seller. It is still the best known story of Jack the Ripper and is, unfortunately for those who seek the truth, quite believable.

Subsequently, however, several books have been published based upon Sickert's hoax and variations thereof. Most notably The Ripper and the Royals by Melvyn Fairclough (1991). In addition to repeating almost all of the Sickert hoax story it adds two quite new, and sensational, pieces of information.

According to Fairclough Prince Eddy, the Duke of Clarence, and heir apparent to the throne, did not die in 1892. He was, instead incarcerated at Glamis castle, in Scotland, the ancestral home of the Earls of Strathmore. Fairclough suggests that the Royal Family were so desperate that Prince Eddy should not ascend the throne that they had him locked away for the rest of his life. In return for this service, to the Royal family, the 13th Earl of Strathmore was promised that one of his descendants would be allowed to marry a future king of England.

This promise was evidently made good, 34 years later, when, on the 26th April 1923 the fourth daughter of the 14th Earl of Strathmore, Lady Elizabeth Bowes-Lyon, married the Duke of York the second son of George the fifth. It would appear that Lady Elizabeth must have known that she would one day become Queen because she had twice refused proposals from the Duke of York since it was his elder brother Edward, the Prince of Wales, who was first in line for the throne. Fairclough suggests, however, that the Prince of Wales had made it privately known, to the Royal Family, that he did not intend to ascend the throne. When this became known to the Lady Elizabeth she promptly married the Duke of York and subsequently became Queen when her husband was crowned King George the sixth after the abdication of the uncrowned King Edward the eighth.

The second new piece of information was the discovery of the diaries of no less a person than, Inspector Frederick George Abberline.

It would appear that these alleged diaries had, all along been in the possession of Joseph Sickert having been given, apparently, to his Father Walter Sickert by Abberline himself. It is not clear as to why Abberline should have entrusted his diaries to Walter Sickert, Neither is it clear why Joseph Sickert did not reveal their existence before, especially to Stephen Knight who had based his book on Joseph Sickerts story. There is no doubt but that Knight would have made much of such a discovery since the diaries, whose provenance has not been tested, appear to support Joseph Sickerts story. Among others the diaries name Lord Randolph Churchill as one of the killers. It is also of some curiousity, however, that F.G. Abberline should have signed the diaries as G.F. Abberline.

In addition to all of this Fairclough tells us that, according to Sickert, Peter Sutcliffe, later convicted as the Yorkshire Ripper, had, in early 1975 visited Sickerts home, while he was out. Sutcliffe apparently caught up with Joseph in a Cleveland Street café where he introduced himself. Joseph claims to have been scared of Sutcliffe especially since he, allegedly, recognised Sutcliffe as the man who had earlier tried to run him over with his car. Sickert claims that he later talked with Sutcliffe and became convinced that he had something to do with the series of murders then taking place in Yorkshire. Sickert claims that he passed this information on to the police but before any action was taken Sutcliffe was arrested.

In May 1992, Melvyn Fairclough, together with Joseph Sickert, interviewed Reg Hutchinson the seventy-four years old son of George Hutchinson, the man who claimed to have seen Mary Kelly enter Millers Court with a man on the night that she was murdered. According to Fairclough Reg Hutchinson told them that he had worked with his Father for many years (even though he was only twenty when his Father died), and that his Father, apparently, knew far more about the Whitechapel murderer than he was ever prepared to say. If his Father was ever asked who he thought was responsible, for the murders, he would say It was far more to do with the Royal Family than ordinary people. It was someone like Lord Randolph Churchill It would appear that Fairclough and Sickert had jogged Reg Hutchinsons memory a little, by showing him the diaries alleged to have been written by Abberline, since the penny suddenly drops and Reg realises that his Father was actually meaning that it was Lord Randolph Churchill that he had seen with Mary Kelly.

Reg Hutchinson further claims that his Father was paid five pounds, presumably, to keep quiet about what he really knew.

In my opinion the whole story is quite preposterous.
Firstly. Is it likely that the 22 years old George Hutchinson would have recognised Lord Randolph Churchill even if he had really seen him? and, secondly, If Hutchinson had recognised Churchill, surely the murdering cartel, Gull, Netley, Churchill etc would have similarly disposed of the unfortunate Hutchinson ? Surely after the careful planning and execution of these murders, and with the Royal Family, and so many eminent persons implicated, Hutchinson would not have been allowed to live. If they had already killed five women in order to cover their tracks Is it really likely, as Fairclough would have us believe that the one man who could have fingered them and blown the whole plot apart was bought off with a fiver.?

The makers of the Michael Caine film had hedged their bets a little by suggesting, early in the film, that Prince Eddy might have had some involvement with the murders, but his movements are checked and he is cleared. They did not find it necessary to mention the secret marriage or the Masonic plot. Yet these were, of course, the very reasons used to substantiate the claim, in Sickert's hoax story, that Gull and Netley were the joint killers.

To compensate for this, the film-makers called into play another character - Robert Lees.

Lees was a well-known philantrophist and scholar. As the leader of a Christian Spiritualist movement he claimed to possess psychic powers in the form of prophetic visions. He was well known to politicians and to the upper-crust society of the day. It has even been suggested that he arranged a seance or two for Queen Victoria, in order that she might be able to make contact with her dear departed husband, the late and much loved Prince Albert.

According to Lees, one day, while he was travelling on an omnibus, he came face-to-face with the killer, whom he was able to identify from one of his visions. He followed the man to a large house in London's fashionable West End. Subsequently the house was said to be the home of Sir William Gull. Lees claimed that the police had taken the occupant of the house away and had him confined to a lunatic asylum.

This story had first appeared as long ago as 1895 in the 'People' (19th May).
The story told how a Doctor Howard had been instrumental in committing the unfortunate 'lunatic' to a mental hospital. Unfortunately for Lees, Doctor Howard claimed to know nothing about this and promptly threatened legal action if the story was repeated. It was repeated though, in 1931 as part of a series of articles published in the Daily Express but this time without the involvement of Doctor Howard . This time the story claimed that Lees had volunteered his story to the police at the time of the murders - but they had told him to go away and stop being silly.

In 1970 Thomas Stowell, a retired brain surgeon, revealed to the 'Criminologist' magazine that the occupant who had been certified was in fact... Prince Eddy. Stowell claimed that he came by this information when examining the private papers of Sir William Gull after they had been loaned to him by Gull's daughter-in-law Lady Caroline Dyke-Acland.

Stowell claimed that the papers revealed that the Prince had contracted syphillis, from a male partner, and that it was this which led him to go out at night killing prostitutes. Stowell suggested that Prince Eddy had been caught after the double murder of Stride and Eddowes, but that he escaped to commit the final murder in Millers Court. He also claimed that the Prince had not died of influenza, in the 1892 epedemic, but had instead died of syphillis in a private mental asylum near Sandringham.

Prince Edward Albert Victor was born, eight weeks prematurely, on the 8th of January 1864 with a condition known as Otosclerosis, a disease which causes deafness. He was described as 'a sickly child'. His weight at birth was less than four pounds. He was also described as being 'backward and sullen'. He and his younger brother Georgie (later King George fifth) used to quarrel a lot and use very strong language to each other. Queen Victoria described them as 'wild as hawks... such ill bred children... I cannot fancy them at all'.
It may be that the Prince's sullenness and apparent autism was due simply to his deafness, which also affected his mother and grandmother.

At the age of sixteen Prince Eddy was sent to train at HMS Brittania, at Dartmouth, and later he was sent on a seven-month sea voyage to the West Indies. It is said that he wore, on his watch chain, a trinket, which had been given to him by Lily Langtry, music hall star, and one of his father's many lovers. The Prince is best described by his Tutor, The Rev John Neale Dalton, who tells us that the Prince was 'listless and vacant... this weakness of brain, this feebleness and lack of power to grasp anything put before him... his inability to concentrate upon anything for more than just a few seconds... a fault of nature'.

Prince Eddy was sent to Cambridge and given rooms at Trinity College. His tutors doubted whether he could 'possibly derive much benefit from attending lectures, as he hardly knows the meaning of the word to read'.
Upon leaving Cambridge, Prince Eddy joined the Tenth Hussars, but showed no more promise as a soldier than he had as a student. In short he was a fop. As such he was often the subject of rumour and mirth. Sarah Bernhardt claimed that he was the father of her son Maurice.

If he was then he evidently swung both ways. This alleged aspect of Prince Eddys private life came to light in 1889 when a fifteen years old telegram boy, Charles Swinscow, was found in possession of a sum of money which was more than he could legitimately account for. When questioned, by the police, the boy explained that he had earned the money by working for a Mr Charles Hammond of 19 Cleveland Street. When asked to elucidate further upon the nature of the work, Swinscow admitted that he had been paid, by Hammond, to go to bed with gentlemen at the house. An investigation uncovered several other telegram boys who all admitted having undertaken similar work for Mr Hammond. One of the boys, Henry Newlove, immediately went to Hammonds house and told him what had happened. Hammond left town the next morning before Chief Inspector Abberline, who Monro had put in charge of the case, could arrest him.

It was said that among those who made regular visits, to Charles Hammonds house, were Lord Arthur Somerset, a close personal friend, and equerry to the Prince of Wales, a Col Jervois, and Lord Euston - a married man, with several mistresses and a close personal friend of Prince Eddy. Lord Arthur Somerset dropped Prince Eddy's name into the frame by telling his solicitor, Arthur Newton, that Prince Eddy often went to Hammonds house with Lord Euston. Lord Arthur Somerset now fled the country. He remained abroad, living on the French Riviera, until his death in 1930. Lord Euston, however, protesting his innocence, decided to stay on in London. He admitted having once visited Mr Hammonds house, believing that it offered gentlemanly delights of a heterosexual nature, and left when he realised that it was a male brothel. He later successfully sued Ernest Parke, the editor of the North London Press, for libel.

The Prince of Wales was obviously very distressed that his close friend, Lord Somerset, whom he called Podge should be involved in such a filthy vice On the 25th October The Prince of Wales wrote, to Lord Salisbury, the Prime Minister, asking that if Lord Somerset should ever dare to show his face in England again, he should be allowed to visit his parents quietly in the country without fear of being apprehended on this awful charge.

Solicitor Newton had made it clear that if the case was proceeded with then Prince Eddy would be implicated. Some sort of deal must have been made since none of the principal characters were charged. Several of the boys were offered, by Newton, the sum of twenty-pounds in cash, a complete set of new clothes, and a pension of one-pound a week for the next three years, together with one-way tickets to Australia. Two of the boys were charged however. Charles Newlove, and his friend, George Veck were charged with having committed unnatural offences with male persons and with having induced others to do the same. They both pleaded guilty. Newlove received a sentence of nine months and and Veck, four months. Considering that, just less than a year earlier, a clergyman had been sentenced to life imprisonment for a similar offence, the sentences were transparently lenient It later came to light that their silence had been bought.

Interestingly we are told that George Veck had claimed to be in Holy orders when in actual fact he was a messenger. It is curious only when we remember that the mesenger who had delivered, what purported to be Eddowes kidney was, according to George Lusk, dressed in clerical garb. I do not make a connection but it is an interesting observation..

Martin Howells and Keith Skinner (The Ripper Legacy - 1987) suggest that Prince Eddy also frequented another upper class male bordello, a house named The Osiers overlooking the River Thames at Chiswick.

The British press stayed quiet about the whole matter and Eddys name was not mentioned in connection with, what now came to be called, The Cleveland Street affair. The foreign press did however publish his name. The Daily Northwestern of 26th May 1890 published an article under the byline Prince Victor.

The article tells us that Prince Eddy had now returned, to England, from India, to where he had been sent until the scandal died down. He is described as a physical and mental wreck - threatening to renounce his succession to the English throne unless he is to be allowed to marry the woman of his own choosing. The article is reprinted, in full, in the appendices.

Notwithstanding these events in 1889 Prince Eddy was, in the same year, given the title of The Duke of Clarence. He wanted to marry Helene d'Orleans the daughter of the Compte de Paris, claimant to the French throne, but she she was a Catholic. The Queen wrote to Eddy that such a match was '...unthinkable'. Lord Salisbury, the Prime Minister expressed the opinion that such a match would be '...injudicious'. The Compte de Paris was adamant that he would not allow his nineteen years old daughter to convert to the Anglican faith. Otherwise he seems to have been mischievously happy to encourage the friendship. Despite these objections Eddy and Helene became engaged at the end of August while staying in Scotland, near Balmoral at Mar Lodge, with the Duke of Fife.

The Prince and Princess of Wales were profoundly grateful to Princess Helene paricularly when she offered to defy her father and renounce her Catholicism. The Queen accepted that the young couple were very much in love and she gave the match her blessing. The Pope, however intervened and the engagement was eventually broken off. Prince Eddy was heartbroken and declared that he wouldn't marry anyone else.

Before the end of the year, however, he was engaged to Princess Mary (May) of Teck.. Queen Victoria, appears to have encouraged the match and was delighted when her Son, The Prince of Wales telegraphed to inform Her Majesty that Eddy had been instructed to propose. So delighted in fact that, shortly after the engagement was announced, the Queen personally took both Eddy and May into the Royal Mausoleum at Frogmore House, Windsor, in order that they might obtain the posthomous blessing of the late Prince Albert. The wedding was fixed for the 27th February 1892. But it was not to be.

Princess Mary and her parents arrived at Sandringham on the 4th of January to join the Royal Family in the celebration of Prince Eddy's twenty-eighth birthday. On the 7th, the day before Eddys birthday, he fell ill with influenza. Two days later Doctor Laking, a Royal physician, diagnosed Pneumonia. For four days Eddy hung between life and death. He became delirious. Again and again he called out Helene! Helene!. In the early hours of the 14th January, on the anniversary of his Grandfathers death, Prince Albert Victor, Duke of Clarence died.

Later the Queen was to assert that 'May never was in love with poor Eddy'.

Princess Mary married Eddy's younger brother Georgie and, in 1910, upon the death of King Edward the Seventh, she was crowned Queen at her husband's Coronation.

Stowell, et al, would have us believe that Prince Eddy roamed around the streets of East London, at night, in a royal coach, murdering prostitutes. He claimed that his source were the private papers of Sir William Gull. But it does not wash.

Sir William Gull suffered two strokes in 1887, a year before the murders. Although the strokes were not severe Doctor Gull was incapacitated to the extent that he had ceased to practice. His infirmities alone would have rendered it difficult, if not impossible, for him to have been involved in the killings.

Furthermore What of Stowells assertion that Prince Eddy died of syphilis, in 1892, and not from influenza? Sir William Gull could not possibly ever have made such a statement in his papers since Gull himself died in 1890 two years before Prince Eddy. According to Stowell Doctor Gulls papers suggested that Gull had, in November 1889, informed the Prince of

Wales that his son, Prince Eddy, was dying of syphilis of the brain. Yet the truth is that Gull, who was in place as one of several Royal doctors, had bever actually attended upon the Royal family, and furthermore by late 1887 the incapacitated Dr Gull was incapable of attending upon the royal family.

And what about John Netley, the coachman who is alleged to have transported Gull/Sickert/Prince Eddy etc to and from the scenes of the murders? In the Michael Caine film Gull is arrested and incarcerated but Netley appears to simply ride off into the gaslit streets and get away with it scot-free.

John Netley certainly existed. He seems to have made no attempt to disguise his identity or to go into hiding. Indeed it appears that he just carried on with his job as a coachman until 1903, when he was thrown from the driving seat of his cab as it went over a stone. According to contemporary newspaper reports, he died instantly under the wheels of his own carriage.

Needless to say there does not exist - contrary to the claim made by the makers of the Caine film - any official or credible record suggesting that Prince Eddy, or Sir William Gull, or John Netley, either alone or in concert with each other, or others, were in any way whatsoever connected with the Whitechapel murders.

The name of Sickert has, alas, not yet been eradicated from the myths surrounding the case of the Whitechapel murders.

The year 2002 heralded a new book 'Portrait of a killer - Jack the Ripper case closed' - (Little, Brown) .The publicity, surrounding the launch of this book was unprecedented. The author, Patricia Cornwell, is a successful writer of crime fiction. That she knows her stuff is without doubt. Doctor Kay Scarpetta is one of Cornwells, fictional heroines. Between 1990 and 2000 eleven Scarpetta novels have been published. Patricia Cornwell is also well up to speed with modern techniques in forensic detection having established the Virginia Institute of Forensic Science and Medicine. She also serves as the Chairperson of the board to that institute.

According to Patricia Cornwell her foray into the realms of the Whitechapel Murders came about as a result of a meeting, in London, between her and John Grieve - a Deputy Assistant Commissioner at Scotland Yard. On a tour of the Ripper sites Grieve gave Cornwell a run-down of the murders and a short list of the major suspects. Grieve also suggested that Patricia Cornwell take a close look at the artist Walter Sickert who had died in 1942. This is the same Walter Sickert whom the modern-day ripper- hoaxer Joseph (Hobo) Sickert claims was his Father.

Walter Sickert , the son of Dutch and Danish parents, was born in Munich on May 31st 1860. After spending three years on the English stage he turned to art. He studied in Paris where he met Degas whose style, for painting low life, he appears to have emulated. In London he studied at the Slade school where he befriended his tutor the artist Whistler. Sickerts love of the theatre is much reflected in many of his paintings which depict music halls. He had many different studios in London and in Paris which he frequently visited. Sickert was a member of the New English Art Club, and in about 1910 the London Group was formed under his leadership. His paintings, and his writings, have had a great influence on later English painters. His autobiography 'A Free House' was published in 1947 five years after his death.

Commander Grieves reason for suggesting Walter Sickert as a suspect in the Whitechapel murders appears to be nothing more than that Sickert had painted a number of canvases featuring women sitting, or lying, on beds. One painting is actually called The Campden Town Murder, another is allegedly called Jack the Rippers bedroom.

Walter Sickert has, of course, been mentioned before as a suspect, but not by any credible source. It is a progression on the Joseph Sickert Story stories and, like so much of anything which emanates from Joseph Sickert, it should be taken with a largepinch of salt.

Notwithstanding this difficulty the narrative of Cornwells book makes it clear that the writer began almost immediately to convince herself that Walter Sickert was indeed Jack the Ripper. In order to substantiate her theory Cornwell called into play the resources of the modern-day forensic technique of DNA matching.

With the permission of the trustees of the Public Records Office, at Kew, in London, Patricia Cornwells team of scientists managed to retrieve, from one of the alleged Jack the Ripper letters, a single-donor mitochondrial DNA (mtDNA) sequence, specific enough to eliminate 99% of the population as the person who licked and touched the adhesive backing of that stamp. Miss Cornwell also tells us that - This same DNA sequence profile turned up as a component of another Ripper letter, and two Walter Sickert letters. Genetic locations, from this mtDNA sequence were also found on Sickerts painting overalls. Other genetic profiles, from other people, was also found.

Miss Cornwell also discovered that one, alleged Ripper letter, was written on art paper. Experts also discovered watermarks on paper used to write the Ripper letters which matched watermarks on paper used by Walter Sickert. Cornwell has also established that the dried blood on Ripper letters is consistent with materials used in the manufacture of etching ground. A material used by artists.

As far as motive is concerned Miss Cornwell states that Walter Sickert was unable to father children and was probably impotent as the result of childhood surgery to correct a fistula of the penis. Miss Cornwell then gives a fairly graphic description of the 19th Century surgeons technique for performing this type of surgery, heavily hinting that this procedure may have been performed without anesthetic.

The seeds of the motive are thus placed in the readers mind. Cornwell suggests that a resulting impotence was a major cause for Sickerts homicidal hatred of women and that this was the driving force behind his serial killing. It is a fact that many serial killers - such as Reginald Christie, for example, are found to be impotent and can only achieve sexual fulfillment during the act of killing.

This then is the basis of Miss Cornwells assertion that Walter Sickert was Jack the Ripper. It is as good as it gets and must rank among the more intelligently contrived Jack the Ripper theories. After all DNA evidence is usually considered conclusive. - But could it be true? Let us look closer at the evidence as presented to us in Cornwells book.

Nuclear DNA tests are considered conclusive. The nuclear DNA tests performed by Miss Cornwells scientists came back negative. It was then that the team performed mitochondrial DNA testing. It was this mtDNA testing, and not Nuclear DNA testing which provided the results upon which Miss Cornwell hangs her case.

MtDNA differs from nuclear DNA inasmuch as it is transmitted matrilineally. A child will only inherit mtDNA from its mother and, unlike nuclear DNA it is not unique. Consequently, the mtDNA tests conducted by Patricia Cornwells forensic team do not prove that Walter Sickert wrote any ripper letters. The results suggest only that the person who left the DNA on Sickerts correspondence can not be eliminated from that percentage of the population who could have provided an mtDNA match.

Unlike nuclear DNA testing an mtDNA match, between two samples does not prove that one person left both. At best it indicates only that a certain percentage of the population could have left both. Given the UK population, at the end of the 19th Century, it can be estimated that 400,000 people could have provided the same mtDNA sequences.

We do not even know if the mtDNA found on Sickerts own letters was his. Since his body was cremated. Furthermore the chances of DNA contamination, on documents of that age, by those who may have subsequently handled Sickerts papers, must be extremely high. Miss Cornwell concedes that her mtDNA test results, far from being conclusive evidence against Sickert, are only a cautious indicator.

As far as the watermarks are concerned Journalist David Cohen discovered that in the late 19th Century there were only about 90 paper-mills manufacturing in the UK. With over 600 alleged ripper letters to sift through the chances of finding manufacturers watermarks similar to that on the many hundreds of Sickerts personal papers are, again, extremely high.

It should also be remembered that even if it could be proved that Walter Sickert had, in fact, authored one or more of the ripper letters it still would not prove that he was the killer since there is no evidence whatsoever that the actual killer wrote any of the 600 or so letters.

Furthermore, Miss Cornwells assertion that Walter Sickerts alleged hatred of women was as a result of a fistula on his penis is not supported by any evidence.
Sickert was treated at St. Marks hospital by Doctor Alfred Duff-Cooper. On page 71, of Miss Cornwells book the author does admit that Doctor Coopers published medical procedures do not mention fistulas of the penis. In fact, Doctor Cooper specialized in anal, rectal, and vaginal surgery, which strongly suggests that if Sickert had a fistula it was probably on his anus or rectum. To simply state that he had a fistula on his penis is perhaps a case of stretching it a little too far.

Moreover, there is no reason to suppose that Sickert was impotent. The contrary is strongly suggested by those who knew him. Sickerts friend Jacques-Emile Blanche described Sickert as 'an immoralist with a swarm of children of provenances which are not possible to count.'

Miss Cornwells case against Walter Sickert is also weakened by the very strong probability that Sickert was, in fact, abroad, in his beloved France, at the time of the first four of the Whitechapel killings. Namely those of Polly Nichols, Annie Chapman, Liz Stride and Catharine Eddowes. Mathew Sturgis, a biographer of Sickert, claimed, in a Sunday Times story (3rd November 2002) that Sickert apparently left England for France sometime in mid-August. His last London Sketch is dated 4th of August.

There is no evidence to suggest that he remained in London after that date. Furthermore, on the 6th of September Sickerts Mother wrote from France describing how Walter, and his brother Bernhard were having such a happy time in France, painting and swimming. Sickerts friend Jaques-Emile Blanche also describes how Sickert visited him in France on September the 16th. Walters own wife also confirms Sickerts presence in France in a letter written to her brother-in-law, dated September 21st she states that her husband, Walter, had been in France for some weeks. Sickert was certainly still in France during early October 1888 since he painted a local scene, a flooded with sunlight boucherie which he entitled 'The October Sun'..

Patricia Cornwell has pioneered the use of modern-day forensic techniques, and invested a considerable personal fortune in her quest to prove that Walter Sickert was Jack the Ripper. Miss Cornwells claims, however, that her evidence would finally close the case, have not, in my opinion, been substantiated by the evidence she has thus presented.

As far as I am aware this was the very first attempt to use a modern day forensic technique as evidence against a Jack the Ripper suspect. It was not to be the last.

The first full-length book, in English, on the subject of Jack the Ripper, was published in 1928. 'The Mystery of Jack The Ripper' by Leonard Matters (W.H.Allen) claimed that the killer was a mad surgeon. Matters claimed to know the true identity of the surgeon but he does not disclose the name. Instead he gives the killer the pseudonym of Doctor Stanley.

Doctor 'Stanley' is said to have killed the women in revenge for his son's death, from syphillis, which he had contracted from... Mary Kelly. Matters claimed that the surgeon confessed to his crimes as he lay dying in an Argentine hospital. The man to whom 'Stanley' confessed had been a student, of 'Stanley' at an unnamed London hospital. It was this student who told Matters the story. However, Matters tells us, on page 110 of his book, that he had checked out the true identity of the surgeon but could find no trace of his existence, either in England or the Argentine. Notwithstanding this crucial point, Matters persisted with his story and it became a best seller.

Interestingly though, and particularly in the light of later research, Matters does come tantalisingly close to what might have been the truth... and then dismisses it. In chapter sixteen, of his book, he discussed the rumour that the body of Jack the Ripper had been fished out of the River Thames shortly after the last murder. He writes: -

'I have searched the columns of 'The Times', 'The Daily Telegraph', 'The Daily News' and 'The Star', and have failed to find any reference, between 9th of November 1888 and March 1889 to this sensational find in the Thames. Surely if the facts could have been substantiated such a discovery would have been a sensation - to say nothing of a great relief to the awe-stricken East End of London.'

He goes on:-

'The finding of a body in the Thames would not, of itself, excite any interest. Bodies are taken from the river almost every day, but not the body of a murderer of the character of Jack the Ripper, for whom the entire police force were still eagerly looking. The suicide of Jack the Ripper is a possibility that cannot be lightly scouted, especially by those who accept the theory of the murders being committed by a lunatic, but to give it its full credence it is first necessary to believe that this lunatic disguised his violent mania for many months... The theory that he was a lunatic, to be incarcerated if examined by a doctor, unaware of anything definite against him to prove his lunacy, will not bear consideration... Many theorists were reluctant to declare that the murderer was quite sane, and they sought a compromise by suggesting that, while he was not mad, he was the victim of delusions and impulses'.

What Matters is telling us here is that there was a story about the body of Jack the Ripper being taken from the River Thames, and that the suspect was insane with apparent periods of lucidity. Matters then dismisses this possibility.

If Matters had, however, extended his search among the periodicals of the day he might well have stumbled across the body in question. For, as we shall see later, a body was indeed pulled from the River Thames during the relevant period. Given Matters' own assertion that such a find would have been 'sensational', I strongly suspect that if Matters had discovered this fact to be true then the fictitious Doctor 'Stanley' would never have appeared in print. As it was the world had to wait for almost another forty years before learning the name of a much more likely, and real, suspect.

Inspector Frederick Abberline, played by Michael Caine in the TV film, was not, the officer in charge of the investigations into the Whitechapel Killings. That dubious honour belonged to Chief Inspector Donald Swanson. Abberline had, however, spent fourteen years, as an inspector, in the Whitechapel division of the Metropolitan Police. He had considerable experience as a police officer, which included a year as an undercover policeman investigating Fenian activities. Abberline was intimately acquainted with the Whitechapel district. It was undoubtedly this type of experienced officer which James Monro needed for his 'special section', Section 'D', known today as Special Branch, at Scotland Yard. The section was headed by Chief Inspector George Littlechild, but it was under the direct control of James Monro, who, as Assistant Commissioner of the Metropolitan police, also controlled the CID. Abberline was transferred to section 'D' at Scotland Yard in 1887.

There can be little doubt but that it was Abberline's intimate knowledge of the Whitechapel area, as well as his ability as an investigator, which made him ideal in the hunt for the 'Ripper'. Abberline, however, was patently not as well informed as some of his colleagues. He clearly had no views as to the identity of Jack the Ripper - until some fifteen years later when George Chapman stood trial at the Old Bailey for murder.

George Chapman's real name was Severin Klosowski. He was born in Poland in 1865. By the age of twenty-three he was working in Whitechapel as a barber-surgeon, removing warts and in-growing toe-nails. He also trimmed bunions. Klosowski married in 1889.

In 1890, together with his wife Lucy and son, Klosowski emigrated to America and settled in New-Jersey. Within a year, however, they had separated. His wife returned to England alone. Klosowski returned shortly afterwards and began living with a woman named Annie Chapman (not to be confused with the Ripper's second victim). He adopted her surname. In 1895 he bigamously married Mary Spinks and went to live in Hastings. Chapman invested some of Spinks' money in a hairdressing business. Chapman attended to the clients while Mary, an accomplished pianist, entertained them at the piano.

The business was evidently quite successful, since Chapman was soon able to purchase a sailing boat. After a few months however, the couple moved back to London where Chapman became the licencee of The Prince of Wales tavern, Bartholomew Square. Mary Spinks became ill and died on Christmas day 1897. Bessie Taylor took on the job as barmaid and the following year she 'married' Chapman. Together they moved to Bishops Stortford where Chapman took on the lease of a pub called The Grapes.

After a little time they moved again, returning to London and the Monument Tavern, in Union Street, Borough. Now Bessie became very ill and died on the 13th of February 1901. The cause of her death was given as: 'exhaustion from vomiting and diarrhoea'.

Maud Marsh was the next barmaid/wife. Her mother seems to have had an instinctive dislike for Chapman. Maud's mother's fears were justified when, in 1902, Maud began to suffer from a similar illness to that of her predecessors. Maud's mother came to stay to nurse her daughter back to health. But, despite her ministrations, Maud died in October of that year.

Maud's mother now confided her worst fears to her own doctor. He contacted Chapman's doctor who refused to sign a death certificate for Maud, until after he had performed a post-mortem. Chapman was subsequently arrested and charged with murder after the doctor found traces of antimony in the body. He went on trial in 1903.

Abberline wrote:

'I have been so struck with the remarkable coincidences in the two series of murders.... that I have not been able to think of anything else for several days past - not, in fact, since the Attorney General made his opening statement at the recent trial, and traced the antecedents of Chapman before he came to this country in 1888. Since then the idea has taken full possession of me, and everything fits in and dovetails so well that I cannot help feeling that this is the man we struggled so hard to capture fifteen years ago.'

What this demonstrates is that Abberline had no firm suspect in mind before 1903. His reasons for believing that George Chapman had been Jack the Ripper fifteen years earlier, were: Chapman's arrival in London before the murders, the cessation of the murders after Chapman's emigration to America, the fact that Chapman had spent five years studying medicine and surgery in Russia, and that the 'series of murders were the work of an expert surgeon'. Chapman's wife Lucy claimed that, while in America, he had attacked her with a long knife. Abberline also claimed that there were other murders, of a similar nature to the Ripper's, in America when Chapman had lived there. According to Abberline Chapman also resembled several of the 'eye-witness' descriptions.

In an interview given to the 'Pall Mall Gazette' in 1903 Abberline aired his views thus:

'You can state most emphatically that Scotland Yard is really none the wiser on the subject than it was fifteen years ago. It is simple nonsense to talk of the police having proof that the man is dead. I am, and always have been, in the closest touch with Scotland Yard, and it would have been next to impossible for me not to have known about it. Besides, the authorities would have been only too glad to make an end out of such a mystery, if only for their own credit... I know that it has been stated in certain quarters that 'Jack the Ripper' was a man who died in a lunatic asylum a few years ago, but there is nothing at all of a tangible nature to support such a theory.'

As far as the 'drowned student' theory was concerned, Mr Abberline had this to say:

'I know all about that story. But what does it amount to? Simply this - soon after the last murder in Whitechapel the body of a young doctor was found in the Thames, but there is absolutely nothing beyond the fact that he was found at the time to incriminate him. A report was made to the Home Office about the matter, but that it was considered 'final and conclusive' is going altogether beyond the truth... the fact that several months after the student's body was found, the detectives were told to hold themselves in readiness for further investigations seems to point to the conclusion that Scotland Yard did not in any way consider the evidence as final.'

There is no reliable source which suggests that Abberline ever wavered from his belief that George Chapman was Jack the Ripper. But there is no evidence that Abberline was correct in his belief. Chapman would have been only twenty-three years of age at the time of the Whitechapel murders. Furthermore, Chapman was a poisoner-for-profit killer, not a psycho-sexual lunatic who butchered his victims in order to possess parts of their body. The thoroughly unpleasant Chapman was hanged on the 7th April 1903.

Eleven years before George Chapman was executed another doctor, Thomas Neil Cream, stood upon the scaffold in Newgate prison. As the executioner, Billington, pushed the lever to open the trapdoors, he heard the prisoner exclaim... 'I am Jack the Ripper'.

Thomas Neil Cream was born in Glasgow in 1850. At the age of thirteen Thomas was taken, by his parents, to live in Canada where he eventually gained a medical degree from McGill University. Cream was, however, a criminal, and became involved in insurance frauds, abortion, blackmail, arson and petty-thieving. In 1881 he was convicted, in Chicago, of the murder of a Mr Stott, with who's wife Cream was having an adulterous affair. Cream had insured Stott's life for a considerable sum of money.
Far from resting upon his laurels Cream himself, rather stupidly, wrote, an anonymous letter to the District Coroner, suggesting that Stott's body be exhumed and re-examined. This was done and a large quantity of strychnine was discovered in the body. By this time, Cream and Mrs Stott had fled. Mrs Stott, however, turned against Cream and gave evidence at the eventual trial. Cream was convicted of second-degree murder and served a ten year sentence. He was released in July 1881. Shortly afterwards his father died leaving him a legacy of £5,000.

Cream arrived in London three months after his release from the American prison. Within a couple of weeks he had poisoned Ellen Donworth a 19 year old prostitute.
A post-mortem revealed that she had died as a result of strychnine poisoning.

Several letters had been received by the Coroner. Undoubtedly they had been written by Cream himself who appears to have had a wish to be captured. A week later he again poisoned another prostitute 27 year old Matilda Clover. This time though Cream attempted to blackmail a Dr Broadbent, of Portman Square, by writing anonymous letters claiming that Broadbent had murdered the girls. The Countess Russell, at that time resident at the Savoy Hotel, also received a letter claiming that her husband, Lord Russell, had murdered the unfortunate girl. Cream returned to America returning six-months later in April 1892.

Towards the end of April two more prostitutes, 18 year old Emma Shrivell, and 20 year old Alice Marsh, were taken to hospital suffering from severe convulsions. Before they died, of strychnine poisoning, they were able to give a clear description of a doctor named 'Fred' who had given each of them three long pills. Cream was eventually caught. Evidence was given against him by Louise Harvey, an intended victim, who had pretended to swallow the pills given to her by Cream.

Some handwriting 'experts' have credited Dr Cream as the author of some of the Jack the Ripper letters. It would appear that their main reason for doing so is because the 'Ripper' letters contain 'Americanisms' of which Cream, presumably, would have been well acquainted. Cream could not possibly have been Jack the Ripper despite his alleged confession on the scaffold. He was in Joliet prison for ten years, from 1881 until 1891. He was not released from that prison until almost two years after the Whitechapel Murders had ceased.

CHAPTER FOUR:

HOAXS , MYTHS AND MORE MAGICIANS

Candidates for the title of the real Jack the Ripper are many and varied. With each new reminiscence, or police memoir, we are confronted with yet another candidate. The private thoughts of retired policemen and those who claim to have been in the know are grist to the mill of those who seek the truth. Unfortunately, the subject has also attracted its share of charlatans and hoaxers. The seeker of the truth needs to be able to distinguish between what is true and what is not. What is fact and what is the product of a genuinely confused memory.

The Sickert hoax implicating the Duke of Clarence as Jack the Ripper, has, as a result of Stephen Knight's book, become so believed and so entrenched in peoples minds, that it has become enmeshed as part of the folk-lore surrounding the Whitechapel murders. Yet the fact is that there does not exist one shred of evidence against Prince Eddy. There does not even appear to be the slightest suggestion that there ever was any evidence against him.

But the most blatant hoax so far was the surfacing, in 1991, of what we were told was the diary of Jack the Ripper.

The story is that - during the spring of 1991, Liverpudlian Mike Barrett, a retired scrap metal dealer, called in at the home of his old friend and drinking partner Tony Devereux. According to Barrett, Devereux gave him a brown paper parcel containing a book. Devereux told Barrett that he wanted him to have it.

Barrett took the package home and found it to contain a Victorian scrapbook. The first forty-eight pages had been cut out of the book with a knife. The remaining sixty-three pages were written in the form of a diary, allegedly by James Maybrick, a wealthy Victorian Liverpool merchant, who had been poisoned to death by his wife Florence, in May 1889.

The book is, basically, an account of the Whitechapel murders written as a series of confessions.

In 1889 Florence, the American born wife of James Maybrick, was convicted, at Liverpool, of her husband's murder. Many still believe that she was wrongly convicted.

Florence, a daughter of the Baroness Von Roques, had married James Maybrick, twenty-three years her senior, in 1891. James Maybrick was a hypochondriac, always taking medicines. He had confessed, to friends, that he often took arsenic as an aphrodisiac. After spending the first three years of their married life in America they returned to Liverpool and moved into Battlecrease House. They had two children.

In 1887 Florence learned that her husband was in some financial difficulty. She also learned that he kept a mistress. She found solace in the arms of Alfred Brierley, a friend of her husband. In March 1889 Florence and Alfred spent a weekend together in London. Maybrick discovered his wife's infidelity and beat her.

Shortly afterwards Florence purchased a dozen flypapers, containing arsenic, from the local chemist. A few days later she purchased another two-dozen flypapers from another shop. In the meantime James Maybrick had re-drawn his will excluding Florence from any legacy. Soon James Maybrick fell ill. Florence told the doctor that her husband had been taking a 'white powder'. Maybrick's health seemed to improve but, suddenly taking a turn for the worse, he died on 11th May.

A post-mortem revealed that his body contained traces of strychnine, hyoscine, and morphine, as well as arsenic. It was argued that Maybrick's death was due to his own experimentation with drugs. Prejudice, against an unfaithful wife, no doubt influenced the case, and the judges biased summing-up led to Florence being convicted and sentenced todeath. Her sentence was commuted and she served fifteen years in prison. She was released in 1904.

Florence eventually returned to America where she died, in squalor and surrounded by cats, in 1941 aged 76.

The scrapbook, now in Mike Barrett's possession claimed to contain James Maybrick's confessional account of his secret life as Jack the Ripper.

One story of the discovery of the diary was that it had been found under the floorboards of Battlecrease House where Maybrick had lived and died. Tony Devereux died not very long after he had given the book to Barrett without, it would seem, ever confiding its existence to his own family. Barrett eventually took the book to a literary agent who eventually sold the rights to publishers Smith Gryphon. It was subsequently published, in October 1993 amidst great publicity.

One of the many problems, with the 'diary', is that, though diligently researched, the ingenious writer was not as well acquainted with the facts of the Whitechapel murders, as the genuine Jack would undoubtedly have been. The most obvious example of this is that the writer repeats myth as fact.

The writer claims that he, as the killer, laid out at the feet of Annie Chapman a number of brightly polished farthings. Several contemporary reports did mention farthings and the farthings have subsequently passed into the folk-lore of Jack the Ripper. But the fact is that no farthings were found deliberately laid out by the body, they were part of the contents of the victims pockets which were found by Doctor Phillips. They had spilled, through the rips in her clothing and had thus formed into what appeared, to Doctor Phillips, to be a neat pile. The items included a piece of muslim and two combs

The diarist also claims to have written some of the letters sent to the Central News Agency. It is now generally accepted that the letters were, in all probability, penned by journalist T.J. Bulling of that agency. It would seem, however, that the diarist was of the belief that Jack the Ripper had himself written the letters..

Furthermore, on line seven of the very first page of the 'diary', the writer claims to have taken refreshment at the 'Poste House'. Unfortunately there was no Poste House in Liverpool. According to writer Roger Wilkes there is now a Poste House but it has only been called the Poste House since the 1960s. Before that time it was known as the 'Old MM' - the Muck Midden. Furthermore in 1888 the site was occupied by a foundry.

The handwriting of the diarist does not match any known sample of James Maybrick's handwriting, including comparison with his will.

In 1993 a number of ripperologists, (a term coined by Colin Wilson) including Paul Begg, Donald Rumbelow, Martin Fido, Colin Wilson and Keith Skinner, gathered, in London, to take part in a video documentary. The result of this was a television film, presented by Michael Winner. The Diary of Jack the Ripper attempted to demonstrate that some details recorded in the diary could only have been known to the killer. But this is not the case. There is not one single new piece of information contained, within the diary. All of the details could have been ascertained by any careful researcher from previously published accounts. For instance, we are told that the diarist refers to a tin box among Catherine Eddowes possessions.

It is suggested that since this tin box was not known about until the 1980s the diarist must have been privy to secret information known only to the killer. But it is not so. The tin box is listed as being among Catherine Eddowes possessions in contemporary reports published in The Times of 1888.

The film also mentions several clues referred to by the diarist. It is pointed out that the scrap of paper, found near Annie Chapmans body, bearing the initial M (for Maybrick) was a clue dropped, or deliberately left, by the killer. Yet we know that, according to Frederick Stevens, Annie left Crossinghams with her pills wrapped up in the same piece of envelope. The clue barrel is really scraped with the suggestion that the cut ∧ (an inverted V) on each of the upper cheeks of Elizabeth Stride can also be joined to make an M.

Pro diarists also seem to be blessed with similar spatial perceptive powers to those who discern hidden gunmen on photographs of the grassy knoll in Dealy Plaza at the time of President Kennedys assasination. They claim that if you study the photographs of Mary Kellys body you will see, written on the wall behind her, the initials, - wait for it - FM.for Florence Maybrick.

It is also suggested that the diarist wrote the Jewes graffiti found on the wall, in Goulston street shortly after the murder of Catharine Eddowes, and erased on Warrens order. It is pointed out that the diarist mentions his Jewish joke. Yet at the same time the pro-diarists suggest that the, somewhat unusual spelling of Jewes was not actually Jewes at all but James. Yet, if this is the case, it no longer makes any sense for the diarist to refer to it as my Jewish joke.

The diarist also claims that he had taken the uterus, from Annie Chapman, and that he had fried and eaten it '-&I ate all off it, it did not taste like fresh fried bacon but I enjoyed it nevertheless.' It is a well documented fact that the uterus was removed from Annie Chapmans body. Why then does the diarist fail to mention the missing heart of Mary Kelly? Surely such a supreme trophy would have been made a meal of by the diarist. In fact the diarist makes a point of telling us, in paragraph 279, that '&Regret I did not take any of it away with me it is supper time, I could do with a kidney or two ha ha.' One answer might be that the diarist was originally unaware that Mary Kellys heart was missing, a fact which only came to light in 1988,when Doctor Bonds original post-mortem report, together with other papers missing from the official files, was returned, anonymously, to Scotland Yard. The diarist does allude to Mary Kellys missing heart in paragraph 302 - the penultimate paragraph of the diary. This strongly suggests an afterthought.

This could also suggest that the diary was probably started before 1988, before Bonds report was known to the diarist, and amended, later at the very end of the diary. I believe that it was a careless omission, by the diarist who, realising his mistake has added a reference to the missing heart later in the narrative. Indeed the whole flow of the narrative, of the diary, tends to undermine the claim that it is a contemporaneous account.

Shortly after the publication of the diary a gold watch was produced. The watch was manufactured in 1846 and had been purchased, in July 1992, from Stewart the Jewellers in Wallasey, Cheshire. The buyer, Albert Johnson, then noticed that the inner case, behind the watch, contained scratches which purport to be the signature J. MAYBRICK, and the words I AM JACK. The initials of the five victims are also scratched. These scratches have been examined by Doctor R.Tursgoose at the University of Manchester Institute of Science and Technology. Using a scanning electron microscope his opinion was that the scratchings are compatible with having been made in 1888 /89 and are unlikely to be recent. Sceptics may wonder how this artifact, which had remained undiscovered for over a hundred years, only came to light after the diary had surfaced. It is also worth remembering that the diary writer claimed that his first victim was murdered in Manchester. If the watch is genuine then it should surely bear the initials of six victims and not five.

None of the evidence presented in the video documentary was conclusive either way, although the video was, predictably, more favourable towards the theory of James Maybrick being the killer and the diary and watch being genuine. It was however acknowleged that if the diary is indeed a forgery it is indeed a very clever one.

Despite the highly dubious, if not non-existent, provenance the diary was published, in book form, together with a narrative by author Shirley Harrison. The book - 'The Diary of Jack the Ripper' was given some credibility when author and Jack the Ripper expert Colin Wilson wrote the foreword with the conclusion that:

'Maybrick is far and away the most likely Ripper candidate so far'.

Yet the 'diary' is, undoubtedly, a brilliant but blatant fake. The black and gilt calf-bound volume is Victorian and is genuine enough. Such volumes can often be found at Jumble sales, auctions, car boot sales, or old bookshops. This volume had evidently been used, at some time, as a scrapbook. Marks of photo corners can be seen on the flysheet. The narrative, of the diary itself, gives the game away by making references to events and descriptions which, despite having been previously published, have subsequently proved to be untrue. The forger of the diary had evidently studied several books on the subjects of the Whitechapel Murders and the Maybrick case, but, had unfortunately for him, or her, taken too much of the contemporary journalistic licence and subsequent media invention as fact.

In June 1994 Mike Barrett, who had claimed that I'll never change my story cos when you're telling the truth you're telling the truth, confessed that the 'diary' was indeed a forgery. His confession was later retracted by solicitors. However it was too late. Barrett had now given the game away. His confession had revealed that he had bought the ink from the Bluecoats Art Shop in Liverpool. The shop confirmed that they had sold a special manuscript ink containing iron salts and nigrosine as colouring agents. The manuscript ink, allegedly sold to Barrett, also contained chloroacetamide, a modern commercial preservative first manufactured in the 1960s.

Subsequent forensic tests, made upon ink samples from the 'diary', confirm that the diary ink also contains chloroacetamide. This fact alone must surely prove, beyond any shadow of a doubt, that the alleged 'diary' of James Maybrick, as Jack the Ripper, is a modern forgery.

Since these tests Mike Barrett has made another full confession of his hoax in a sworn affidavit copied below

Michael Barrett's Confessions

January 5 1995

From a sworn affidavit:

I MICHAEL BARRETT, make oath and state as follows:-

That I am an Author by occupation and a former Scrap Metal Merchant. I reside alone at XXXXXXXXXXXXXXXXX, and at this time I am incapacitated due to an accident., for which I am attending Hospital as an out-patient. I have this day been informed that it may be neccessary (sic) for them to amputate two of the fingers on my right hand.

Since December 1993 I have been trying, through the press, the Publishers, the Author of the

Book, Mrs Harrison, and my Agent Doreen Montgomery to expose the fraud of ' The Diary of Jack the Ripper ' ("the diary"). Nobody will believe me and in fact some very influential people in the Publishing and Film world have been doing everything to discredit me and in fact they have gone so far as to introduce a new and complete story of the original facts of the Diary and how it came to light.

The facts of this matter are outlined as follows:-
I Michael Barratt (sic) was the author of the original diary of 'Jack the Ripper' and my wife, Anne Barrett, hand wrote it from my typed notes and on occasions at my dictation, the details of which I will explain in due course.
The idea of the Diary came from discussion between Tony Devereux, Anne Barrett my wife and myself, there came I time when I believed such a hoax was a distinct possbility. We looked closely at the background of James Maybrick and I read everything to do with the Jack the Ripper matter. I felt Maybrick was an ideal candidate for Jack the Ripper. Most important of all, he could not defend himself. He was not 'Jack the Ripper' of that I am certain, but, times, places, visits to London and all that fitted. It was to (sic) easey (sic).
I told my wife Anne Barrett, I said, "Anne I'll write a best seller here, we can't fail".

Once I realised we could do it. We had to find the necessary materials, paper, pens and ink. I gave this serious consideration.
Roughly round about January, February 1990 Anne Barrett and I finally decided to go ahead and write the Diary of Jack the Ripper. In fact Anne purchased a Diary, a red leather backed Diary for L25.00p, she made the purchase through a firm in the 1986 Writters Year Book, I cannot remember their name, she paid for the Diary by cheque in the amount of L25 which was drawn on her Lloyds Bank Account,
Water Street Branch, Liverpool. When this Diary arrived in teh post I decided it was of no use, it was very small. My wife is now in possession of this Diary in fact she asked for it specifically recently when I saw her at her home address XXXXXXXXXXXXXXX
At about the same time as all this was being discussed by my wife and I. I spoke to William Graham about our idea. This was my wifes father and he said to me, its a good idea, if you can get away with it and in fact he gave me L50 towards expences which I expected to pay at least for the appropriate paper should I find it.

I feel sure it was the end of January 1990 when I went to theAuctioneer, Outhwaite & Litherland, XXXXXXXXXXXXXXXXXXXXXXXX. It was about 11.30am in the morning when I attended the Auctioneers. I found a photograph Album which contained approximately, approximately (sic) 125 pages of phootgraphs. They were old photographs and they were all to do with teh 1914/1918 1st World War. This Album was part of lot No.126 which was for auction with a 'brass compass', it looked to me like a 'seaman's Compass', it was round faced with a square encasement, all of which was brass, it was marked on the face, North South, East and West in heavy lettering. I particularly noticed that the compass had no 'fingers'.

When the bidding stated (sic) I noticed another man who was interested in the itmes (sic) he was smartly dressed, I would say in his middle forties, he was interested in the photographs. I noticed that his collar and tie were imaculate and I think he was a Military man. This man big up to L45 and then I bid L50 and the other man dropped out.
At this stage I was given a ticket on which was marked the item number and the price I had bid. I then had to hand this ticket over to the Office and I paid L50. This ticked was stamped. I woman, slim build, aged about 35/40 years dealt with me and she asked me my name, which I gave as P Williams, XXXXXXXXXXXXX I think I gave the number as 47. When I was asked for details about me the name Williams arose because I purchased my house from a Mr P Williams, the road name I used is in fact the next street to my mums address, XXXXXXXXXXXXXXX.

64

I then returned to the Auction Room with my stamped ticket and handed it over to an assistant, a young man, who gave me the Lot I had purchased.
I was then told to return return (sic) my ticket to the Office, but I did not do this and left with the Photograph Album and Compass.

When I got the Album and Compass home, I examined it closely, inside the front cover I noticed a makers stamp mark, dated 1908 or 1909 to remove this without trace I soaked the whole of the front cover in Linseed Oil, once the oil was absorbed by the front cover, which took about 2 days to dry out. I even used the heat from the gas oven to assist in the drying out.

I then removed the makers seal which was ready to fall off. I then took a 'Stanley Knife' and removed all the photographs, and quite a few pages. I then made a mark 'kidney' shaped, just below centre inside the cover with the Knife. This last 64 pages inside the Album which Anne and I decided would be the Diary. Anne and I went to town in Liverpool and in Bold Street I bought three pens, that would hold fountain nibs, the little brass nibs. I bought 22 brass nibs at about 7p to 12p, a variety of small brass nibs, all from the 'Medice' art gallery.

This all happened late January 1990 and on the same day that Anne and I bought the nibs we then decided to purchase the ink elsewhere and we decided to make our way to the Bluecoat Chambers, in fact we had a drink in the Empire Pub in Hanover Street on the way.

Anne Barrett and I visited the Bluecoat Chambers Art shop and we purchased a small bottle of Diamine Manuscript ink. I cannot remember the exact price of the Ink. I think it was less than a pound.
We were now ready to go and start the Diary. We went home and on the same evening that we had purchased everything, that is the materials we needed, We decided to have a practise run and we used A4 paper for this, and at first we tried it in my handwriting, but we realised and I must emphasie (sic) this, my handwriting was to (sic) disstinctive (sic) so it had to be in Anne's handwriting, after the practise run which took us approximately two days, we decided to go for hell or bust.

I sat in the living room by the rear lounge window in the corner with my word processor, Anne Barrett sat with her back on to me as she wrote the manuscript. This pose was later filmed by Paul Feldman of MIA Productions Limited.

Several days prior to our purchase of materials I had started to roughly outline the Diary on my word processor.
Anne and I started to write the Diary in all it took us 11 days. I worked on the story and then I dictated it to Anne who wrote it down in the Photograph Album and thus we produced the Diary of Jack the Ripper. Much to my regret there was a witness to this, my young daughter Caroline.

During this period when we were writing the Diary, Tony Devereux was house-bound, very ill and in fact after we completed the Diary we left it for a while with Tony being severly (sic) ill and in fact he died late May early June 1990.

During the writing of the diary of Jack the Ripper, when I was dictating to Anne, mistakes occurred from time to time for example, Page 6 of the diary, 2nd paragraph, line 9 starts with an ink blot, this blot covers a mistake when I told Anne to write down James instead of thomas. The mistake was covered by the Ink Blot.
Page 226 of the Book, page 20, centre page inverted commas, quote "TURN ROUND THREE TIMES, AND CATCH WHOM YOU MAY". This was from Punch Magazine, 3rd week in September 1888. The journalist was P.W. WENN.

Page 228 of the book, page 22 Diary, centre top verse large ink blot which covers the letter 's' which Anne Barrett wrote down by mistake.

Page 250 book, page 44 Diary, centre page, quote: "OH COSTLY INTERCOURSE OF DEATH". This quotation I took from SPHERE HISTORY OF LITERATURE, Volume 2 English Poetry and Prose 1540-1671, Edited by Christopher Ricks, however, Anne Barrett made a mistake when she wrote it down, she should have written down 'O' not 'OH'.

Page 184 in Volume 2 referrs (sic).
When I disposed of the photographs from the Album by giving them to William Graham, I kept one back. This photograph was of a Grave, with a Donkey standing nearby. I had actually written the "Jack the Ripper Diary" first on my word processor, which I purchased in 1985, from Dixons in Church Street, Liverpool City Centre. The Diary was on two hard back discs when I had finished it. The Discs, the one Photograph, the compass, all pens and the remainder of the ink was taken by my sister Lynn Richardson to her home address, XXXXXXXXXXXXXXX.
When I asked her at a later date for the property she informed me that after an article had appeared in the Daily Post, by Harold Brough, she had destroyed everything, in order to protect me.

When I eventually did the deal with Robert Smith he took possession of the Diary and it went right out of my control. There is little doubt in my mind that I have been hoodwinked or if you like conned myself. My inexperience in the Publishing game has been my downfall, whilst all around me are making money, it seems that I am left out of matters, and my Solicitors are now engaged in litigation. I have even had bills to cover expenses incurred by the author of the book, Shirley Harrison.

I finally decided in November 1993 that enough was enough and I made it clear from that time on that the Diary of Jack the Ripper was a forgery, this brought a storm down on me, abuse and threats followed and attacks on my character as Paul Feldman led this attack, because I suppose he had the most to gain from discrediting me.
Mr. Feldman became so obsessed with my efforts to bare the truth of the matter, that he started to threaten me, he took conttrol (sic) of my wife who left me and my child and he rang me up continuously threatening and bullying me and telling me I would never see my family again. On one occasion people were banging on my windows as Feldman threatened my life over the phone. I became so frightened that I sort (sic) the help of a Private Detective Alan Gray and complaints were made to the Police which I understand are still being pursued.

It was about 1st week in December 1994 that my wife Anne Barrett visited me, she asked me to keep my mouth shut and that if I did so I could receive a payment of L20,000 before the end of the month. She was all over me and we even made love, it was all very odd because just as quickley (sic) as she made love to me she threatened me and returned to her old self. She insisted Mr Feldman was a very nice Jewish man who was only trying to help her. My wife was clearly under the influence of this man Feldman who I understand had just become separated from his own wife. It seemed very odd to me that my wife who had been hidden in London for long enough by Feldman should suddenly re-appear and work on me for Mr Feldman.

I have now decided to make this affidavit to make the situation clear with regard to the Forgery of the Jack the Ripper Diary, which Anne Barrett and I did in case anything happenes (sic) to me. I would hate to leave at this stage the name of Mr. Maybrick as a tarnished serial killer when as far as I know, he was not a killer.
I am the author of the Manuscript written by my wife Anne Barrett at my dictation which is known as The Jack the Ripper Diary.

66

I give my name so history do tell what love can do to a gentleman born,

Signed)

Yours Truly -- Michael Barrett.

Sworn at Liverpool in the   (
County of Merseyside, this 5th day of January 1995.

Before me: (Signed)

A Solicitor Empowered to Administer Oaths

D.P. HARDY & CO.,
Imperial Chambers,
XXXXXXXXXXXXXX

Yet despite all of this there are many who still remain convinced that the Maybrick diary is genuine. There is still considerable debate on the matter and literally gigabytes of cyberspace have been devoted to the matter on the Jack the Ripper Website. (www.casebook.org) .

The prize however for the most unsubstantiated theory must however be awarded to author James Tulley who, in his book 'The Secret Of Prisoner 1167 - Was this man Jack the Ripper' (1997) suggests a James Kelly as the Whitechapel murderer. The theory was originally postulated by John Morrison, the man responsible for recently erecting the headstone above Mary Kellys grave. Morrison had published a photostated forty-page document titled Jimmy Kellys Year of The Ripper Murders 1888. Although Morrison sub-titled his publication as the most authentic account ever of the Whitechapel murders there is absolutely nothing whatsoever to connect the unfortunate James Kelly with the Whitechapel murders.

The facts are that on the 21st June 1883 James Kelly murdered Sarah his young bride of just Seventeen days. He was tried, at the Old Bailey, for murder and on the 1st August 1883 was found guilty and sentenced to death. The date set for his execution was the 20th August, but, just three days before he was to suffer execution he was certified insane. One week later on the 26th August he was admitted to Broadmoor Asylum. He escaped from Broadmoor on the 23rd January 1888. He remained at large for thirty-nine years until 1927. He had evidently emigrated to America in the meantime. Kelly had volunteered himself for repatriation to the British Consul in New-Orleans in 1896 but successfully evaded the British Police when his ship arrived at Liverpool. He appears to have remained at large until he eventually gave himself up thirty-one years later at the gates of Broadmoor. He claimed that he gave himself up because he wanted to die among friends. His wish was granted James Kelly died at Broadmoor on Tuesday 17th September 1929.

Morrison claims that Kelly had murdered his wife because she had discovered that he was having an affair with Mary Jane Kelly, and, that he escaped from Broadmoor in order to join Mary Kelly in London. It is alleged that Jimmy discovered that Mary Kelly had, in the meantime, aborted his child and turned to prostitution. Jimmy made enquiries as to her whereabouts finally discovering her in her Millers Court lodgings. He killed her. Morrison claims that Kelly had to murder the other women since they had assisted him in finding Mary.

The characters are all genuine but there is not one shred of evidence put forward to substantiate Mr Morrisons story.

Furthermore Jimmy Kelly does not figure in what we do know of Mary Kellys life. If Kelly had, as Tulley suggests, a relationship with Mary we would almost certainly have heard of it from Joseph Barnett. He had lived with Mary for the last two years of her life and it was he who has supplied most of the information on her life to the police. Had Barnett known of any relationship Kelly may have had with another man, particularly if this other man had only recently escaped from Broadmoor. Barnett would surely, and unhesitatingly have told the police. Such a man would have been the prime suspect.

For Tulleys story to be true we would have to believe that Mary Kelly had her affair with Jimmy Kelly when she was twenty. Yet at this time Mary was, according to Barnett, newley-widowed and living in Cardiff. Barnett claims that Mary Kelly had told him that she had not come to London until four years earlier in 1884 by which time Jimmy Kelly was already in Broadmoor. There is no evidence, nor even a suggestion, that Jimmy Kelly had ever been to Cardiff.

How then could he have had an affair, let alone make pregnant, a young woman whom he could never have met?

We have already seen how even high-ranking police officers who were closely involved with the investigations into the Whitechapel murders were divided in their opinions regarding not only some of the facts of the case but also in their opinions as to the 'likely suspects'. Their letters, memoirs, and marginalia, ambiguous, inaccurate, and in many cases written years after the events, are still being discovered and seized upon as gospel, and often hailed as the final answer.

In 1993 Stewart Evans, a serving policeman and student of the Whitechapel murders, was contacted by the late Mr Barton, a highly respected bookseller and manuscript dealer. Barton had discovered, amongst his stock, a bundle of letters which' had been written to journalist George Sims.

In 1888 Sims, who used the pseudonymn 'Dagonet', had taken a close interest in the Whitechapel murders. He was friendly with, and enjoyed the confidences of, both Monro and MacNaghten. He shared MacNaghten's views on the identity of the killer. Sims, like MacNaghten, believed that Jack the Ripper had put an end to his own life soon after the last murder. Given that Sims enjoyed such close personal relationships with the two men who knew most about the Jack the Ripper crimes his words should not be easily dismissed. Extracts of his writings are reproduced in the appendix. In 1911 he wrote:

'There was ample proof that the real author of the horrors had committed suicide in the last stages of his maniacal frenzy'.

Two years later, in 1913, he had written to John Littlechild, an ex-Metropolitan Chief Inspector Littlechild one-time head of the Special Branch. As a direct subordinate of Monro George Littlechild had been involved with the Ripper investigations.

Sims had evidently written to Littlechild to ask him if he had ever heard of a Dr 'D' in connection with the murders. Littlechild had replied to Sims' enquiry and it was his reply, dated 23rd of September 1913, which was now found among the papers in Mr Bartons bookshop. The relevant passage, of Littlechild's reply, is here reproduced:

'I have never heard of a Dr. 'D' in connection with the Whitechapel murders, but among the suspects, and to my mind a very likely one, was a Dr.'T' (which sounds much like 'D'). He was an American quack named Tumblety. (Tumblety)... was at one time a frequent visitor to London and on these ocassions constantly brought under the notice of police, there being a large dossier concerning him at Scotland Yard. Although a 'sycopathia (sic) sexualis' subject he was not known as a 'sadist' (which the murderer unquestionably was) but his feelings towards women were remarkable and bitter in the extreme, a fact on record'.

The letter concludes that:

'Tumblety was arrested at the time of the murders in connection with unnatural offences and charged at Marlborough Street, remanded on bail, jumped his bail, and got clean away to Boulogne and was never heard of afterwards. It is believed he committed suicide but certain it is that from this time the 'Ripper' murders came to an end&...'

It is just possible that Sims may have been enquiring about the activities of a certain Doctor Davies, of the Whitechapel hospital, or even a 'Doctor' D'Onston both of whom more later. But given the fact that Sims had, through his friendship with both MacNaghten and Monro, been privy to their beliefs, it would seem more obvious that the subject of Sims' letter, Dr 'D', was none other than Montague Druitt, a suspect who was described, by MacNaghten, as 'said to be a doctor'. I shall deal with Druitt later but, in the meantime we must ask who was Tumblety? and why should Chief Inspector Littlechild consider him to be a 'more likely' suspect than Sims' Dr 'D', whom Littlechild had never heard of?

Stewart Evans, a serving police officer, and a colleague, Paul Gainy have, as a result of finding the 'Littlechild letter', attempted to show that Tumblety could have been the Whitechapel killer. The results of their studies culminated in a book called 'Jack the Ripper, First American Serial Killer'. The book was published in 1995.

I fail to understand how Evans and Gainey should consider that Tumblety could be described as American, since he was Canadian. Furthermore even if he had been a serial killer he would, by no means have been the first. The Bender family of Cherryvale Kansas were systematically murdering travellers, who stayed at their 'inn' during 1873. A full fifteen years before Jack the Rippers first murder.

Notwithstanding these slight inaccuracies Evans and Gainey, with the assistance of author and researcher Keith Skinner, were able to throw some considerable light on the identity, and life, of Tumblety.

Francis J. Tumblety was born in Canada around 1833. Soon after 'Frank' was born, the family moved to Rochester, New York. Of Irish descent, Frank was the youngest of eleven children. At the age of twenty-five Frank Tumblety was passing himself off as a medical doctor in Toronto. A flamboyant and colourful character he was often seen riding through the city streets upon a white horse followed by a pack of thoroughbred hounds. Tumbletys 'medical career', in Toronto, came to an a sudden and abrupt end when one of his patients, James Portmore, died as a direct result of the treatment which he had recieved from Tumblety. By the time that the doctor was found guilty of Portmore's manslaughter he had already fled south, across the border, to the American city of Boston.
In Boston his flamboyancy found a different expression. He took to wearing pseudo-military uniforms and decorations to which he was not entitled. He claimed to have been an army surgeon during the Civil War, but now he concentrated upon the dispensing of patent medicines for pimples.

No record has yet been found of Tumbletys medical qualifications. He may well have gained some knowledge from employment in hospitals. He was, in fact, just as George Littlechild described him in his reply to Sims, a 'quack doctor'. A medicine man. It had been one of his own patent 'concoctions' which had killed old Portmore.

Tumblety was known to use many aliases. He was, in short, a con-man and prolific self-publicist. He was prone to draw attention to himself in the strangest of ways. He once managed to talk his way into being arrested as a suspect in the assassination of President Abraham Lincoln. The newspaper coverage of his various antics, and publicity stunts, are legion and have been heavily drawn upon by Evans and Gainey.

Tumblety's hatred of women, particularly of prostitutes, was well known if for no other reason than the fact that he was a homosexual sadist. Notwithstanding these unpleasant facts, Tumblety does appear to have made a considerable living and, as such, it is claimed he was often readily accepted into the various New York and Washington society circles.

Evans and Gainey quote at length the observations of a Colonel Dunham, a New Jersey lawyer and contemporary of Tumblety, who, in an article published in 1888 describes Tumblety as 'an adventurer' who would do almost anything under heaven to achieve notoriety. Dunham tells us how he and a fellow officer were invited to dinner in Tumblety's rooms.

'Tumblety... 'then invited us into his office', where 'quite a museum was revealed - tiers of shelves with glass jars and cases... filled with all sorts of anatomical specimens'. Tumblety placed upon the table a dozen jars, or more, which he claimed contained the wombs of every class of women.

According to Dunham Tumblety had told him that he had once been married to a woman older than himself but that he had eventually discovered that she was a practising prostitute. Since that discovery Tumblety had forsaken womankind.

Such then is the character and personality of Francis Tumblety. But how does this wealthy American con-man/quack doctor fit in with what we know about the Whitechapel murderer? Evans and Gainey have pieced together the following scenario.

'Doctor' Francis Tumblety arrived in Liverpool, from America, around June 1888. He may well have visited England previously to attend to family and business interests which he claimed to have. Evans and Gainey suggest that Tumblety might have been the mysterious medical person who had tried to purchase the anatomical specimens referred to by Coroner Wynne-Baxter, at the inquest summing-up upon Annie Chapman. They further suggest that Tumblety might even have been the mysterious lodger, with the bloodstained shirtsleeves, who, so it had been reported, had fled his lodgings in nearby Batty Street, shortly after the murders of Catherine Eddowes and Elizabeth Stride.

The contention is that Tumblety had a double-motive. His hatred of all women and his desire to possess parts of the female reproductive organs provide the motivation for the murders. Tumblety, presumably unable to obtain his anatomical specimens legitimately, murdered the women, obtained his specimen (except in Stride's case), and then went to ground in lodgings at 22 Batty Street.

The theory is tantalising. But, alas, apart from the mention of Tumblety's name in Littlechild's letter to Sims, there are no mentions of Tumblety's name in any dossier, or other papers, connected with the Whitechapel killings, and not one shred of evidence that Frank Tumblety was Jack the Ripper.

Let us examine the facts on Coroner Wynne-Baxter's mysterious American would-be buyer of anatomical specimens.

At the inquest summing-up upon Annie Chapman, Wynne-Baxter had referred to Doctor Phillips' suggestion that it was the killer's desire to possess the missing organs. Phillips' testimony had been widely reported in the press. Following publication of this evidence Wynne-Baxter had evidently received some new information. He had told the court:

'Within hours of the issue of the morning papers, containing a report of the medical evidence given at the last sitting of the court, I recieved a communication from an officer of one of our great medical schools, that they had information which might or might not have a distinct bearing on our enquiry. I attended at the first opportunity, and was told by the sub-curator of the pathological museum that some months ago an American had called upon him, and asked him to procure a number of specimens of the organ (the uterus) that was missing in the deceased. He stated his willingness to give £20 for each and explained that his object was to issue an actual specimen with each copy of a publication on which he was engaged. Although he was told that his wish was impossible to be complied with, he still urged his request. He desired the organs to be preserved, not in spirit of wine, the usual medium, but in glycerine, in order to preserve them in a flaccid condition, and he wished them sent to America direct. It is known that the request was repeated to another institution of a similar character. Now is it not possible that the knowledge of this demand may have incited some abandoned wretch to possess himself of a specimen. I need hardly say that I at once communicated my information to the Detective department at Scotland Yard.'

Wynne-Baxter was not suggesting that the American was the killer. He was making the point that there was a possible market for the missing uterus and that the killer may have been cashing in on this market.

Whether there really was any basis for the Coroner's assumption, or not, the story was followed up a week later by the 'British Medical Journal'. In the issue of 6th October 1888 it reports that.

'It is true that enquiries were made at one or two medical schools early last year by a foreign physician, who was spending some time in London, as to the possibility of securing certain parts of the body for the purpose of scientific investigation. No large sum, however, was offered. The person in question was a physician of the highest reputability and exceedingly well accredited to this country by the best authorities in his own, and he left London fully eighteen months ago. There was never any real foundation for the hypothesis, and the information communicated, which was not at all of the nature the public has been led to believe, was due to the erroneous interpretation by a minor official of a question which he had overheard and to which a negative reply was given. The theory may be dismissed, and is, we believe, no longer entertained by its author.'

There is, of course, no evidence that the American doctor was Frank Tumblety, although it may well have been. We have already seen that Tumblety was quite capable of using a false identity and it would not have been beyond him to use forged documents to give him the necessary accreditation. But the events between the foreign doctor's enquiries and the Whitechapel murders was at least eighteen months and, on the face of it, there is no real reason to suppose that the two events were, in any way, related.

Coroner Wynne-Baxter evidently decided not to place any weight on this 'Burke and Hare' theory since he did not refer to it at all at the subsequent inquest, three weeks later, upon the body of Elizabeth Stride. It must be remembered however that no organs were removed from Elizabeth Stride's body.

But what about the Batty Street lodger?
There are a number of contemporary newspaper reports relating to reports of a mysterious lodger who 'fled' his lodgings at number 22 Batty Street immediately after the murders of Stride and Eddowes. Batty Street was next to and ran parallel with Berner Street, where Elizabeth Stride had been murdered.

Before considering the fleeing lodger of Batty Street we should first consider this newpaper report which appeared in 'The Globe' on Wednesday 10th October 1888:

'DETECTIVES ON A NEW SCENT
A well informed correspondent states that he has gleaned the following information from an undeniably authentic source, and from careful and persistent inquiries in various quarters he is able to relate the news as fact, though for obvious reasons names and addresses are for the present suppressed:
A certain member of the Criminal Investigation Department has recently journeyed to Liverpool and there traced the movements of a man which have proved of a somewhat mysterious kind. The height of this person and his description generally are fully ascertained, and among other things he was in posession of a black leather bag. This man suddenly left Liverpool for London, and for some time occupied apartments in a well-known first-class hotel in the West End. It is stated that for some reason or another this person was in the habit of 'slumming'. He would visit the lowest parts of London and scour the slums of the East End. He suddenly disappeared from the hotel leaving behind the black leather bag and its contents, and has not returned. He left a small bill unpaid, and ultimately an advertisement appeared in the 'Times', setting forth the gentleman's name and drawing attention to the fact that the bag

would be sold under the Innkeepers' Act to defray expenses, unless claimed. This was done last month by a well-known auctioneer in London and the contents, or some of them, are now in the possession of the police, who are thoroughly investigating the affair. Of these we, of course, cannot make more than mention, but certain documents, wearing apparel, cheque books, prints of an obscene description, letters &c., are said to form the foundation of a most searching enquiry now on foot, which is being vigilantly pursued by those in authority. It has been suggested that the mysterious personage referred to landed in Liverpool from America, but this so far is no more than a suggestion.'

Yet there is nothing here to suggest that the runaway guest was the Whitechapel murderer. What it does suggest is that the obscene material, and other contents of the bag, was of a type sufficiently to be of interest to the police. The certain documents and cheque books might well have attracted the attention of the police particularly if they were in different names. The letters may well have been potential blackmail material. There are any number of reasons why the police might want to interview such a man.

Evans and Gainey suggest the possibility that Tumblety could have been this man, and, that during his 'slumming' trips to London's East End, he took lodgings. There is some evidence that a lodger did attract the attentions of the police.

The 'Daily News' of Tuesday 16th October tells us that:
'...the police are watching with great anxiety a house at the East End which is strongly suspected to have been the actual lodging, or a house made use of by someone connected with the East End murders. Statements made by the neighbours in the district point to the fact that the landlady had a lodger, who, since the Sunday morning of the last Whitechapel murders has been missing. The lodger, it is stated, came in early on the Sunday morning, and the landlady was disturbed by his moving about. She got up very early, and noticed that her lodger had changed some of his clothes. He told her he was going away for a little time, and he asked her to wash the shirt he had taken off, and get it ready for him by the time he came back. As he had been in the habit of going away now and then, she did not think much at the time, and soon afterwards he went out. On looking at his shirt she was astonished to find the wristbands and part of the sleeves saturated with wet blood. The appearance struck her as very strange, and when she heard of the murders her suspicions were aroused. Acting on the advice of some of her neighbours, she gave information to the police and showed them the bloodstained shirt. They took possession of it, and obtained from her a full description of her missing lodger. During the last fortnight she had been under the impression that he would return, and was sanguine that he would probably come back on Saturday or Sunday night, or perhaps Monday evening. The general opinion, however among the neighbours is that he will never return. On finding out the house and visiting it, a reporter found it tenanted by a stout, middle-aged German woman, who speaks very bad English, and was not inclined to give much information further than the fact that her lodger had not returned yet, and she could not say where he had gone or when he would be back. The neighbours state that ever since the information has been given, two detectives and two policemen have been in the house day and night. The house is approached by a court, and as there are alleys running through it into different streets, there are different ways of approach and exit. It is believed from the information obtained concerning the lodger's former movements and his general appearance, together with the fact that numbers of people have seen this same man about the neighbourhood, that the police have in their possession a series of most important clues, and that his ultimate capture is only a question of time.'

We have here then someone who would have been a prime suspect. A man who only occasionally stayed at a lodgings in the heart of the area where the murders took place. On the night of the double murder he turned up at the lodging wearing a bloodstained shirt. He then promptly disappeared. If the landlady's story is true, and given that the first of the double murders had taken place in the very next street shortly before the lodger arrived home, it is not surprising that the police should take an exceptional interest in this man.

The day following the above 'Globe' report the 'Manchester Evening News' brought us up to date with events in Batty Street. The following item appeared in the issue of Wednesday 17th October 1888:

'The story is founded on some matters which occurred more than a fortnight ago. It appears that a man, apparently a foreigner, visited the house of a German laundress at 22 Batty Street, and left four shirts tied in a bundle to be washed. The bundle was not opened at the time, but when the shirts were afterwards taken out, one was found to be considerably bloodstained. The woman communicated with the police, who placed the house under observation, the detectives at the same time being lodged there to arrest the man should he return. This he did last Saturday, and was taken to Leman Street Police Station where he was questioned, and within an hour or two released, his statements having been proved correct.'

Evans and Gainey suggest that this report may have been contrived by the police who wished to cover-up their investigation of this particular individual. But why ?

It seems quite obvious that whoever the Batty Street lodger was he was arrested and was able to satisfy the police of his movements. It would also appear that he was able to account, to the satisfaction of the police, for the bloodstains on his shirt.

There is nothing at all to identify Frank Tumblety as either the Batty Street lodger, or the guest who fled the hotel leaving his bag and the unpaid bill.

Frank Tumblety was, however, arrested on Wednesday 7th November 1888 and charged with four counts of gross indecency. The charges were as follows:

On Friday 27th July 1888, with force and arms in the County of Middlesex, unlawfully did commit an act of gross indecency with another male person, to wit Albert Fisher.
On Friday 31st August 1888, with force and arms in the County aforesaid unlawfully did commit an act of gross indecency with another male person, to wit Arthur Brice.
On Sunday 14th October 1888, with force and arms in the County aforesaid unlawfully did commit an act of gross indecency with another male person, to wit James Crowley.
On Friday 2nd November 1888, with force and arms in the County aforseaid did unlawfully commit an act of gross indecency with another male person, to wit John Doughty.
Four other charges of indecent assault against the same men were also made.

On Friday 16th of November Frank Tumblety was granted bail, at Marlborough Street Police Court. He promptly fled to France where, on the 24th November, using the alias of Frank Townsend, he boarded the French steamer 'La Bretagne' at Le Harve and returned to America. Once back in America, Tumblety, who we already know thrived upon his talent for notoriety and self-publicity, proclaimed to all and sundry that he had been arrested on suspicion of being Jack the Ripper. His feigned indignation may have been contrived to mask the fact that he had in fact been arrested for violent homosexual offences.

That Tumblety craved attention through self-publicity is an established fact perfectly illustrated by Colonel Dunham. He tells us that:

'Tumblety would do almost anything under heaven for notoriety, and although his notoriety in Washington was of a kind to turn people from him, it brought some to him. At the time there was a concert saloon known as the Canterbury Music Hall. One day, Tumblety told me, apparently in great distress, that the management of the Canterbury Hall had been burlesquing him on the stage. An actor, made up in imitation of himself, strutted about the stage with two dogs something like his own, while another performer sang a topical song introducing his name in a ridiculous way. I went with some friends to this concert hall, and, sure enough, about ten o'clock, out came a performer the very image of Tumblety. In a minute, a dog that did not resemble the doctor's, sprang from the auditorium upon the stage and followed the strutting figure. The longer I examined the figure the greater became my surprise at the

perfection of the make-up.
Before I reached my hotel I began, in common with my companions, to suspect that the figure was no other than Tumblety himself. The next day the Lieutenant-Colonel told the 'doctor' of our suspicions. The fellow appeared greatly hurt. He at once instituted an action against the proprietor of the hall for libel. The action was another sham, and three or four nights afterwards the 'doctor' was completely unmasked. When the song was under way a powerful man suddenly sprang from the auditorium to the stage, exclaiming at the figure, "See here, you infernal scoundrel, Doctor Tumblety is my friend, and I wont see him insulted in such an effigy as you are. Come, off with that false mustache and duds."
The false beard and cap were torn from the figure revealing it to be none other than Tumblety himself.'

Such a self-seeking publicist, as Tumblety has been shown to be, could not resist the temptation to suggest that he himself was the notorious Jack the Ripper.

The American newspapers carried a number of refutations by Tumblety. Under the circumstances it is not surprising that such publicity would attract the attention of Scotland Yard. Evans and Gainey tell us that Scotland Yard sent a posse of policemen hot-foot after Tumblety. What is the basis for this claim?

The 'Pall Mall Gazette' of 31st December 1888 reported:

'Inspector Andrews, of Scotland Yard, has arrived in New York from Montreal. It is generally believed that he has received orders from England to commence his search in this city for the Whitechapel murderer. Mr Andrews is reported to have said that there are half a dozen English detectives, two clerks, and one inspector employed in the same chase. The fact that a man suspected of knowing a good deal about this series of crimes left England for this side of the Atlantic three weeks ago, has, says the Telegraph correspondent, produced the impression that Jack the Ripper is in that country.'

Inspector Andrews, an officer seconded from Monro's Special Branch had, in fact, gone to New York from Montreal. He had escorted two men, Roland Gideon and Israel Barnet who were suspected of a terrorist attack upon a bank. Furthermore, as we have seen Tumblety fled from England some seven weeks earlier and not three weeks earlier as Inspector Andrews' quarry appears to have done.

There is no doubt, however, that Tumblety was watched upon his return to New York. But that is not surprising since he was wanted by the English police for violent sexual offences against men. But there really is nothing of any substance to connect Tumblety with the Whitechapel murders except the press reports, undoubtedly generated by Tumblety himself upon his return to America, and the mention of his name in George Littlechild's letter to George Sims.

Tumblety's name does not appear anywhere in any of the remaining Scotland Yard files or internal memos. More significantly there is no mention of him in any police memoir, marginalia or private notes other than the Littlechild letter.

Furthermore at the time of Mary Kelly's murder on the 9th November 1888, Tumblety was in police custody. He had been arrested on the 7th of November and does not appear to have been bailed until the 16th. It has however been suggested however, that, since the charges which Tumblety faced were misdemeanours, he may have been bailed when he was charged and, returning to the court a week later was bailed again. But there really is nothing to support this. There is no record of Tumblety having been released between his arrest, on the 7th of November, and his bail granted at his court appearance nine days later later on the 26th November. If Tumblety had been released during this period he would have, surely, not hesitated to flee the country. This is precisely what he did immediately upon his release from custody on the 16th.

John Littlechild, in his letter to George Sims only mentions Dr 'T' (Tumblety) because it sounded like Dr 'D' the subject of Sims' enquiry. Littlechild does no more than suggest that Tumblety was a 'likely suspect'. Littlechild is in error though when he suggests that Tumblety had committed suicide. Given that after Tumblety's return to America he was hardly out of the American newspapers it is difficult to understand how Littlechild had formed the opinion that Tumblety was dead.

Francis Tumblety was 55 years of age at the time of the Whitechapel murders. He died aged 73 on the 28th May 1903 in St. Louis. He is buried in Rochester, New York.

Tumblety is a fascinating character. He was in London during Jack the Ripper's autumn of terror. His eccentric dress, his flamboyancy, his craving for notoriety all drew attention to himself. These were not the characteristics of the swift, silent and invisible murderer. But the killings were grist to Tumblety's mill and upon his return to America he cashed in on them as only somebody of Tumblety's disposition could do.

The Littlechild letter is an important recent discovery. Even with its inaccuracies it is fascinating inasmuch as it throws another name into the arena of suspicion. But it is not evidence. There is no evidence to support any suggestion that Frank Tumblety was ever seriously considered as the Whitechapel murderer.

Four years before Littlechild wrote his letter. George Sims had published an article in 'Lloyds Weekly News'. Shortly after the article appeared Sims was contacted by a lady. He recalled the meeting in a subsequent article, published in the 'Yarmouth Independent' on 25th February 1911.

'She called upon me late one night. She came to tell me that the Whitechapel fiend had lodged in her house. On the night of the double murder he came in at two in the morning. The next day her husband, going into the lodgers room after he had left it, saw a black bag and, on opening it, discovered a long, sharp knife, and two bloodstained cuffs. The lodger was a medical man, an American. The next day he paid his rent, took his luggage, and left. Then the police were communicated with but nothing more was heard of the American doctor with the suspicious black bag. "But," said my lady visitor, "I have seen him again this week. He is now in practice in the North West of London." She gave his name and addresses of two people who were prepared to come forward and identify him as the lodger with the black bag, the knife and the incriminating cuffs. The next day I took the information, for what it was worth, to the proper quarters. But the doctor was not disturbed in his practice. There was ample proof that the real author of the horrors had committed suicide in the last stage of his frenzy.'

Could this have been the Batty Street landlady now telling her story first-hand to George Sims? If it was then there are some differences from her story of nearly twenty years earlier. But the story is so similar in other respects that it could be assumed that she was the Batty Street landlady. If it was then her lodger could not have been Tumblety since he had already been dead for four years, at the time that she claimed to have seen him again.

Evans and Gainey, who accept that this lady was the same as the Batty Street Landlady, circumvent this difficulty by suggesting that the lady's current interest had been aroused by fresh press interest in the case, and, that after nearly twenty years her memory was impaired and that she must have been mistaken in her identification of the doctor as being one and the same as her 1888 lodger. Presumably her two witnesses must also have suffered from the same difficulties.

An alternative view is that the doctor, now identified by the Batty Street landlady, was indeed one and the same as the Batty Street lodger, and that by the fact that, as we have seen, he had already been questioned and exonerated of any suspicion of involvement in the Whitechapel murders, it was considered unnecessary for the doctor to be disturbed at his practice twenty years after the event.

It is obvious that John Littlechild could not have seen the MacNaghten memorandum or heard of the three principal suspects named in that vitally important document. If Littlechild had been as well informed, as we have been led to believe he was, then he would surely have heard of at least one Dr 'D' - Montague Druitt one of the three suspects named in the memorandum, and described by MacNaghten as a doctor. It is almost certain that Druitt was the subject of Sims enquiry to Littlechild. But Littlechild makes it quite clear, in his letter to Sims, that he had never heard of a Dr 'D'.

This strongly indicates that Littlechilds boss, Monro, despite being requested, by Home Secretary Henry Mathews, to drop a hint to the CID, had not, subsequently, made any of his subordinate officers privy to any of the information relating to Druitt.

During the mid 1960s I was commissioned, as a researcher, by Brian Desmond-Hurst a film director. During the following fifteen years, or so, as a regular visitor to Brians' Belgravia mews house I met many interesting people from the world of film and the arts. Among these was an elderly, and somewhat impoverished old gentleman upon whom Brian had taken pity. I spent many evenings making soup for this old man and was rewarded by some of the most interesting conversations of my life. The old mans' name was Gerald Hamilton. The writer Christopher Isherwood had characterised Hamilton as Mr Norris in his book 'Mr Norris Changes Trains'. Hamilton, a Rugby-educated Irishman, had befriended Roger Casement in 1913 and, during the Great War he had offered his services to Sinn Fein. During the second world war, despite attempting to flee to Ireland disguised as a nun he was arrested and interned for his pro-nazi views.

Gerald Hamilton had once shared a flat with Alestair Crowley, the black magician, in Victoria Street, Central London. Gerald knew of my fledgling interest in Jack the Ripper. According to him Crowley had very firm ideas on the identity and motive of Jack the Ripper, and had often discussed it with him. Alas, at 75 years of age, Hamiltons memory had faded somewhat and he could not recall any of the precise details.

It was not until some years later that I again came upon the Crowley/Jack the Ripper connection through Richard Egans excellent 'Casebook on Jack the Ripper'. Crowleys' theory, it would seem was that Jack the Ripper was a high-ranking black magician whose mission was to sacrifice women at certain places which would form the seven points of a magical cross. The black magician was said to have been granted the power of invisibility as the result of his ritualistic murders.

The whole story is, of course, quite ridiculous, as were so many of Crowleys' claims. However, according to Richard Whittington Egan there does exist an unpublished manuscript written by the late Bernard O'Donnell, a respected Fleet Street crime reporter. O'Donnell names the black magician referred to by Crowley as Roslyn D'Onston, author of 'The Patristic Gospels' published by Grant Richards in 1904.

The source of O'Donnells' information was the Baroness Vittoria Cremers, widow of Baron Louis Cremers a one-time diplomat at the Russian embassy in Washington. She now lived at Marius Road, Balham.

Her story began in 1886 when she lived in the United States. She had read a book called 'Light on the Path' written by Mabel Collins a leading member of the American Theosophical Society. Vittoria Cremers was so impressed by the content of the book that she joined the society. In 1888, the now widowed Cremers came to England and reported to Madame Blavatsky, the societys founder, at her offices at Holland Park. She was given the job of looking after the business interests of the societys monthly journal 'Lucifer'. One of the editors of the magazine was none other than Mabel Collins, whose book had first introduced Cremers to the ideas of the society. The two women became neighbours and close friends.

The story is that one afternoon, in December 1888, Vittoria Cremers discovered Madame Blavatsky and two other prominent theosophists, Doctor Archibald Keightley and his cousin Bertram, poring exitedly over an article in the 'Pall Mall Gazette' a London evening paper. The article, subsequently tracked down by O'Donnell had been written by Lord Crawford, himself an occultist, had suggested the Jack the Ripper was a black magician.

Crawford had revealed that - 'In one of the books by the great modern occultist Eliphas Levi 'The Doctrine and Ritual of Magic' there are given elaborate direction for the working of all kinds of magical spells.' Crawford wrote that 'Levi gives the fullest details of the substances required for the successful working of such spells.' Among this list are such things as candles made from human fat and a preparation made from certain portions of the body of a harlot. Crawford pointed out that 'This last point is insisted upon as essential, and it was this extraordinary fact that first drew my attention to the possible connection with the black arts. Further, in the practice of evocation, the sacrifice of human victims was a necessary part of the process, and the profanation of the cross and other emblems considered sacred, was also enjoined. Leaving out the last murder committed indoors...we find that the sites of the murders form a perfect cross.'

Some months later Vittoria Cremers had to return to America and it was not until March 1890, upon her return to England, that she again met up with Mabel Collins. Mabel had become infatuated with the author of another article in the 'Pall Mall Gazette and was now living with the man at Southsea. Mabel described her paramour as 'a marvellous man... a great magician who has wonderful magical secrets..' His name was Roslyn D'Onston.

A short time after the reunion of Cremers and Collins they, together with D'Onston' returned to London where they went into business together manufacturing beauty creams and potions. They acquired premises in Baker Street. The company' which they formed' was named the Pompadour Cosmetique Company. The venture was financed by the two women using D'Onstons alleged expertise in devising the recipes for the potions.

According to Vittoria Cremers D'Onston was full of colourful stories about himself. He had been a Doctor in Garibaldis' army, a gold prospector in California. He even hinted that he had murdered his wife. Vittoria Cremers suspected that D'Onston was not his real name. As a writer he had used the pseudonym 'Tautriadelta'. Cremers had asked him why he used such a strange name. D'Onstons' reply was that the name meant a devil of a lot. His explanation was that the Hebrew Tau was always shown in the form of a cross. It was the last letter of the sacred alphabet. Tria is the Greek for three, while Delta is the Greek letter D, which is written in the form of a triangle. The completed word, Tautriadelta, represents "cross-three-triangles". He explained that 'There are lots of people who would be interested to know why I use that signature. In fact the knowledge would create quite a sensation. But they will never find out, never".

Mrs Cremers also remembered going into D'Onstons room and finding some dirty pieces of candle burning on the mantlepiece. D'Onston claimed to have made the candles as an experiment. Mabel Collins later astounded Vittoria Cremers by confiding in her that she believed D'Onston was Jack the Ripper. Mabel did not say how she had arrived at this conclusion other that to tell Vittoria that it was 'Something he said to me. Something he showed me. I cannot tell even you. But I know it, and I am afraid.' By now Mabel had had enough of her lover D'Onston. She appears to have distanced herself from both he and the cosmetic company.

Vittoria Cremers evidently decided to attempt to discover the truth for herself. She had noticed, in D'Onstons room, a black enamelled deed-box. D'Onston had told her that he kept a few first editions and some private papers in it. One day, while D'Onston was out Vittoria Cremers had unlocked the box and opened it. Apart from some books the box contained some old ties. She noticed that each one was stained and stiff and hard in the area of the staining which was just behind the ready-made knot.

Vittoria Cremers became convinced that D'Onston was Jack the Ripper when, in July 1890 he discussed with her a newspaper article he was reading about Jack the Ripper. He told Cremers that he had known Jack the Ripper who had been a doctor at the Whitechapel hospital. According to D'Onston the doctor had killed the women from behind and after removing the organs he tucked them away in the space between his shirt and his tie. It was the recollection of her discovery of the bloodstained ties which convinced Vittoria Cremers that it was D'Onston himself who was the killer. D'Onston also told her that the killer had always selected the spot where he intended to kill his victim for a very special reason. He told her it was 'A reason which you would not understand'.

In September 1891 Vittoria Cremers wound up the Pompadour Cosmetic Company. She never saw or heard from D'Onston again.

Bernard O'Donnell had already heard the story of the stained ties but from a different source. In 1925 he had written a series of articles dealing with the life of Betty May. She had been one of Epsteins models and had married Raoul Loveday a disciple of Alestair Crowley. In her book, 'Tiger Woman' said to have been ghosted by O'Donnell, she spoke of her time spent at Crowleys Abbey of Thelema, at Cefalu, in Sicily. Her story is remarkably similar to that of Vittoria Cremers. She claims that:

'..one day I was going through one of the rooms in the abbey when I nearly fell over a small chest that was lying in the middle of it. I opened it and saw inside a number of men's ties. I pulled some of them out, and then dropped them, for they were stiff and stained with something. For the moment I thought it must be blood. Later I found the Mystic (Crowley) and asked him about the ties..... "Sit down," he said, "and I will tell you about them." He then went on to say that these were the relics of one of the most mysterious series of murders that the world had ever known. They had belonged to Jack the Ripper....Jack the Ripper was before your time," he went on. "But I knew him. I knew him personally, and know where he is today. He gave me those ties. Jack the Ripper was a magician. He was one of the cleverest ever known and his crimes were the outcome of his magical studies. The crimes were always of the same nature, and they were obviously carried out by a surgeon of extreme skill. Jack the Ripper was a well known surgeon of his day. Whenever he was going to commit a new crime he put on a new tie. Those are his ties, every one of which was steeped in the blood of his victims. Many theories have been advanced to explain how he managed to escape discovery. But Jack the Ripper was not only a consummate artist in the preparation of his crimes. He had attained the highest powers of magic and could make himself invisible. The ties that you found were those he gave to me, the only relics of the most amazing murders in the history of the world.'

It is clear that the 'black magician' to whom Alestair Crowley refers is none other than D'Onston Since Crowley had annotated this passage in his own copy of 'Tiger Woman' with the words 'Victoria (sic) Cremers' story!!! O'Donnell knew Crowley and he had asked him about Betty Mays discovery of the ties in the box and what had happened to them.

'I destroyed them,' replied Crowley 'When I left the Abbey in Cefalu I had to get rid of a lot of things.' Apart from confirming that they had been given to him Crowley was reticent to give any further details.

The above is all that comprises the case against D'Onston. The story of Vittoria Cremers and the word of Alestair Crowley. They both appear to have been convinced that D'Onston was indeed Jack the Ripper. D'Onston himself never claimed to be Jack the Ripper neither did he pretend to be. He told Vittoria Cremers that he knew who Jack the Ripper was, and Crowleys' story is nothing more than a regurgatation of Cremers' story as he himself attests in his marginalia.

In the Home Office files there are three documents which cast some light on the mysterious D'Onston.

It would seem that on Christmas Eve 1888, a man named George Marsh of 24 Pratt Street, Camden Town called at Scotland Yard where he made a statement. He claimed that about a month earlier he had met a man named Stephenson at the Prince Albert public house in Upper St. Martins Lane. The two men had fallen into casual conversation about the Whitechapel murders. They had subsequently met two or three times a week to further discuss the latest developments. Marsh had told Stephenson that he was an amateur detective hoping to solve the Jack the Ripper mystery. His statement claims that 'Stephenson explained to me how the murders were committed. He said they were the work of a woman-hater, that the murderer would induce a woman to go up a back street or into a room, and to exite his passion would bugger her and cut her throat at the same time with his right hand, holding on with the left. He illustrated the action, and from his manner I am sure that he is the murderer. Today Stephenson told me that Dr. Morgan Davies, of Houndsditch, is the murderer, and he wanted me to see him. He drew up an agreement to share the reward on the conviction of Dr. Davies, and also to go to Mr. Stead of the 'Pall Mall Gazette' with an article for which he expected to get two pounds. He wrote the article in the 'Pall Mall Gazette' about the writing on the wall about Jews. He got four pounds for that. Stephenson has shown me a discharge as a patient from the London Hospital. He is now living at the common lodging-house at 29 Castle Street, St. Martins Lane, W.C., and has been there three weeks.

His description is: Age 48. Height 5 feet 10 inches. Full face. Sallow complexion. Moustache heavy, mouse-coloured, waxed and turned up. Hair brown, turning grey. Eyes sunken. When looking at a stranger generally has an eyeglass. Dress- Grey suit and light brown felt hat, and all well worn. Military appearance and says he has been in forty-two battles. Well-educated. He is not a drunkard. He is what I call a regular soaker - can drink from eight o'clock in the morning until closing time but keep a clear head.'

Two days later - December 26th, 1888 the man described by Marsh himself turned up at Scotland Yard. His name was ... Roslyn D'Onston Stephenson. D'Onston Stephenson had come to Scotland Yard to draw the attention of the police to the attitude of Dr. Morgan Davies, of Castle Street, Houndsditch, to the Whitechapel Murders. He claimed that his suspicions were mainly in connection with the murder of Mary Kelly. He produced a five-page statement. He explained that he had been a patient in a private ward at the London Hospital suffering from typhoid. He claimed that he had been visited nightly by Dr Davies during which times they had discussed the Whitechapel murders. D'Onstons' statement went on:

Dr Davies always insisted on the fact that the murderer was a man of sexual powers almost effete, which could only be brought into action by some strong stimulus - such as sodomy. He was very positive on this point, that the murderer performed on the women from behind - in fact per ano. At that time he could have no information, any more than myself about the fact that the post-mortem examination revealed that semen was found up the womans rectum, mixed with her faeces. Many things, which would seem trivial in writing, seemed to me to connect him with the affair - for instance - he is himself a woman-hater although a man of powerful frame, and, (according to the lines on his sallow face) of strong sexual passions. He is supposed, however, by his intimates never to touch a woman.

One night when five medicos were present, quietly discussing the subject, and combatting his argument that the murderer did not do these things to obtain specimens of uteri (wombs) but that in his case it was the lust of murder developed from sexual lust - a thing not unknown to medicos, he acted (in a way which fairly terrified those five doctors) - the whole scene - he took a knife, 'buggered' an imaginary woman, cut the throat from behind: then, when she was apparrantly laid prostrate, ripped and slashed her in all directions in a perfect state of frenzy. Previously to this performance, I had said: 'After a man had done a thing like this, reaction would take place, and he would collapse and be taken at once by the police, or would attract the attention of the bystanders by his exhausted condition.' Dr D said 'No! he would recover himself when the fit was over and be as calm as a lamb. I will show you!' Then he began his performance. At the end of it he stopped, buttoned up his coat, put on his hat and walked down the room with the most perfect calmness. Certainly his face was as pale as death, but that was all.

It was only a few days ago, after I was positively informed by the editor of the 'Pall Mall Gazette' that the murdered woman last operated on had been sodomized - that I thought - 'How did he know?' His acting was the most vivid I ever saw. Henry Irving was a fool to it.

Another point. He argued that the murderer did not want specimens of uteri, but grasped them, and slashed them off in his madness as being the only hard substance which met his grasp, when his hands were madly plunging into the abdomen of his victim.

I may say that Dr Davies was for some time House Physician at the London Hospital, Whitechapel; that he has a house in Castle Street., Houndsditch; that he has lived in the locality of the murders for some years; and that he professes his intention of going to Australia shortly should he not make a success in his new house.

Roslyn D'O Stephenson

P.S. I have mentioned this matter to a pseudo-detective named George Marsh of 24 Pratt St., Camden Town, NW with whom I have made an agreement (enclosed herewith), to share any reward which he may derive from my information.

Roslyn D'O Stephenson

P.P.S I can be found at any time through Mr Iles of the 'Prince Albert', St Martin's Lane - in a few minutes- I live close to; but do not desire to give my address.

Roslyn D'O Stephenson

The enclosed agreement, the second document in the file, did however give his address. Dated the 24th December it said:
-I hereby agree to pay to Dr R D'O Stephenson (also known as"Sudden Death") one half of any or all rewards or monies received by me on a/c of the conviction of Dr Davies for wilful murder. (signed) Roslyn D'O Stephenson MD, 29 Castle St, WC, St Martin's Lane.'

D'Onston was clearly drunk when he wrote the above agreement since it seems to be an agreement with himself to pay himself half of any reward money.

The third document in the file is a report on the matter written by Inspector J. Roots and sent to Chief Inspector Swanson. It states:

'When Marsh came here on the on 24th I was under the impression that Stephenson was a man I had known twenty years. I now find that impression was correct. He is a travelled man od education and ability, a doctor of medecine upon diplomas of Paris and New York, a major from the Italian army - he fought under Garibaldi, and a newspaper writer. He has led a bohemian life, drinks very heavily, and always carries drugs to sober him and stave of delerium tremens. He was an applicant for the Orphanage secretaryship at the last election.'

D'Onston/Stephenson was incorrect in his belief that the victims of Jack the Ripper were sodomised. He was however convinced that Davies was Jack the Ripper. It would seem that his references to Vittoria Cremers and Mabel Collins, two years later, were quite probably misunderstood by them to be references to himself. Crowley had presumably got the story from Cremers.

As for the ties, if they ever really did exist, and if Crowley really had believed them to have once been used by a great magician it is extremely unlikely that he would have casually discarded them when he vacated his abbey in Sicily. There remains no reason whatsoever to consider Roslyn D'Onston/Stephenson as a suspect in the Whitechapel murders.

. We do know that in 1904 D'Onston, having by now embraced Christianity, published a full-length book entitled 'The Patristic Gospels', a critical analysis of the four gospels. It is said to be a brilliant and deeply religious work written, as D'Onston himself said - 'with the undeniable guidance of the Holy Spirit.

Crowley had told O'Donnell that D'Onston had died in 1912. In fact D'Onston died, of throat cancer, on the 9th October 1916 at the Islington Infirmary. He is buried in the East Finchley Cemetery.

CHAPTER FIVE:

THE MACNAGHTEN PAPERS

During the 1950s, the late Daniel Farson presented a television series called 'Farson's Guide to the British'. Several of the programmes dealt with the Whitechapel murders.

Whilst researching for his programmes, Farson happened to mention to a friend, Lady Rose MacLaren, that he was busy preparing a programme on the subject of Jack the Ripper. It so happened that Rose MacLaren was the daughter-in-law of Lady Aberconway - the daughter of Sir Melville MacNaghten. Christabel Aberconway still had some of her late father's private papers. Among these papers was a draft copy of a confidential report which Melville MacNaghten had prepared, for the Home Secretary, in 1894.

It would appear that the 'Sun' newspaper had published a series of stories on the Whitechapel murders in which they had named a certain Thomas Cutbush as the killer.

Thomas Cutbush, the nephew of a police superintendent who later committed suicide had suffered a mental breakdown around 1888 and, after giving up his job, took to rambling the streets. At first he appeared to be in the habit of pinching ladies bottoms but he had subsequently progressed to the more painful, and dangerous, pursuit of stabbing ladies bottoms with a sharp pair of scissors. As a result of this he was now in Broadmoor where he died in 1903.

The 'Sun' articles, naming Cutbush as the Whitechapel murderer, had caused a small sensation, and the Home Secretary, in anticipation of being questioned upon the matter, had asked MacNaghten to prepare a brief on the matter. There are at least two versions of MacNaghten's report. The final, and official version (see appendix), and, MacNaghtens draft version, though the gist is the same in each. In the draft version, which Farson now held, MacNaghten tells of three men, either of whom, in MacNaghten's opinion would have been much more likely to have been the Whitechapel killer than Thomas Cutbush.
They are:

Montague John Druitt - a doctor of about 41 years of age and of good family, who disappeared at the time of the Millers Court murder, and whose body was found floating in the River Thames on the 31st December, ie; 7 weeks after that said murder. The body was said to have been in the water for a month or more. On it was found a season ticket between Blackheath and London. From private information, I have little doubt that his own family suspected this man of being the Whitechapel murderer; it was alleged that he was sexually insane

Kosminski - a Polish Jew and resident in Whitechapel. This man became insane owing to many years indulgence in solitary vices. He had a great hate of women, especially of the prostitute class, and had strong homicidal tendencies, he was removed to a lunatic asylum in about 1889. There were many crimes connected with this man which made him a strong suspect.

Michael Ostrog - a Russian doctor, and a convict, who was frequently detained in a lunatic asylum as a homicidal maniac. This man's antecedents were of the worst possible type, and his whereabouts at the time of the murders could never be ascertained.

.

In the same document MacNaghten also writes:

'...personally, and after much careful and deliberate consideration, I am inclined to exonerate the last two, but I have always held strong opinions regarding option number one and the more I think the matter over, the stronger do these opinions become. The truth however will never be known, and did indeed at one time lie at the bottom of the Thames, if my conjectures be correct.'

Both Kosminski and Ostrog are positively described as homicidal maniacs with criminal backgrounds. Whereas suspicion seems to fall upon Druitt as the result of allegations voiced by Druitt's own family. For MacNaghten to be so convinced that Druitt was the killer he must have known more. We can be sure therefore that he is suppressing some known details, in contrast with the information he gives on the other two suspects.

Even if that is not the case, there is still some suggestion that MacNaghten altered some of the details in the case of Druitt by adding ten years to his actual age, and, by describing him as a doctor when in fact Druitt, a fully qualified barrister, had spent his working life as a schoolmaster. It can, however, be argued that Druitt was, in fact, a Doctor - of Law. Furthermore the term 'Doctor' was often used as a form of address to schoolmasters.

The importance of the discovery of the MacNaghten papers has rightly been acknowleged as the starting point for all subsequent research into the Whitechapel murders.

It has been suggested that the names contained within the MacNaghten papers may have been drawn at random from a much larger list. No other list has been found in the police records, though both Sims and Major Griffithst refer to a shortlist. However, given MacNaghten's assertion that, in his opinion, Druitt was the likeliest suspect, it can be assumed that even if a more comprehensive list did exist he would still have been of the same opinion.

Major Griffiths had been a professional soldier before joining the prison service. He was also a crime historian, and a close personal friend of Melville MacNaghten. Four years after MacNaghten penned his now famous memo, Griffiths wrote:

'...the police, after the last murder, had brought their investigations to the point of strongly suspecting several persons, all of them known to be homicidal lunatics, and against three of these they held very plausible and reasonable grounds of suspicion. Concerning two of them the case was weak, although it was based on certain colourable facts. One was a Polish Jew, a known lunatic, who was at large in the district of Whitechapel at the time of the murders, and who, having afterwards developed homicidal tendencies, was confined to an asylum. This man was said to resemble the murderer by the one person who got a glimpse of him - the police constable in Mitre Court.
The second possible criminal was a Russian doctor, also insane, who had been a convict in both England and Siberia. This man was in the habit of carrying about knives and surgical instruments in his pockets; his antecedents were of the very worst, and at the time of the Whitechapel murders he was in hiding, or at least, his whereabouts were never exactly known.
The third person was of the same type, but the suspicion in his case was stronger, and there was every reason to believe that his own friends entertained grave doubts about him. He was also a doctor in the prime of life, was believed to be insane or on the borderland of insanity, and he disappeared after the last murder, that in Millers Court, on the 9th November 1888. On the last day of that year, seven weeks later, his body was found floating in the Thames, and was said to have been in the water for a month. The theory in this case is that after his last exploit, which was the most fiendish of all, his brain gave way, and he became furiously insane and committed suicide.'

There is no room for doubt that Griffiths is endorsing, and elaborating, upon MacNaghten's suspicions. There is no conflict between Griffiths' description of MacNaghten's suspects; Kosminski, Ostrog, and Druitt, with the facts which have subsequently been discovered about them.

Until the 1980s very little was known about Kosminski apart from the scant details contained in MacNaghten's papers. But diligent, and exhaustive research, by writers Paul Begg and Martin Fido, has unearthed one Kosminski who seems to fit the bill.

During Paul Begg's research into the Whitechapel murders he was handed a copy of Sir Robert Anderson's biography 'The Lighter Side of My Official Life'. Sir Robert had been the head of the CID at the time of the murders although he was hardly involved due to his absence abroad on sick leave. He had only been appointed to the office the day before he left for his holiday to fill the vacancy left by Monro's departure to the Home Office. For operational purposes Anderson did not effectively take up his post until the 1st October the day after the double murder.
In his book Anderson is nonetheless able to recount how:

'...the conclusion... we came to was that he (the killer) and his people were certain low-class Polish Jews... I will merely add that the only person who ever had a good view of the murderer unhesitatingly identified the suspect... but refused to give evidence against him....'

While Anderson's views on the matter are well known, the real importance of Paul Begg's find was that the actual volume of Anderson's memoirs, which he now held, had once belonged to Inspector Donald Swanson.

Donald Swanson was born at Geise, in the Scottish highlands, in 1848. He grew up in Thurso - the mainland's most Northerly town. His ambition was to be a teacher and he became proficient in both Latin and Greek. At some time he decided against an academic career and travelled South to London. In April 1868 he joined the Metropolitan Police. He was married with five children. He died in New Malden, Surrey, aged 76, on the 24th November 1924. Swanson was one of the few officers involved in this investigation who did not go into print with his memoirs, and, until Paul Begg was shown Swanson's personal copy of Anderson's book, his views on the case were largely unknown.
In the margin of the book next to Anderson's description of the low-class Polish Jew, Swanson had pencilled:

'Kosminski was the man'.

At the bottom of the page he had noted that:

'...because the suspect was also a Jew and also because his evidence would be the means of the murderer being hanged which he did not wish to be on his mind.'

On the same page:

'...and after his identification which suspect knew, no other murder of this kind took place in London.'

On the end papers of the book Swanson elaborates:

'...after the suspect had been identified at the Seaside Home where he had been sent by us with difficulty, in order to subject him to identification, and he knew he was identified. On suspect's return to his brother's house in Whitechapel he was watched by police (City CID) day and night. In a very short time the suspect with his hands tied behind his back, was sent to Stepney Workhouse and then to Colney Hatch and died shortly afterwards. Kosminski was the suspect... DSS.'

Swanson appears, at first, to be clarifying the identity of Anderson's Polish Jew. He tells us that Kosminski was taken, or tricked into going, to a seaside home, where he was identified by a witness, also a Polish Jew, who was the only person to have a good view of the killer. The witness identified Kosminski but refused to give evidence against him because he was a fellow Polish Jew and the witness did not want to be responsible for giving Kosminski over to the hangman. Yet, notwithstanding this identification Kosminski was released, and allowed to return to his brother's house, where he was watched by the City Police. Very soon though he is bound and taken off to a workhouse before being sent to an asylum.

Working on this information, writer and broadcaster Martin Fido, discovered, in the records of the Colney Hatch asylum, one Aaron Kosminski. This was the only entry for this name. From this we may assume that this is the Kosminski to whom Anderson alludes, and to whom Swanson, Griffiths and MacNaghten refer.

Fido reveals that Aaron Kosminski had been admitted to the Colney Hatch Asylum on the 7th February 1891. After three years at Colney Hatch he was transferred, in 1894, to the Leavesden Asylum for imbeciles where he eventually died on the 24th March 1919 aged 54.

So what kind of character was Aaron Kosminski ?
We are told by Melville MacNaghten that Kosminski:

'...became insane owing to many years indulgence in solitary vices.'

The asylum records show that Jacob Cohen of 51 Carter Lane, St Pauls, made a statement in which he said that Aaron Kosminski had practiced:

'..self abuse... refused to wash... and had not attempted work for many years.'

Solitary vices ?... Self abuse ?... Aaron Kosminski was a prolific masturbator.
The prevailing Victorian belief was that masturbation could cause insanity. This, it is clearly suggested, was the case with Aaron Kosminski.
The author of the 'Clinical Manual of Mental Disease', Dr A. Campbell Clark, gives us, in his manual published in 1897, a contemporary insight into this condition:

'...the first signs of its evil influence are depression and hypochondria... such people seek solitude and secrecy... and... if they possess any moral sense at all they will engage in self-reproach and a loss of self-respect. Such persons display sexual antipathy and a fierce unreasoning hatred of the opposite sex.'

Dr Clark tells us of a case under his care at the Lanark County Asylum.

'...a determined masturbator, who acts as a mason's labourer, and is a most useful man. He indulges in self-abuse every morning, and for some hours afterwards is so dangerous that he has to be kept in the asylum until after breakfast. By that time he has cooled down and is safe to go out to work. He is a case of impulsive homicide.'

Doctor Tuke, the noted psychiatrist and founder of the York retreat, which pioneered the humane treatment of the insane, described the physical signs of the prolific masturbator as:

'...anorexia, atonic dyspepsia, palpitations, peculiar head sensations, skin pale and cold, circulation sluggish, susceptible to disease; boils eruptions etc. He also notes that the masturbator is unsociable, lies long in bed and especially avoids the opposite sex.'

These observations can, of course, only be food for thought in considering the personality, and overall physical appearance of Kosminski, given the scant information available on him at present. But if one accepts the medical description of him it does become difficult to readily accept that the 23 years old Kosminski, who, according to the Asylum records only spoke Yiddish, could ever have been seen as a reasonable prospect by even the most desperate prostitute.

Paul Begg has suggested that Kosminskis' illness may not have afflicted him until after his detention two years after the Whitechapel murders. But the only support that I can find for this suggestion is MacNaghten's assertion that Kosminski 'became insane', and Griffiths' observation that '...after the murders', ie; after the end of 1888, Kosminski developed 'homicidal tendencies'.

But MacNaghten goes on to say that Kosminski's insanity was due to '...many years indulgence.'
By 'many' we may assume that MacNaghten must mean more than two. The fact that Aaron Kosminski was eventually transferred to an asylum for imbeciles strongly suggests that his illness had been finally diagnosed as imbecility - a condition of congenital origin. In other words a condition present from birth, and not, as has been suggested, an illness which took hold of him when he was 25 years of age. Furthermore the killer was, without doubt, someone who was insane at the time of the murders and not someone who developed homicidal tendencies 'after the end of 1888'.

If one compares the information we have on MacNaghten's Kosminski, and the Aaron Kosminski discovered by Martin Fido, the inescapable conclusion must be that they are one and the same person. Yet MacNaghten describes Kosminski as a 'homicidal maniac', whereas the Colney Hatch asylum records tell us that Aaron Kosminski was '...no danger to himself or others'. MacNaghten also tells us that:

'There were many crimes connected with this man which made him a strong suspect.'

Yet no record exists, in any official document, apart from MacNaghtens notes, which indicates that Kosminski ever commited any criminal offence whatsoever.

If we knew where Kosminski was, and the nature of the 'homicidal tendencies' which he had developed after the murders, and in the period up to his detention in January 1891, fourteen months after the last-known Ripper murder, we may be on firmer ground. Though one is bound to ask why, if Kosminski was Jack the Ripper, did he stop killing?
The real Jack the Ripper had not displayed any intention of slowing down - indeed each murder had increased in ferocity until the 'awful glut' at Millers Court.

It is of course quite possible that Kosminski, the harmless imbecile, developed his homicidal tendencies as a direct result of the Whitechapel murders. We are told that he was there in the thick of it. If so then he must have been aware of the activities of Jack the Ripper, as well as of the increased activity of the police in the area in which he frequently roamed.

In Robert Anderson's book he tells us that he came to his conclusions 'as a result of a house-to-house search' following the double murder of Elizabeth Stride and Catherine Eddowes.

So what did come out of this search other than the 'eye-witness accounts' given by Joseph

Lawende and Joseph Levy? Lawende claimed to have had a good look at the killer, as had Israel Schwartz earlier on the same night. Either of these two men, who were both Jewish, could have been the unidentified witness who refused to testify against the unhappy Kosminski, who according to Swanson had been taken to the seaside home for that very purpose.

One problem with these events is the time lapse between them.
Anderson is clearly referring to contemporary events which took place in 1888, whereas Swanson, if his marginalia is to be accepted, must be writing of a much later period.
Swanson tells us that the suspect (Kosminski) was identified at the 'seaside home'. Paul Begg suggests that this is a reference to the police convalescent home at Brighton. Paul Begg acknowledges that the difficulty here is that the Police Seaside Home, at Brighton had not even been built at the time of the events being described by Anderson.

It is quite possible though that Kosminski was, at some later time, taken to the seaside home and identified, but this explanation does not explain the time lapse between the two described events. Neither does it help to identify the 'witness', who presumably had some reason for being at the police convalescent seaside home.

The only clues which we have as to the identity of the 'witness' who, according to Swanson's marginalia, identified the suspect is Anderson's description of him as being of the same '...low class Polish Jew' and that he was the only person to '...have had a good look at the killer.' Lawende? Levy? Harris? Or Schwartz? One can take their pick.

But if it were any of these men, one must surely ask what they were doing at the seaside convalescent home for policemen. None of them were policemen, it is indeed unlikely that there were any 'low-class Polish Jewish policemen', and why take a suspect all the way to Brighton from Whitechapel if the witness himself lived in Whitechapel, unless, of course, the witness was a member of the staff at the seaside home.

Anderson is however, clearly in error when he describes the 'witness' as being the one person who had a good look at the killer. George Hutchinson gave a very clear description of a man entering Mary Kelly's room with her just a few hours before her butchered body was found there. Curiously enough Hutchinson had not been called as a witness at the inquest upon Kelly. It is possible, though unlikely, therefore that Anderson did not know of Hutchinson's evidence.

Hutchinson was not a low-class Polish Jew and he could not have been the witness at the seaside home. But, if one, sensibly, discounts the various sightings of Mary Kelly some hours after her death, then Hutchinson was almost certainly the last person to see her alive.
If the Anderson/Swanson 'witness' was either Lawende, Harris or Levy, then their theories' credibility is further called into question when one recalls that Lawende himself claimed that he would not be able to recognise the man again.

It is possible that Lawende and Levy were playing a game with the police and had no doubt coloured their observations somewhat in order to gain some sort of notoriety. Griffiths certainly mentions that the case against the first two suspects (of MacNaghten's list of three) Kosminski and Ostrog were based on '...certain colourable facts.'

It is also worth remembering that Harris, the somewhat reticent companion of Lawende and Levy, had strongly hinted that none of them had actually seen anything other than the back of a man and a woman. The sensible Harris had no doubt realised what the consequences might be for wasting the time of the police during this important investigation.

If we accept the Swanson marginalia then we must accept it warts an' all. The problem here though is that Swanson has displayed a remarkable lack of knowledge as to Kosminski's fate, for he tells us that the 'suspect', Kosminski, died shortly afterwards. As we know Aaron Kosminski lived on for a further thirty-one years until 1919 without, it would appear, any attempt to question him about the Whitechapel murders.

Some writers have laid great emphasis on the fact that Swanson was not senile or forgetful. But, in his marginalia, written at least 22 years after the events described, he has quite definitely, at least in one respect, confused one suspect, Kosminski, with another Montague Druitt. If he is clear that the killer was Kosminski then he is wrong when he describes him as dead. If Swanson is correct in his assertion that the killer died shortly afterwards then he may have meant Druitt who did put an end to his life shortly after the last murder, and at about the same time that the events being described by Anderson were taking place.

The possibility that Swanson had confused some of the known facts, relating to Kominski and Druitt, as he appears to have done with the seaside home scenario, cannot be discounted.

Moreover Martin Fido discovered that, on the 7th December 1888, another resident of Whitechapel, 23 years old Aaron Cohen, of 86 Leman Street, had been taken before Thames Magistrates Court for being a lunatic wandering at large. He was sent to the Workhouse infirmary for observationas a result of which two weeks later he was admitted to Colney Hatch asylum. He had no known relatives. Cohen was a foreign Jew, a tailor, and had no known relatives. He is described as dangerous, dirty, mischevious and destructive. He died of exhaustion of mania and pulmonary phthisis on the 20th October 1889 aged only 24. Although there is no reason whatever to suspect that Cohen was the Whitechapel Murderer his antecedents and subsequent history fit more closely with the Swanson marginalia suspect than does the unfortunate Kosminski.

. The Seaside Home may not have been a reference to Brighton at all. It might have alluded to Gravesend. Abberline had gone to Gravesend and returned with Pigott. It is the only documented instance of the police investigation, into the Whitechapel murders, in which the police had any cause to go to the coast, and return with a suspect under restraint.

The 'great difficulty' with which the suspect was brought to Leman Street police station was caused by the enormous number of onlookers who had gathered there in anticipation of Abberlines return from Gravesend, with the suspect Pigott. Pigott was identified, at Leman Street police station' by Mary Chappell, a friend of Mrs Fiddymont, landlady of the Prince Albert. Furthermore Pigott had, unlike Kosminski, died by the time Swanson wrote his marginalia.

There is no suggestion that Pigott was a 'low class Polish Jew', but these events took place at precisely the same time that Pizer, who was sometimes referred to as Leather Apron, and who was a low-class Polish Jew, was also being detained at exactly the same time, and at the same police station.

It is my contention that Swanson has confused a number of events. Swansons' story appears to be a composite of a number of different events and personalities. As such his marginalia must be discounted as unreliable.

Notwithstanding these difficulties it was announced in 2014 that a DNA examination had proved beyond doubt that kosminski was the killer. This sensational claim was made by Russell Edwards author of a book 'Naming Jack the Ripper.'

Edwards claimed, amid wide press coverage, that he possessed the only piece of forensic evidence in the whole history of the case and that after fourteen years of research into the case he had finally solved the mystery of the identity of Jack the Ripper.. He further claimed, somewhat arrogantly, that only those who wished to perpetuate a myth would doubt his findings. So what is this evidence.

The story surrounds the existence of a piece of printed silk material described, variously as a shawl, or table runner. According to Edwards the item was found, in Mitre Square, next to the mutilated body of Catherine Eddowes by Acting Police Sergeant Amos Simpson.. The claim is made that Simpson was given permission to take the shawl home as a gift for his dressmaker wife. We are told that the garment, though stained, was left unused and unwashed and simply packed away in the attic of the family home where it remained apparently unseen by the public for the next 100 years.

The shawl passed down the family until it came into the possession of David Melville Hayes a great great nephew of Amos Simpson. The oral tradition which had also passed down the family line along with the shawl was this; Amos Simpson, on special duties from his own division, was the first Police officer to discover the body in Mitre Square. He had simply picked up the shawl and kept it. David Melville Hayes recalls seeing the shawl, at his Grandmothers house, for the first time when he was a young boy. It was kept in an old sea chest along with Sunday best family clothes.

Having been loaned in 1991 to the Metropolitan Police Black Museum (now the crime Museum) the shawl was returned to Melville Hayes in 2001 at his own request. It subsequently made several appearances at Jack the Ripper conferences and meetings. It was swabbed, for genetic material twice for two separate TV documentaries as well as subjected to psychic investigation. Melville-Hayes sold the shawl in 2007. The proceeds of the sale were donated to the RNLI charity. The purchaser was businessman, and Ripper enthusiast, Russell Edwards

Having purchased the Shawl Edwards sought to have it tested for any genetic material. The analysis was conducted, in 2011, by Jari Louhelainen, a genetic expert form the John Moores University of Liverpool. Louhelainen, is a respected scientist specializing in historical crime scene analysis, He conducted the research in his spare time using a technique he himself had devised. He was assisted in this work by Dr David Miller.

They photographed the staining on the shawl using an infra red camera. This primary analysis revealed arterial blood consistent with blood spatter associated with slashing. They also found semen stains. Usually such bloodstains can yield DNA but these samples were too old for swabbing. Instead Louhelainen devised his own method, which he calls vacuuming. Using a pipette containing a buffering liquid he was able to lift some samples. He then duplicated those samples using a chain reaction by the use of a conventional polymerase in order to create a large enough amount for sequencing. No peer group validation of Louhelianens work has yet been undertaken because the precise details of his techniques have not yet been revealed.

However we are told that Louhelianen was able to extract several complete mtDNA profiles from the shawl. Doctor Miller found surviving epithelium cells, a type of cell which coats organs. In this case it was suggested that they had come from the urethra during ejaculation.

The next step was to trace descendants of both Eddowes and Kosminski to whom they could match the mDNA.

Mitchocondrial DNA or mtDNA is passed down from mother to her children. It is described as a maternal marker. As a male I have my mothers mtDNA but my children do not. They will have their mothers mtDNA. Multiple individuals can have the same mtDNA type, which means that unlike Nuclear DNA unique identifications are not possible using mtDNA analysis.

But before we consider the validity of Louhelainens findings let us just question the provenance of the shawl itself.

There is not one scrap of evidence that the shawl was in anyway connected to the victim Eddowes. There is no record of the shawl having been found in, or even near, Mitre Square and no item of that description is listed in the items which were found in her possession. Contemporary police records do not support Amos Simpsons story that he was on duty anywhere near Mitre Square on the night of the murder contradicting Simpsons claim that he was the first police officer to discover the body.

The eyewitnesses who claim to have seen Eddowes shortly before her murder are consistent in their description of her clothing, a black jacket and black bonnet and chintz skirt, with no mention of any silk shawl. Moreover it is also extremely unlikely that Eddowes would have been in possession of such an expensive item given that she had earlier had to pawn her husbands boots in order to obtain beer money. Furthermore it is inconceivable that if such an item been found on, or even close by, the body of Eddowes, that Simpson would have simply been allowed to take it home. Notwithstanding these difficulties the shawl took on the persona of the myth surrounding it.

Subsequent to Louhelianens examination of the shawl Russell Edwards announced that a segment of mitochondrial DNA, from the blood had a sequence of variation which was a match with that of Karen Miller a descendant of Catherine Eddowes and that this variation is known as Global Private Mutation 314.1C a rare gene variation usually found only in a single family or in a small population. According to the database of the Institute of legal Medicine and based on the latest information available, the variation of both Millers DNA and the DNA from the bloodstains on the shawl shared a frequency estimate of only 0.000003506, this means it is present in only 1 in 290,000 of the worlds population. With the current population of the UK at roughly 64 million Karen Miller would be only one of 233 people who would have this genetic variation. Since Catherine Eddowes would also have possessed this variation, when the UK population in 1888 was about half of what it is now she would have been one of about 136 people with that genetic profile. On the face of it these results would seem to confirm a connection between the shawl and Catherine Eddowes. No such connection could be claimed for Kosminski however. Semen stains on the shawl showed only that it was a very common subtype T1a1.

But all is not as it would seem. Experts, with a detailed knowledge of the mtDNA database claim that Dr Louhelianen had made an "error of nomenclature" because the mutation in question should be written as 315.1C and not 314.1C. If standard forensic practice had been followed and the variation had been described properly Louhelianen would have discovered that the mutation was not rare but shared by more than 99% of people of European descent. This error, by Louhelianen, has been subsequently confirmed by Professor Sir Alec Jeffreys, the forensic scientist who invented DNA fingerprinting in 1984.

It must also be pointed out that the shawl itself had been in contact with many human hands, as well as having been kept in a trunk with Amos Simpsons family Sunday clothes, and that at least two of Eddowes descendants had been in contact with the shawl in 2007 during the making of a television documentary. All of these factors make the probability of cross-contamination a highly likely possibility thus rendering any DNA present unworthy of consideration as evidence. This together with the uncertain provenance of the shawl itself, currently at auction once more with a reserve price said to be over two million pounds, and not least the unsatisfactory forensic evidence, strongly suggests that the blurb on Russell Edwards book claiming 'Case Closed' is not justified.

However, in leaving Kosminski to those who will, hopefully, discover more about him, I will add the following for their consideration:

Doctor Campbell Clark tells us, in his manual, that he discovered, among his masturbators, four cases where a...

'...low type of inflammation over one knee-cap came on, the result of long prolonged attitudes of prayer and supplication. In one case the inflammation became gangerous but the patient recovered and has since resumed his vicious indulgence.'

Interestingly enough the cause of death shown on Aaron Kosminski's death records is: 'gangrene of the left knee'.

MacNaghten's second suspect is Michael Ostrog.

A con-man and a thief born in 1833, it would appear from police records that he was a Russian/Polish Jew. In his chosen career as a confidence trickster he employed many aliases. He came to the attention of the authorities twenty five years before the Whitechapel murders when he was sentenced to ten months imprisonment in Oxford for swindling local hotels. Upon his release he seems to have travelled around the country stealing and swindling whenever the opportunity presented itself. In December 1864 he served eight months in Exeter Gaol for fraud. In 1866 he was sentenced to seven years. He served all but three months of this sentence before being released in May 1873.

Within a few weeks of finishing this long sentence he stole some silver from an officer at Woolwich Barracks and fled to Windsor where he took rooms at the South Western Railway Hotel. He managed to ingratiate himself with Oscar Browning the assistant master at Eton College. From Browning's library he stole two valuable books and fled. He was pursued by police to London but evaded capture by escaping over the roof of a building. He returned to Eton where he tried to shoot the arresting officer. For these, and other offences, he was sentenced at the Buckingham Assizes to serve a term of ten years imprisonment. He was evidently paroled before he completed this sentence for in 1833 he was wanted, by police, for failing to report.

In 1887 Ostrog turned up again at the Woolwich Barracks where, dressed in cricketing whites and carrying a black Gladstone bag, he attempted to steal a tankard. While in custody he made several half-hearted attempts at suicide. At this time he was described, by Police Superintendent Dunham, as 'one of the most desperate criminals who ever lived'. In September 1887 Ostrog pleaded insanity at the Old Bailey. He was not believed and he was sentenced to six months' hard labour. He did, however, serve this sentence at the Surrey Paupers Lunatic Asylum. From there he was discharged in March 1888. In May 1889 he was back at Eton. Using the Alias of H.Weber he now posed as an assistant master. He conned three gold watches from a local jeweller and promptly disappeared again. Three months later, on August 9th 1889, the 'Police Gazette' sought information on Ostrog's whereabouts. He was still wanted for failing to report but he was now being described as 'dangerous'. He was eventually captured in April 1891.

After several appearances at Bow Street Magistrates Court he was committed, on the 1st May 1891, to the St Giles Workhouse, Endell Street. Three days later Ostrog was examined so as to ascertain his mental condition. The doctor, W.C. Sheard certified him insane:

'He has delusions of exaggeration... he says he has 20,000 houses and half-a-million francs in

Paris, and... he intends to commit suicide.'

Ostrog was sent to Banstead Lunatic Asylum, in Surrey, on the 7th May, as a lunatic found 'wandering at large'. A covering letter, from the Relieving Officer of the Strand Poor Law Union, stated that Ostrog was suicidal but was not considered a danger to other people. The Banstead admissions register describes Ostrog's physical condition as '...much impaired' and that he has '...delusions of various kinds and is paralyzed on one side of (his) face, muscular tremor due to sclerosis'. He was discharged, as 'recovered', two years later on 29th May 1893. Just one month after Ostrog's release from Banstead, he was arrested at Canterbury for robbery. He may have duped the police into believing that he was French since they evidently decided to deport him to France. While en route to Dover and deportation, he escaped and committed yet another robbery at Maidstone. Once again Ostrog decided to try his luck at Eton College, Windsor, where, it is believed, he stole a silver cup and two books. He was again captured and arrested, in June 1894. He appeared at the Buckingham Quarter Sessions and in July 1894 he was convicted of the theft of the gold watches, which he had stolen from the Windsor jeweller. He was sentenced to five years penal servitude with an order for a further seven years police supervision.

Ostrog turned up again in September 1898, at Woolwich, when he was convicted at the Magistrates Court for theft of books from the room of a cadet at the Woolwich Royal Military Academy. He was sentenced to six weeks hard labour.

In August 1900 Ostrog pawned a microscope at a pawnbrokers in Lewisham High Road. He then tried to sell the ticket to one of the pawnbroker's neighbours. The pawnbroker's suspicions were aroused and it was discovered that the microscope had been stolen from the London Hospital Medical College. Three months later, in December, the pawnbroker recognised Ostrog in the street and had him arrested. He was sentenced to five years penal servitude. He began his sentence in Wormwood Scrubs Prison and was eventually transferred to Parkhurst Prison on the Isle of Wight.

He was released from Parkhurst on the 17th of September 1904. He told the prison authorities that he would be working as a doctor and he gave his address as 29 Brooke Street, London. It is the last we know of Michael Ostrog.

A convict photograph of Ostrog shows a villianous-looking bearded man with a large nose and baggy eyes yet the truth may well belie the image. Ostrog was evidently a fairly cultured and well-mannered man. How else could he have passed as an assistant master at Eton? Or ingratiated himself with the likes of Oscar Browning. Brownings tendency towards muscular male bedfellows might, however, provide the answer to that question.

Ostrog may well have possessed some medical knowledge since it is known that he sometimes passed himself off as a doctor. Could he have been Jack the Ripper? And what were MacNaghten's reasons for including him in his list of suspects?
MacNaghten, in his memorandum, gives his reasons thus:

'Michael Ostrog, a Russian doctor and a convict who was subsequently detained in a lunatic asylum as a homicidal maniac. This man's antecedents were of the worst possible type, and his whereabouts at the time of the murders could never be ascertained.'

These then are MacNaghten's reasons for having suspected Ostrog. MacNaghten does no more than to indicate that Ostrog had at sometime been suspected of being the Whitechapel murderer.

MacNaghten is wrong when he describes Ostrog as a 'homicidal maniac'. Although to be fair he had threatened to shoot Police Superintendent Tom Oswald when the latter had arrested him at Burton-on-Trent. By the time that MacNaghten came to write his memorandum, in 1894, he had already encountered Ostrog.

On the 7th of May, 1891, MacNaghten had written to the Medical Superintendent, at Banstead Asylum, on behalf of the Convict Supervision Office:

'I shall feel obliged if you will cause immediate information to be sent to this office in the event of his (Ostrog's) discharge.'

MacNaghten's reasons for requesting this information are that:

'...the magistrate had adjourned the case sine die, in order that he (Ostrog) might be again brought up and dealt with for failing to report himself if it is found that he is feigning insanity.'

There is not one single shred of evidence to link this fascinating confidence trickster and thief with the Whitechapel killings. MacNaghten's concern appears to be from the fact that Ostrog's whereabouts, at the time of the Whitechapel Murders, could '...never be satisfactorily accounted for'.

The fact is that MacNaghten does not suggest that either Ostrog, or Kosminski, was the Whitechapel killer. He is merely indicating three examples of 'more likely' suspects than the unfortunate Cutbush.

The MacNaghten memorandum, like Anderson's biography, Swanson's marginalia, Littlechild's letter and the countless reminiscences of police officers and journalists, are not free from error.

Sir Basil Thompson, who as MacNaghten's successor would surely have known the contents of the MacNaghten memorandum, writes in his book 'The Story of Scotland Yard' that it was:

'...the belief of CID officers at the time that (the murders) were the work of an insane Russian doctor and that the man escaped arrest by committing suicide at the end of 1888.'

This is clearly then a composite image of at least two of the three MacNaghten 'suspects'.

It is quite possible of course that MacNaghten, and others, might have indulged in a certain amount of deliberate disinformation in order to protect the identity of the killer. Whilst this may appear to be, at first sight, an incredible statement to make, there is some evidence that it does happen. It used to be common practice that if a suspect died before being convicted he, or she, would not be named. This was largely to protect innocent relatives.

Such 'disinformation' was used successfully in concealing the identity of a more recent prostitute serial killer who operated in West London seventy years after Jack the Ripper's reign of terror in London's East End.

During the 1960s a number of prostitutes were found murdered in and around the West London area. They had not been mutilated, but the manner of their deaths was no less harrowing. 'Jack the Stripper', as the unknown killer was dubbed, asphyxiated his victims during the act of fellatio. The bodies of the victims were then stored, sometimes for just a few hours and at other times for a few days before they were dumped in the streets or gardens of West London. Forensic evidence indicated that the bodies had been used for the killer's sexual gratification after rigor mortis had set in. Several of the bodies had had their front teeth removed after death, and, at least one had been sodomised sometime after she had died.

John Du-Rose, in charge of the investigations, tells us in his autobiography that, by using the media he was able to communicate with the killer. He announced to the press that he had a list of suspects. Soon afterwards he appeared on national television and announced that he had whittled his list down to just three suspects. Later Du-Rose announced that one of his suspects, worn down by the psychological pressure, which he Du-Rose, had applied had committed suicide. Du-Rose claimed that he did not intend to reveal the name of his dead suspect because he wanted to spare the suspect's family the pain of knowing that he was the prostitute killer known as 'Jack the Stripper'.

Du-Rose, in his book, which was serialised by a Sunday newspaper, then tells us that the killer was aged 45 and worked for a security company which regularly patrolled the trading estate where the last body had been found. He claimed that his suspect lived in South London and that he had left a suicide note saying that he could no longer cope with the pressure. Yet, having told us that he would not reveal the suspect's identity, Du-Rose has given away an awful lot of information. Certainly there is enough information here for any of the suspect's family, reading the newspapers, to know exactly to whom Du-Rose refers.

My own investigations into the 'Jack the Stripper' case confirms that Du-Rose's description of the suspect, as given above, in no way resembles the true description of the real killer. The information' which Du-Rose published' was simply not true. The killer was not a night security guard at all. He was much more likely to have been a prizefighter, a pipe fitter or a priest.

A similar technique may have been used in the hunt for Jack the Ripper.

Journalist George Sims was a close friend of James Monro. He was also known to MacNaghten. Just three weeks after the slaying of Mary Kelly, Sims, writing of the re-appointment of James Monro, to the position of Commissioner, had this to say:

'It would be strange if the accession of Mr Monro to power were to be signalised by such a universally popular achievement as the arrest of Jack the Ripper. From such information which has reached me, I venture to prophesy that this will be the case.'

This article was published on the 2nd of December 1888 and it is clear that Sims' purpose is to let the reader know that Monro is on to someone. Writing in 'The Referee' fifteen years later, Sims tells us that a shortlist of seven suspects existed. He writes:

'This list was reduced by a further exhaustive enquiry to three, and we were about to fit these three persons movements in with the dates of the various murders when the only genuine Jack saved us the trouble, by being found dead in the Thames, into which he had flung himself, a raving lunatic... But prior to this discovery the name of the man found drowned was bracketed with two others as a possible 'Jack' and the police were in search of him alive when they found him dead. It is perfectly well known at Scotland Yard who 'Jack' was, and the reasons for the police conclusions were given in a report to the Home Office, which was considered by the authorities to be final and conclusive.'

The list of suspects, to which Sims refers in his December 1888 article, could not have been the MacNaghten memorandum since MacNaghten had not yet been appointed to his office. It was to be a further three and a half years before MacNaghten was to write his notes. Yet somehow Sims knew of the list of suspects. In his later article Sims mentions a report made to the Home Office which was considered '...final and conclusive'. This must be the report to which Abberline alludes. Sadly though there remains no trace of this important report in the Home Office files. It vanished along with so many other important documents associated with this case.

The shortlist of seven suspects was almost certainly drawn up by Monro, and, if Sims is to be believed, Monro must have divulged its contents to Sims. If this was the case then there can be no doubt but that James Monro was indeed, as early as the beginning of December 1888, already hunting for a named individual. Perhaps it was this individual who committed suicide before he could be caught.

Furthermore, it is reasonable to assume that the final shortlist of three whittled down from seven, are the same three more likely suspects named by MacNaghten in his memorandum.

CHAPTER SIX:

MONTAGUE JOHN DRUITT

Montague John Druitt, the first name on MacNaghten's list of three, was last seen alive just one day after George Sims' article appeared in print. It was Montague Druitts body which was pulled out from the River Thames at Chiswick. It is clear from MacNaghtens own words that, unlike Kosminski and Ostrog, he considered Druitt much more than a likely suspect.

In MacNaghten's memorandum Druitt is described as a doctor aged 41. Druitt was, in fact, a barrister aged 31. But he also worked as an assistant schoolmaster. Teachers were often addressed as 'Doctor'.

If MacNaghten's erroneous description of Druitt had been deliberate, as was Du-Rose's seventy-five years later, in order to conceal, or at least to blur the identity of the killer, who like Jack the Ripper was never caught, then MacNaghten, like Du-Rose, was, at least until his memorandum was made public, successful.

Remember Leonard Matters? There can be little doubt but that he had read George Sims' articles on the subject. Matters had looked for a drowned doctor aged forty one and could not find him. Consequently Matters discounted the story of the drowned suspect - but he had been looking for a forty one year old doctor and not a thirty one year old barrister.

Montague Druitt first 'surfaced' as a suspect in Daniel Farson's TV programme, 'Farson's Guide to the British', in 1959. In deference to the wishes of MacNaghtens daughter, Lady Aberconway, who had given Farson a copy of her father's notes, Farson did not name Druitt. Instead he showed a blanked-out death certificate revealing only the initials MJD. Six years later, however, in 1965, Druitt was named in Tom Cullens book 'Autumn of Terror'.

As a Chiswick born person I was intrigued by this 'new' revelation of a piece of previously unknown local history. My exitement heightened when I realised that Druitts body had been found only two hundred yards from my birthplace.

I checked out the local Chiswick newspapers for 1888 and there it was. The now much quoted report of Montague Druitts Inquest. I contacted Tom Cullen and subsequently visited him at his home in Hampstead. It was the first of several convivial visits. Tom was impressed at my, hitherto unknown find.

Dan Farson was also a profound influence upon my interest in Jack the Ripper. So in 1970 I jumped at the chance to meet him. The meeting was arranged and we met at the house of a mutual friend in Chiswick.

I had hoped to get access to Dans notes but they had, apparently, long since been lost. Dan initially claimed that they had been stolen from his office by an American gentleman who he named. He later, however, admitted that he had probably left them in a pub. We agreed to collaborate on a book about Jack the Ripper.

Many people found Dan a difficult person to get along with. He was a skilled photographer, an excellent writer and raconteur, a first-class host and one of Francis Bacons couterie of heroic drinkers. We had many wonderful sessions at his favourite London pub –The Watermans Arms, on the Isle of Dogs in Londons East End. He had once owned it.
We met one Sunday morning at the Barbican. We had been invited to meet Professor Francis

Camps another heroic drinker. We were guided to Camps' flat by a young, thin City of London Police Constable, and Ripperologist, Donald Rumbelow.
The gin and the conversation flowed in equal quantities. Camps was a fascinating man and full of wonderful stories. I recall that Don had already left before Dan and I eventually staggered to the Barbican underground station and went our different ways home.

I did much of the London end of the research. At the time I was employed by a Westminser firm of solicitors so I had easy access to all parts of London including Somerset House, the High Courts, the Public Records office and the probate registry.

Dan claimed that, after his original television programme had been transmitted he had been contacted by a Mr Knowles, an elderly London resident, who told him of a document, published in Australia, in the early 1900's, written by Lionel Druitt, a Doctor and cousin of Montague. The document was allegedly called 'The East-End Murderer - I knew him.

The document was said to have been published privately, in 1890, by a Mr Fell of Dandenong. This tantalising lead appeared to be strengthened when it was dicovered that Doctor Lionel Druitt, a first cousin of Montague, had at one time, practised, at a Doctor Thynnes surgery in The Minories, particularly since The Minories is mentioned in one of the alleged Jack the Ripper letters. Furthermore Doctor Lionel Druitt had emigrated to Australia in 1886.

Dan was desperate for this document, which, if actually written by a member of Druitts own family could be considered as conclusive evidence, to be brought to life so as to strengthen his case against Druitt. On one of my visits to Dans house, in North Devon, he confided to me that he was even prepared to say that he had actually seen the document. I cautioned against such a suggestion and, after some discussion about integrity, he relented. I was relieved when he did not make the claim in print.

The fact was that such a document had never existed. Notwithstanding this Dan pursued this red-herring all the way to the Dandenong ranges in Australia, and staked his belief, in Montague Druitts guilt, upon its existence. Subsequent findings have suggested that the alleged pamphlet was in fact no more than a supplementary article about an East-End landlady who had claimed that Jack the Ripper had, at sometime, been her lodger. It had been published in the St Arnaud Mercury 29th November 1890.

The subsequent book 'Jack the Ripper' (Michael Joseph 1972) by Dan Farson based its conclusions mainly on the MacNaghten memorandum and the discovery that Lionel Druitt, Montagues cousin had, two years before the murders, held the post of locum at a Doctor Thynnes surgery in The Minories, in the heart of Londons East End.

The book was, however, a landmark publication inasmuch as it contained, previously unpublished, photographs of the victims and of Montague Druitt. Dan Farson had chased the spectre of Jack the Ripper all over Australia. None of it was necessary. The truth was much nearer home : -

The 31st of December 1888 was a very cold day. A dense fog hung over the flooding river at Chiswick, then a small village on the western outskirts of London. A local man, Henry Winslow, was in his boat, just off Thorneycrofts Wharf, when he saw, through the mist, a body floating in the river. He brought the body ashore and summoned assistance. Shortly afterwards, Police Constable George Moulsom arrived at the scene and the body was eventually taken, on a cart to the St Mary Magdelene chapel of peace, in nearby Bennett Street, where it was examined and the contents of the pockets noted. The body was that of a well-dressed man thought to be about forty years of age. The body was badly decomposed but it was soon identified as that of Montague John Druitt.

Three days later, on Wednesday the 3rd of January 1889, the inquest upon Druitt's body was held at the Lamb Tap, a public house in Church Street, just a few yards from where the body had been brought ashore.

In 1970 I discovered the report in an archive copy of the local paper for 1888. This is from the 'Acton Chiswick and Turnham Green Gazette':

'FOUND DROWNED
Shortly after mid-day on Monday (31st December) a waterman named Winslade (sic) found the body of a man, well dressed, floating in the River Thames off Thorneycrofts. He at once informed a Constable, and without delay the body was conveyed on the ambulance to the mortuary. On Wednesday afternoon, Dr Diplock, Coroner, held the inquest at the Lamb Tap, when the following evidence was adduced:
William H. Druitt said that he lived at Bournemouth and that he was a solicitor. The deceased was his brother, who was 31 last birthday. He was a barrister-at-law and an assistant master at a school in Blackheath. He had stayed with witness at Bournemouth for a night towards the end of October. Witness heard from a friend on the 11th of December that deceased had not been heard of at his chambers for more than a week. Witness then went to London to make enquiries, and at Blackheath he found that deceased had got into serious trouble at the school and had been dismissed. That was on the 30th December. Witness had property of the deceased searched where he resided and found a paper addressed to him (produced). The Coroner read the letter, which was to this effect:
'Since Friday I felt I was going to be like mother, and the best thing for me was to die.'
Witness continuing, said deceased had never made any attempt on his life before. His mother became insane in July last. He had no other relative.
Henry Winslade was the next witness. He said he lived at number 4 Shore street, Paxton Road, and that he was a waterman. At about one o'clock on Monday he was on the river in a boat when he saw a body floating. The tide was at half-flood running up. He brought the body ashore, and gave information to the police.
PC George Moulsom 216T said he searched the body which was fully dressed excepting the hat and collar. He found four large stones in each pocket in the top coat; 2 pounds 10 in gold, 7 shillings in silver 2 pence in bronze, two cheques on the London Provincial bank (one for fifty pounds and the other for 16 pounds), a first class season pass from Blackheath to London (South Western Railway), a second half return Hammersmith to Charing Cross (Dated 1st December), a silver watch, gold chain with a spade guinea attached, a pair of kid gloves and a white handkerchief.
There were no papers or letters of any kind. There were no marks of injury to the body, but it was rather decomposed.
A verdict of suicide whilst in an unsound mind was returned.

Druitt's body was then transported to Wimborne in Dorset where, on the afternoon of the day following the inquest Montague Druitt was buried in Wimborne Cemetery. Relatives and a few friends attended the funeral.'

Montague Druitt was born at Wimborne on the 15th of August 1857. His parents were well-to-do and very well known in the area. Montague was the second son. William Druitt, Montague's father, was a Justice of the Peace, as well as being the town's leading surgeon.

Montague's grandmother was Jane Mayo of the founding family of the Mayo clinic. Montague's uncle, Robert Druitt, was the author of the 'Surgeons Vade-Mecum', and editor of the 'Medical Times and Gazette'.

Montague and his six brothers and sisters lived with their parents at 'Westfield', the largest and most imposing house in the town.

Montagues passion was cricket. His boyhood hero was the famous cricketer Nicholas Wanostrocht also known as Nicholas Felix who lived in Wimborne for some time and was believed to have coached many of the local boys.

At the age of thirteen Montague was sent to Winchester College as a fee-paying student. He entered Fearons house. Two terms later, however, he won a scholarship which relieved his Father of paying further fees. .He was said to be bright and extrovert and active at sports, debating and literature. He bypassed the junior part of his schooling and was under the personal tutorlege of Winchesters Headmaster Dr George Ridding for the last three years of his schooling. He was a first rate cricketer and he played for the school team as their opening bowler. He was an outstanding Racquets player. In 1874, with his partner, he won the senior doubles Fives, and, the following year he won the championship to become the school's Fives champion.

Montague seemed, however, to also enjoy the gentle pursuit of debating and in this he displayed a remarkable radicalism by expressing support for Gladstone. It is evident from his defence of the French Republic, and his suggestion that 'States should be made for men as they are now', that Druitt may have embraced Socialism. All of this seems to have been in stark contrast to his father's staunch Conservatism.

In his final year at Winchester, Montague was elected Prefect of the Chapel, one of the school's top honours. He was also one of only nineteen successful candidates from the school in the Oxbridge examinations.

Once at New College, Oxford, Druitt's sporting activities flourished. He played for the New College eleven. In the 1877 Freshmans match he took five wickets for thirty in the second innings. He also played Rugby for the college, and was the University Fives champion in 1877. However, his earlier promise of high academic achievement does not appear to have been fulfilled. He took a second-class honours in classical moderations in 1878, but by 1880 he could only manage a third-class honours in classics. He was, however, elected Steward of the junior common-room, which certainly attests to his popularity among his fellow undergraduates

Until recently it was unknown how Druitt spent the 12 months, or so, between the summer of 1880, when he graduated, and the summer of the following year when he commenced his job at Mr Valentines Blackheath School. Some writers have suggested that his original intention may have been to study medicine and to follow in the family tradition by qualifying as a Doctor. This suggestion, if it had been true, is important inasmuch as it may have provided Druitt with some knowledge of anatomy which some claim was displayed by the killer. Anatomy is an important part of first year medical studies. But there is no evidence that Druitt ever formally studied medicine, and as yet no record has been found of his attendance at any medical school.

In fact in the six months immediately following Druitts graduation from Oxford he is known to have studied for the entrance exam for the Civil Service. Several of his contemporaries from Oxford, including his old pal Evelyn Ruggles-Brise sat the same exam on the 14th January 1881.

Civil Service Commission^ January 20, 1881.
THE Civil Service Commissioners hereby give notice, that the "Candidates hereinafter named have passed the Preliminary Examination for situations in the Civil Service (Class I), viz.:—
Of the Candidates examined on January 1-f, 1881—

Archer, Charles
Badenoch, George
Bassett, Frank Pickering
Berkeley,. Herbert
Bourchier, Henry
Brise, Evelyn John Ruggles
Burrell, Peter George
Clarke, Edward Ashley Walrond
Cohn, John Rougier
Connolly, James Henry
Cook, Edward Tyas
Cox, Homersham
Crowly, Joseph Patrick
Cuthbertson, Norman William
De .la Bere, Henry De La B&re
Druitt, Montague John
Ferard, Arthur George
Fiddes, George Vandeleur
Fincham, Francis Warren Xavier
Fraser, James Wilson
Gee, Raymond
Hammond, Francis
Hand, Cecil Sturges
Herington, Stuart
Hoskyns-Abrahall, Bennet
Johnson, Hugh
Jones, John Francis
Kains-Jackson, Charles
La Brooy, Justin Theodore
Lees, George Turbayne
Liebich, Max Alfred Oscar
Lord, Robert Harley
Matthews, George Frederick
Orr, Thomas Morris Hamilton Jones .
Pynn, John Henry.
Scott-Langley, Harley Edward
Stebbing, George Alexander
Thiselton, Herbert Cecil
Tidey, Stuart Alexander

There is some evidence which suggests that Montague, along with several hundred other new graduates, from both Oxford and Cambridge, swept into the East End of London to offer their expertise and talents to The Peoples Palace and later to Toynbee Hall which opened in 1883. Toynbee Hall was.overseen by the Rev Barnett and his wife. Barnett was the man who later met the costs of Mary Kellys funeral. Toynbee Hall, in Commercial Street was based in the very heart of Whitechapel and rescue and social work among the local poor of the area was one of the fundamental activities of its staff and volunteers.

The Peoples Palace had been the brainchild of social reformer John Beaumont who provided funding for the building in the 1830's. The Peoples Palace, situated in the Mile End Road provided entertainment along with sporting and debating activities as well as social and educational facilities, which catered for several hundred students and pupils. In todays language it may also had a very useful social networking function

From what we do know of Montagues school and University interests such activities, and study facilities which were offered by the Peoples Palace would have been of some considerable interest.. That this was the case is further strengthened by the fact that 'The Times April 1st 1886 (pp 12) lists among the contributors to the Peoples Palace a Mr Montague Druitt as subscribing the sum of £1.00 (£75 approx in todays money) to the Peoples Palace fund. Other contemporary contributors included Montagues old school chums, from Winchester, E.T. Cook and Reginald.Dyke-Acland, Druitts old 'fives' opponent

Many of the, almost exclusively Oxford and Cambridge students and graduates who flocked to the Peoples Palace took lodgings either at the Palace itself or in one of the many 'soriety' houses which they set up in the area. Eighty graduates lived at 88 Commercial St, adjoining George Yard, in one year alone. Another such house was in Berner St and was overseen by a Mr Henriques. Even a disused alehouse in Leman Street was utilised for accommodating the 'Oxford Settlement' The Rev Canon Barnett, wrote in his memoir 'Life and Work'

"After they graduated some of the men who had visited us came to reside in the East End of London.They lived together in twos and threes in lodgings or in the model dwellings. One group of five took a disused beer-shop in Leman Street -where they established a delightful bachelor household and termed it "The Friary". They themselves often went back to Oxford to recruit for the East End work."...........

Having now established at least a positive connection between Druitt and the Peoples Palace it is reasonably safe to assume that he may have spent his post graduate year as one of the many Oxford graduates residing and working in the area.

Tom Cullen touches on this possibility. In 'Autumn of Terror' in a chapter entitled ' A sense of Sin.'

'Answering "The Call from the East", the undergraduates now flocked to Whitechapel….with more enthusiasm than practical sense, they helped to administer the "top boots and blankets" fund which the Barnetts had founded. They assisted at flower Shows, concerts, conversaziones, which were designed to bridge the gulf between classes and masses by bringing culture to the latter. When Toynbee Hall opened its doors as a residential settlement in 1885, a majority of its settlers were Oxonians…It would be natural therefore that, that Druitt should turn to Toynbee Hall not only as a means of recreation, but as an opportunity to do good. With his love of polemic, it would be natural that he should take part in the weekly "Smoking Conferences", or "Tobacco Parliaments", as they were called, where social questions were heatedly discussed by clerks in cloth caps and earnest settlement workers wearing old school ties. Here Druitt would have been exposed to Fabian Socialism, for Bernard Shaw and the Webbs were frequent visitors to Toynbee Hall.'

Arthur Pillans Laurie 1861 – 1946 was the Principal of Heriot Watt College Edinburgh, from 1900 until 1928. He writes in his memoir 'Pictures and Politics' 1934 of his time as a graduate of Kings College Cambridge and of his experiences in Whitechapel at the time of the Ripper murders.

'There was an atmosphere about Toynbee Hall which irritated us. . . We were supposed to be noble young men engaged in trying to do good to the poor. We did not feel noble and we had no desire to do good to anybody, and were quite incapable of doing so. We wished a closer contact with the people and lives of East London. . . Toynbee Hall was very much in the limelight then, and irritating flocks of gaily arrayed young men and women used to descend upon us from the West End. Slumming became a fashionable amusement. After a good dinner, a crowd of men and women would be personally conducted through the worst slums known, prying into people's homes and behaving in an intolerable manner. We wanted to get away from all that. I was teaching at the People's Palace. . '…………….'In the days I speak of, Whitechapel was inhabited by two types of residents in the main – foreign Jews mostly from Poland, and a shifty, semi-criminal population, in the dark and narrow closes and courts behind Toynbee Hall. The two populations were divided by Commercial Street. For neither of these populations had Toynbee Hall any message.

'On one side of Commercial Street there was a rabbit warren of slums, hardly lighted at all at night, and consisting of narrow streets, with passages and courts opening off which had no lighting, making easy the ghastly murders of Jack the Ripper. Here and there the wide-open doors showed the kitchen and living room of a common lodging house heated by a huge fire where a bloater could be cooked, and with a collection of ruffians round the door whose faces would have made the fortune of a film of the underworld. The respectable inhabitants of Whitechapel complained that this slum district was getting very riotous at night and the police were getting very slack, and suggested a watch committee and nightly patrols between eleven and one.'

This was undertaken by the Toynbee Hall men, who were organised to patrol the district, and to note events without interfering. Often they patrolled alone, and without even the protection of a walking stick. 'The semi-criminal has no more courage than a rabbit, and behaved accordingly. No Toynbee man was ever molested, and I have always been completely sceptical of the stories of places in London which were not safe to enter at night. I have picked out of the gutter an occasional respectable grocer from the provinces in nothing but shirt and trousers, and in a state of stupor, which suggested drugging, but either drink or love had led to his undoing.

'Hideous shrieks of "police!" and "murder!" used occasionally to arise, but we learnt to treat them with indifference. I never found that there was any reason for complaining of the police. In those dark and primitive regions they resembled the cadi in the Arabian Nights, kept order, administered a rough justice and were appealed to on all sorts of occasions. A conversation between a thief and a policeman in the midnight hours is very amusing – the thief all oily obsequiousness, the policeman grimly sarcastic.
'Obtaining a lodging at the police-station was not an unknown device. I watched an old lady one night dancing a wild fandango in the middle of the road, and shrieking out a torrent of obscene abuse at three policemen, watching her and muttering curses. They knew her game. She had no money and was determined to compel them to arrest her. She was disturbing the whole neighbourhood, and sooner or later they would have to run her in.

'It was during the winter of our patrol that the horrible Jack the Ripper murders began in Whitechapel. . . A cry for help would receive no attention when it was so common. It became our rule to strike a match and light up dark courts and passages and open stairways, with a shudder at what we might see. Occasionally we unearthed a detective standing in a corner, silently waiting. Whitechapel was swarming with detectives hoping to trap the murderer. The strange thing was that a new murder was known in Whitechapel before the police heard of it. One murder was committed in a room. I was told of it at 1am, while patrolling the slums. The police did not know of it it till seven.

The settlement workers often formed themselves into street patrols to deal with local street crimes. Other groups sought to evangelise to the fallen women of the area. There can be little doubt but that many of them would have become acquainted with the intricate local geography of the immediate area around Toynbee Hall. After the Murder of Martha Tabram, just yards from Toynbee Hall, they formed into a vigilance committee to hunt for Jack the Ripper.

Whatever connections, or associations Montague may have had with the Peoples Palace or la at Toynbee Hall there is no reason to suppose that he discontinued them once he obtained work in nearby Blackheath. This is evident from the fact that Druitts subscription to the Peoples Palace was made some years after he commenced to work at the Blackheath School.

Despite Druitts success in passing the Civil Service entrance eaxamination he appears to have dismissed any idea of entering the Civil Service since the national Census of 1881 shows that Montague was, by then, employed at George Valentines' school, at 9 Eliot Place Blackheath, as an assistant schoolmaster. However in 1882 Montague applied for admission to the inner temple to study for his bar exams. His decision to continue to work at the school while, at the same time, studying for the bar may have been influenced by the many sporting activities which were played on the heath at Blackheath overlooked by the school.

It is also quite possible that his choice may have been influenced by the frequent presence, of his boyhood sporting hero Nicholas Wanostrocht who had frequently played upon the nearby Heath as well as running a local school.

George Valentine was of mixed race. Born in Bombay India his father was the Rev George Valentine, a church missionary. His mother was Louisa Stather who came from the West Indies
The school, at Eliot place seems to have been a successful enterprise with students from all across the world. There were 38 boarders each with their own cubiculed bed space in a dormitory. Their ages ranged from eleven to seventeen.
It seems to have catered to the wealthier classes. The register of 38 boarders at the school show five names which were eventually listed in Who's Who.

In May 1882 Montague was admitted to the Inner Temple. He borrowed the sum of £500 from his father, set against his inheritance, in order to pay his tuition fees. He continued to work at Valentines school.

Three years later, on the 29th April 1885, dressed in white wig and black gown, he was called to the Bar and admitted to the Inn as a fully-fledged barrister. He took chambers at 9 Kings Bench Walk, Temple, joined the Western circuit, and opened for business.

Apart from the documents which Montague had to sign when he was called to the Bar, shown above, and which are preserved at the Treasury of the Inner Temple, and only three known court appearances no full contemporary record of Druitt's legal career has yet been found. This has led some writers to state that he was a 'failed barrister'. But there is no evidence that he was a failure. The following newspaper report, from, of one of Druitts cases demonstrates that Druitt had a very keen, and dry, sense of humour, and, where he was quite capable of reducing the court to fits of laughter.

The Daily News – 22nd May 1886
AN AMUSING BREACH OF PROMISE CASE
In the Middlesex Sheriffs' Court, Red Lion square, before Mr. Under Sheriff Burchell and a Common Jury, yesterday, the case of Mildon v Binstead was heard, it having been remitted from the Queen's Bench Division of the High Court of Justice for purpose of assessing the

amount of damages, if any, to which the plaintiff was entitled, the defendant having allowed judgement to go by default. Mr. Montague Druitt, who was counsel for the plaintiff, said that this was an action for recovery of damages for a breach of promise of marriage. His client, Miss Marion Mildon, when she first made the acquaintance of the defendant was a lady's maid in the service of a titled family near Selborne, and the defendant was employed as a draper's assistant in a neighbouring town. In September, 1883, she was walking out one evening, and she met the defendant, who seemed fascinated by her good looks, and he asked her if she would allow him to accompany her for a short distance. She assented, and from that time forward he paid her the most marked attentions; he wrote her a number of letters, breathing sentiments of undying love and attachment, telling her that her darling image and lovely form occupied his waking hours and sleeping dreams. (Laughter.) She had so bewitched him that feared he was rather negligent in the performance if his duties as a draper's assistant, for it was Cupid, and not calico or cambric, that was uppermost in his mind. (Renewed laughter.) The correspondence that passed between them was voluminous, but the learned counsel said that he should content himself with a few samples. Writing from Odiham on March 8th., 1884, he says:-

My dearest Marion, - You can hardly imagine how your lovely letter of this morning relieved my poor dull brain of all the weary thoughts that generally occur in bachelor solitude. (A laugh.) But thanks, darling, your sweet, loving,. little epistle has acted as an emetic, and has carried the black bile off. (Roars of laughter.) You must always allow me to think about you in my daily work, but do not be afraid that I shall omit doing my ordinary duties; it will be the reverse, for in having your loving angelic face always in my memory it will inspire me with the everlasting hope of gaining my chief desire on this earth - namely, darling, your own sweet self. (Laughter.) With you, my lovely one, my honeysuckle, my incomparable "Maid Marion", as my wife and partner in all my joys and sorrows, I will be an English Ajax, defying the thunders and lightnings of mundane tribulation. (Continued laughter.) In our wedded life, darling (and oh!, do I not wish the happy auspicious day of our nuptials was now at hand!), I hope sorrows will be, as the poet says, few and far between. I suppose we must wait a little while longer for that glorious day which will consummate all my thoughts of terrestrial bliss.

In another of these effusive epistles. glowing with the tender and rapturous feelings of love, he wrote:

The 8th. March was your birthday, and strange to say I was wondering and thinking about you all the way along the road from Alton, whilst I was driving in the low backed car. I kept looking at my watch every ten minutes or quarter of an hour, wondering if you had got home in time ..... Sorry you were so awfully hungry! What a pity you had not some of those apples I had with me! Would I not be superlatively pleased to present, like another arbitrator of beauty, on a Hampshire Mount Ida, the prize to the fairest goddess on earth - my own darling Marion. (Laughter.) I had a favourable reply from Yateley yesterday, and I am very glad of it, because now I shall not be so far from you. I shall try and get the chance to see you often, as it is a beautiful road for walking along. Indeed, I do not know of any more secluded or appropriate promenade for two find hearts to coo and bill in. (Laughter.)

During his holidays he took her, said the learned counsel, to the home of his parents, by whom she was accepted and treated as their future daughter in law; she was the honoured guest of his numerous friends and relatives in Hampshire and Sussex, who invited her to balls, dancing parties, penny readings, and other forms of mild dissipation in which unsophisticated country folks like to indulge. He told her his wages amounted to £2 a week, besides commission on whatever sales he effected, and these latter, according to his own representation, were occasionally very considerable. In addition to these brilliant prospects he assured her that his father and mother were thrifty people, the former being for many years a coachman in the service of the Right Hon. George Sclater-Booth, and the latter a housekeeper to a nobleman in Hampshire; and at his mother's death, he told Miss Mildon, he would be entitled to a large sum of money. In the first week of March, 1884, with the full approval and sanction of his parents and friends, he solemnly ratified the promise he had previously made to her, by giving her an engagement ring, and telling her that she might regard herself as his betrothed wife. He removed from Selborne to Petersfield, and from the latter place he wrote her a letter in which he stated that his life was incomplete, cheerless and melancholy, because she was not near to solace and soothe the weary, languid hours. (Laughter.) "Marion," he gushes forth -

My Sweet and darling Marion, - When I take my solitary walks abroad I am ever fondly thinking of you. (Continued merriment.) At church yesterday, when the parson preached from the old familiar text, "Love one another," my thoughts were wandering from the subject of his discourse, and where were they? Aye, where? They were nestling in your fond bosom. (Roars of laughter.) Life has lost its charms for me; and why? The response is, because my darling is away. Some moonstruck poet once wrote, "Absence makes the heart grow fonder," and I have bitterly realised the full truth of that assertion, for without you I am pining and wasting away. (Laughter.)

This letters concluded, said the learned counsel, with 60,000 kisses, and with a number of geometrical figures which he understood were, in the language of love, emblematic of undying attachment and perennial love. (Laughter.) In a subsequent letters, dated from Yateley and addressed to his "Darling Marion," he beseeches her to remember him in her prayers, and at the same time, while he is at Pulborough, near Brighton, to send him some of those amatory notes that she had lately been in the habit of writing to him. Away from her, his lovely, idolised one, he felt disconsolate and lonely, for without her he often thought he was like a ship without a captain or a boat without a rudder. A very short time after these gushing letters were written the plaintiff received a letter from the defendant expressing sentiments the reverse of those which characterised his previous communications; and in this note he coolly informed her that he must break off the engagement, as his parents did not approve of the intended marriage. Miss Mildon was naturally horrified at this sudden and astounding revulsion of affection on his part, and, as might be expected, she indignantly wrote back, asking for an explanation, but (said the learned counsel) the quondam amorous swain did not deign to give any excuse or exculpation for his despicable treatment of this poor young woman, and for such disgraceful trifling with the affections of a chaste and virtuous woman he hoped the jury would award his client not a vindictive or an immoderate amount of damages, but such a sum as would be some solution for her wounded feelings and the wrong done to her womanly pride.

The plaintiff gave evidence in support of the opening statement of her counsel.
The defendant did not appear nor was he legally represented.
The jury assessed the damages at £50.

On the 19th September 1888 Druitt appeared in court at the Old Bailey as defence counsel for Christopher Powers who was accused of maliciously wounding by stabbing Peter Black. Powers and Black had been work colleagues for some years but Powers had suffered some sort of illness which had affected his work as a draughtsman. He had been dismissed from his job in 1886. Powers had evidently though subsequently bombarded Black with letters, which were considered to be offensive and disgusting, with references to sodomy.

It would appear that Druitt argued that Power was suffering from diminished responsibility. Powers landlady, Mrs J Cameron appeared for the defence and testified that Powers behaviour had been very odd. Powers had claimed that he was being watched and that his conversations were being listened to by people outside the window. On one occasion he jumped out of his bed and started fighting with an invisible assailant. He often broke furniture and glasses when engaging in imaginary fighting. He had also been caught attempting to choke Mrs Camerons young daughter. The prison doctor also testified that Powers was suffering from audio and visual hallucinations and that Powers believed he was being followed by a gang who were making suggestions about his victim Black and sodomy.
Powers was convicted and committed to an asylum.

As well as occasional appearances in court Montague Druitt may well have worked as a special pleader, a kind of behind-the-scenes junior counsel, advising and teaching pupils, as well as assisting in the preparation of civil proceedings. The fact that he was allowed to retain his chambers, at number 9 Kings Bench Walk testifies to his continuing legal career, even if it was in tandem with his employment at Mr Valentine's school.

More telling is the fact that when Druitt died he left an estate valued at £2,600 in cash. This did include a sum of £1,083 inherited posthumously from his mother, but even so, by 1888 standards it is still a vast amount. Montague had received nothing in his late father's will. As an assistant schoolmaster he would not have earned more than £100 per annum so his total earnings from Valentine's school would not have exceeded £800. We know that he was well dressed and moved in fashionable, and expensive, society. His sporting subscriptions alone were considerably more than the average worker earned.

Since 1881 Montague had regularly played cricket for the Mordern Cricket Club. In 1885 he became the Club Secretary and the following year he was elected Honorary Secretary and Treasurer. He was also a member of the Blackheath Hockey Club, having been proposed for membership by no less than the head of the school, his employer George Valentine. Another master from the school, George Lacey, seconded the proposal.

Tragedy was soon to intervene upon Druitt's halcyon existence.
In September 1885, Montague's father suddenly collapsed and died of a heart attack. William Druitt left an estate of £17.000, which was divided, between the families. All that Montague received was release from the £500 debt, which he had borrowed from his father to finance his legal studies, and which had been set against his inheritance.

Montague's mother Anne was devastated by her husband's death. She never recovered. Ten years her husband's junior, she had borne him seven children. Not a strong woman, she was diabetic, and frequently suffered bouts of melancholia. Her depression appears to have been an hereditary condition. Annes mother, Elizabeth Harvey, had become insane before committing suicide and Annes own sister had attempted to kill herself on more than one occasion. (She eventually succeeded). In later life Georgiana, Montagues younger sister was also to commit suicide.

Widowhood appears to have accelerated Anne's downward spiral. Her mental and physical health had deteriorated to such an extent that by July 1888 she had to be admitted, as a private patient, to the Brooke House Asylum at Clapton, under the care of Dr. Josiah Adams. She was certified insane by a Doctor Perry.

Anne Druitt was however given frequent leaves of absence from the Brooke House Asylum. During one of these leaves of absence Anne had been placed under the care of Doctor Gasquet at Brighton. These leaves had expired at the time of her son's death and she was not certified again until April 1889 when she was returned to Dr Gasquet's asylum at Brighton. On May 31st 1890, apparently at the insistence of her eldest son William, she was removed from Brighton and admitted to the Manor House Asylum at Chiswick. She died there a little over six months later on the 15th of December 1890.

Until the publication of 'The Ripper Legacy' by Martin Howells and Keith Skinner, it had been assumed that Montague's final visit to Chiswick must have been to visit his mother at the Manor House Asylum. But, with the realisation that Montague's mother was not moved to the Chiswick Asylum until after his death the obvious question was why did Montague Druitt travel all of the way to Chiswick? He did not appear to have any obvious connection with the area. I felt that the answer to this question might help to shed some light on the reasons why he was suspected of being Jack the Ripper.

We do know that the Montague John Druitt referred to in MacNaghten's notes is, without any doubt, the same Montague John Druitt discussed above regardless of the differences in age and occupation. Yet, just as it is with all of the suspects so far discussed, there is not one shred of evidence, which could prove that he was the White chapel murderer. But, unlike any of the other suspects, there are clear indications that evidence against Druitt did, at one time, exist. What could this evidence have been? And how did the police discover this evidence?

MacNaghten gives us two vital clues. He tells us that '...from private information I have little doubt that his own family suspected (him) of being the White chapel murderer.'

Who could the 'private information' have come from?

Montague's elder brother William seems to be the obvious possibility. But there are other possibilites.
Evenly Ruggles-Brise would have known Druitt. They played in the same university cricket team.
Ruggles-Brise was now the liason man between the police and the Home Secretary. William Druitt may have confided in Ruggles-Brise. What could have caused William to suspect his brother?   What could he have discovered?

Another possibility presents itself with the discovery of a list of papers which were, at one time or another destroyed by the Home office. The list referred to a large number of communications from members of the public mostly offering suggestions regarding the Whitechapel murders. One such name on this list attracted my attention.

A communication was received by the Home office on the 24th November 1888, just ten days before the date given for Montagues death e do not know the contents of the communication other than it offered some kind of suggestion regarding the murders. The author of the communication was painter Henry Scott-Tuke the son of Thomas Hack-Tuke the proprietor of the Hanwell asylum and friend and colleague of fellow alienist Thomas Seymour Tuke of the asylum in Chiswick. The two Tuke families were unrelated even though they shared the same surname and profession.

Henry Scott-Tke did not follow in his Fathers profession as a doctor. He became a painter of some repute. He seems to have specialised in painting pictures of naked young men and boys/ One of his paintings hangs in the Red House museum in Christchurch Dorset. The museum, a former workhouse was gifted to Christchurch by the Druitt family.

The timing of Tukes' communication is interesting arriving as it did just five days before Montagues flight from Valentines school and just a week before George Sims announced that Monro was on to someone.

William had travelled to London to search for his brother Montague when he went missing almost three weeks before his body was found. It was William who had searched Montague's lodgings. It was William who learned, from Mr Valentine, that Montague had been dismissed from the school at Blackheath for a 'serious offence.' It was William who produced Montague's suicide note at the inquest, and it was William who gave what has proved to be perjured evidence at that inquest.

William held all the cards. William was well acquainted with Inquest procedures. Apart from being a solicitor William was also the Deputy Coroner for the Liberty of Westover, an area of Bournemouth and was thus perfectly placed to manipulate, or at least affect, the outcome of Diplocks Inquest upon his brother Montague. It is also worth mentioning that Dr Diplock had trained at St Georges Hospital under the tutorage of Druitts Uncle Robert Druitt.

What else had William discovered? Had Montague left a confession? It is clear that only the gist of Montague's suicide note was read out at the inquest. It could have contained a confession. But even if it had, would the suicide note confession of a lunatic have been considered evidence unless it could be corroborated?

According to Inspector Abberline a report into Montague Druitt's death was made and forwarded to the Home Office. Someone obviously felt that the circumstances of Druitt's death were considered important enough at the time to deserve a report to the Home Office.

Regarding Druitt as Jack the Ripper, MacNaghten tells us that:

'...Certain facts pointing to this conclusion were not in the possession of the police until some years later.'

If this was the case then he is telling us that factual evidence pointing to Druitt's guilt did exist, but, at the time when the the Home Office report on Druitt's death was being prepared, ie: January 1889, they were not yet in possession of the 'evidence of a factual nature.' Whatever the 'factual' evidence was, it did not materialise for 'some years'.

Let us consider, with caution, what we are told by Donald McCormick, that in March 1889, just seven weeks after Montague Druitt's funeral, a prominent member of the Whitechapel Vigilance group, Albert Bachert, approached the police to voice the concern of his committee that the police patrols in Whitechapel had been wound-down on the grounds that there had been no Ripper murder for almost four months. McCormick, who claims to have discovered this information from Doctor Duttons elusive 'Chronicles of Crime', tells us that Bachert, after being sworn to secrecy, was told that the Whitechapel murderer was dead and that his body had been fished from the river seven weeks earlier. Bachert was further advised to disband the Vigilantes.

Even if one considers McCormick as an unreliable source his information is, on this point at least, fairly accurate. It fits perfectly with the known facts. Consider the actions of James Monro. On the 26th of January, just three weeks after Druitt's funeral, he ordered a reduction in the police presence in Whitechapel.

Seven weeks after Druitts death, Monro ordered the winding-down of the manhunt for Jack the Ripper. He reported to the Home Office saying:

'I am gradually reducing the number of men employed on this duty as quickly as it is safe to do so, but such reduction cannot be effected all at once.'

The winding down of the special patrols took seven weeks. On 15th March, Monro reported the cessation of all the special patrols.

Monro must have had very good reason to believe that there would be no more Jack the Ripper killings. Since the evidence 'of a factual nature' had not yet come to light, Monro must have arrived at his conclusions as a result of the report on Druitt. George Sims described the report as 'final and conclusive.' The un-informed Abberline naturally disagreed with this view. Nevertheless Monro did stop looking for Jack the Ripper - and the killings did stop.

Could Montague Druitt have been Jack the Ripper?

If he was, then he must have been a very cool fellow indeed for we know that on the day following the murder of Polly Nichols, Druitt turned out for his team, to play cricket at Canford in Dorset. We know too that he was playing cricket at Blackheath just six hours after Annie Chapman was murdered.

I have shown here Druitts' cricketing fixtures for the relevant period:

Saturday 21 July......................Blackheath
Friday 3/4 August...................Bournemouth
Friday 10 August....................Bournemouth
Saturday 1 September.............Canford. Dorset
Saturday 8 September.............Blackheath

Some writers have commented that it is inconceivable that anyone could commit such crimes and then cooly turn out to play a game of cricket. I disagree. Such coolness, and detachment from the crime, is a prime characteristic of the Psychopathic sexual serial killer.

Peter Sutcliffe, the so-called Yorkshire Ripper, lived an outwardly normal existence with his wife and friends. None of them ever suspected that he was a serial killer. Yet, in a period of five years he brutally murdered more than a dozen women.

Peter Kurten, the mass killer of Dusseldorf, led an overtly blameless life until it was discovered that he had murdered at least nine women, each time in a frenzy of sexual sadism. The youngest of his victims was only nine years old.

Denis Nielsen murdered more than a dozen young men. Some of his victims were disposed of by burning. Others were dismembered and boiled before the remains were flushed into the public sewers. Nielsen's crimes came to light when the drain outside his house became clogged up with rotting human flesh.

During the days, Nielsen would go off to his job as a civil servant in a social security office. At weekends he socialised in the local pubs and gay bars of West London. Although essentially a loner he did form relationships. But when not in a relationship he killed, as he himself has intimated, for company. His most recent victim would often be left sitting upright in an armchair as if waiting to welcome him home from a hard day at the office. Until the bodies started to smell he would treat them as a living companion. Yet no one could have guessed that this outwardly normal-looking, inoffensive clerk was a serial sexual murderer. All three of these men killed more often than did Jack the Ripper.

The fact that Montague Druitt played cricket, and displayed normal behaviour, in between murders does not exclude him from the capabilities required of such a killer.

Did Montague have the opportunity?

Yes. Polly Nicholls body was discovered before 4.00am on August 31st. Montague next plays cricket, the following day, in Wimborne. If we assume that the match did not start before 9.00 am Montague would have had thirty hours to make the two-hour train journey to Wimborne.
Annie Chapman was killed before 6.00am on September 8th. Montague played cricket, in Blackheath later that day, the match commencing at 11.30 am. This would give him, at least five and a half hours to make the thirty minute train journey from the East-End to Blackheath. Trains from London to Blackheath were frequent. They ran, from Charing Cross platforms three and four every ten minutes during the morning and evening rush-hours, and, every twenty minutes during the rest of the day. The same was true of Cannon Street Station.

No cricket was played on either the 31st September – Stride and Eddowes, or on November 9th the day of Mary Kellys murder.

Druitt's chambers, at 9 Kings Bench Walk in the Inner Temple, are situated close by the Thames Embankment and are within easy walking distance of Whitechapel. If Montague had

110

ever visited his mother, during her times at the Brooke House Asylum at Clapton, he would have travelled through, or very close by the same area. He may, or may not, have known the area well but he was within easy reach of it. It is, however, doubtful that Druitt actually lived at his chambers, and, there is no reason to suppose that he did not live at 9 Eliot Place, Blackheath, Mr. Valentine's School. Druitt certainly used this as his address as the electoral roll confirms. He would, of course, have had access to his chambers at all times, and he may well have stayed overnight from time to time.

Furthermore, given Montague Druitts known association with the Peoples Palace, in nearby Mile End Road, and the very strong likelihood of an association with the 'Oxford' settlement in and around the environs of Toynbee Hall, in the Commercial Road, it is easily within the realms of probability that he may have made use of these resources if requiring a bolt-hole.

The railway season ticket found upon Druitts body confirms that he travelled regularly between Blackheath and Charing Cross. In those days the underground railway ran from very early in the morning until late at night for the convenience of market traders. Montague could easily have travelled from Blackheath to New Cross and then on the underground directly to Whitechapel. The journey is only five stops and such a service had been in operation since 1884.

Montague Druitt does not have an alibi. His exact whereabouts, at the precise times of the Whitechapel murders, remain unknown. It may even be that Druitt was one of the many Vigilantes which patrolled the dark streets and alleyways, of the area, looking for the killer. In plain sight and with a perfect alibi for being on the streets at night

Did Montague possess the skills to commit murder?

When not at school, Montague's youth had been spent at 'Westfields', the family home at Wimborne. He would have had access to his surgeon father's text-books. He may even have read his uncle Robert's 'Vade Mecum', and he would almost certainly have been familiar with surgical instruments. He may even have had a rudimentary knowledge of anatomy.

It is also worth recalling that medical opinion was divided as to whether Jack the Ripper possessed any surgical skill at all. The killer may have possessed a sufficient knowledge of anatomy to know where the organs were, but his means of obtaining them appear more akin to slash and grab than to surgical skill.

Montague's excellence at the game of Fives strongly suggests that he may have been ambidexterous. It is a two-handed game which requires the player to have strong arms and hands. An ambidexterous Jack the Ripper could explain the infliction of those cuts, which appear to have been made by a left-to-right sweep of the knife.

Look again at the statement made by George Hutchinson. He claimed to have seen Mary Kelly go into her house with a man. Hutchinson had waited outside Millers Court, he was seen still waiting there at 2.30am by Sarah Lewis who was visiting the occupant of number two. According to Hutchinson the man was still in Kellys room. This man was almost certainly the killer of Mary Kelly. Hutchinson describes the mans 'dark eyes and eye lashes'.

The first thing which one notices when looking at a photograph of Montague Druitt are his very dark eyes and very long dark eyelashes. The description is that of a young man about town. Button boots and gaiters, he 'wore a very thick gold chain, white linen collar, black tie respectable.and Jewish looking. Obviously he was a man of some substance. It could so easily be a description of Montague Druitt

There can be little doubt but that Montague had the means, the physical abilties, and, from his associations with the Peoples Palace the geographical knowledge of the area to commit the Whitechapel killings. If Druitt had been part of any of the several Oxbridge groups patrolling the area at night he would have had a perfect reason for being there.

What about desire? Or motive? What kind of insanity could turn this handsome, popular, well-connected, well-heeled, athletic and professional man on the ascent of what promised to be a brilliant legal career into a frenzied serial killer of prostitutes?

His motive was not the thrill of the kill. It was more.

In the case of Elizabeth Stride the killer had not had the opportunity to satisfy his motivation. He had killed but it was not enough. He had not time to obtain his trophy. So he made his way to Mitre Square where he butchered Catharine Eddowes and started to reap his blood harvest.

It is evident, from the phrase quoted from Druitts alleged suicide note, - since Friday I felt I was becoming like Mother.., that Montague must have recognised his own insanity as similar to that of his mother. She had been certified insane in July 1888 just a few weeks before the first Whitechapel murder. He would have already known of his grandmother's suicide, as well as of his Aunt's several failed attempts. He would have recognised the insanity which had afflicted three generations of his family.

We do not know what kind of relationship Montague had with his mother. Whether he doted upon her, or hated her for the feelings which he felt she had now passed onto him. We may never know. But either way it was, according to Montague himself, his Mothers madness which was the direct cause of his own decline and death.

Could Anne Druitts insanity also have been indirectly responsible for the Whitechapel murders?

All of Jack the Ripper's victims, with the exception of Elizabeth Stride, suffered severe mutilation of the pelvic region. It was almost as if the womb itself, the symbol of motherhood, was the central target of the killer's knife, and possession of the female reproductive organs appears to have been the object of the killer's desire.

Coroner Wynne-Baxter had put his finger on the very point of Jack the Ripper's murders with his comment that '...it was the killer's desire to possess the missing organ.'

Montague Druitt himself has told us that he was '...feeling like mother.' But, apart from the brief reference, at Montague's inquest, to his mother's insanity, we are not told any details of her illness. How much more light could be thrown upon Druitt's own condition if we knew more of his mother's illness?

Anne Druitt's case papers, together with other papers from the Manor House Asylum, are preserved in the archives of the Wellcome Institute. They comprise of nine sheets, hand-written by the doctors at the Manor House and a two-page typed letter, written by Doctor Gasquet, who had attended to Anne Druitt at the Brighton Asylum.

The case notes cover only the last six months of her life spent at the Manor House. Doctor Gasquets letter does however provide a thumbnail history of her medical condition:

127 Eastern Road
Brighton

June 6 1890

Dear Mr Tuke,

I will gladly accede to Mr Druitt's wish that I should give you a short account of her case, so far as I know it.

She was brought down to Brighton on leave of absence from Brooke House in the summer of '88, and placed under my care.

I never had any history of her case from the asylum authorities, but I gathered she had had an attack of melancholia with stupor, from which she was slowly emerging. I was told she had diabetes, and that Dr Pavey had ordered her a special diet; but the urine, frequently examined since, has never shown more than slight signs of sugar and occasional traces of albumen. She slowly improved, and the leave was prolonged from time to time until it was inadvertenly allowed to run out at the beginning of '89. It was then impossible to recertify her, her condition being one mainly of apathy with an unreasonable refusal to spend money; but these symptoms increased, so that she was placed under certificates in April of last year.

She continued more or less in the same state till this winter when she had, as I believe, an attack of influenza. Her mind was quite clear for some days during the attack; but the symptoms of melancholia and stupor became much worse after. Especially her refusal of food became more obstinate, and for the last two months she has been almost entirely fed with the stomach-tube.

She has always been very obstinate, and latterly has been violent when thwarted. When in this condition, bromides have appeared to suit her; otherwise she seemed to gain most from the occasional use of Indian Hemp for a week or two. The bowels have been regulated by Jalapine and glycerine enemata. Last year when she was communicative, she evidently had hallucinations that she was being electrified, latterly it has been difficult to elicit anything, but her refusal of food has been justified by her alleging there is no oesophageal passage. If there is any other point which you wish me to tell you, I shall be happy to write again, and am,

Yours faithfully,
Gasquet (signed)

The case papers, subsequently compiled by Doctor Tuke at Chiswick, elaborate further upon Anne Druitt's condition. She is still described as 'troublesome.' Sometimes lucid but very withdrawn. She was physically very weak and was incontinent. She spat frequently and copiously. If she spoke at all it was in a low whisper. She still refused food on the grounds that she had no throat-pipe. I have reproduced the notes here below.

Case papers written by Dr T.S. Tuke
at the Manor House Asylum Chiswick
May 31st to Dec 15th 1890

(Blanks refer to undecipherable words in the original papers)

Page one

> Admitted may 31st 1890 transferred from private care at Brighton.
> Aged 60. Widow of Wimborne Dorset has had a family 5 sons
> 2 girls. General good health till 18 years ago when her last child was
> born. She then became sleepless and restless and for some time was
> ---- in 1888 was in care again for two months.
> In the habit of taking ---- and sleeping draughts of bromide
> of ---- ----- which she prescribed and took in brandy. This illness
> lasted for about 12 months and was ---- ---- ----

and she recovered fairly well, till 4 years ago when her
husband died suddenly of angina ---- ---- ---- ----
---- ---- and she became queer and was noticed doing odd things.
Was always lamenting whether she had done the right thing or not
then after this ---- ---- ---- ---- ---- developed delusions. Not
lots of money ---- ---- ---- and was placed in 1888 in Brooke
House Clapton where she remained for some months, but being
No better was sent to Brighton under the charge of a lady and a man
Being ---- ---- ---- for a year has been losing flesh. For
the last three months has been fed artificially by ---- ---- once
daily. She has been till quite recently sitting up in
the day and going out for drives 2 or three times a week.

family history. Patients mother died insane (suicide). Patients
sister an attack of ---- she recovered

Page two.

Was carried out of carriage having driven over from -.Acton
Station.
Is of middle height hair grey and ----, ----dull and ---
General appearance of extreme illness and weakness face pale
and ----. Eyes partly closed well manicured hands and nails.
Whole body very much emaciated ---- ---- ---- ---- ----
and the joints of the knees stiff and evidently ---- and I am
informed that she has been aware of the rigidity for some years
shin clean and not too dry ---- ---- ---- ---- ----.
Typhoid condition Bones seem well developed no obvious deformity
Heart ---- complicated ---- ----.

Mental condition dull and apathetic is apparently ----
conscious of what goes on about her. Speaks a very little
in a whispering voice. Dribbles and spits saliva from her
mouth in considerable quantities, and on being fed with a
spoon spat everything out of her mouth.
Was put to bed ---- at 6.30 was fed with the stomach
tube some little difficulty owing to her ----
---- ---- 1 pint of milk with   two eggs
½ pint of strong beef tea ---- ---- ---- -------------
---- water freely.

Page 3

June 1st Somewhat sleepless night but altogether
Plenty of sleep ----- urine ---- ---- to bed
Refused food was fed as before with ---- added
whispered a few words ---- ---- ----
talked with ------------- pharynx which rattles
and makes a noise in her throat and I think she has
---- cough up. Tea again later in the day 6.30
---- noted.
      C.M. Tuke

June 2nd ---- ---- much sleep and changed four times
---- ---- again --- loose motion.
Refused food and was fed twice in the day by stomach tubes
---- ---- ---- ---- is very weak indeed.

C.M. Tuke

3rd from 11.30 to 3.15 coughing feebly
---- ---- ---- wet in bed again.
Refused food and was fed twice ---- bowels active.
Not much sleep
Is kept in bed there she has ---- ---- spits
a good deal for a few ---- ---- at a time.---

6th A better night has slept a good deal ---- ---- ---- ----
sitting up in bed and talking a little says she is full of soup
---- ---- ---- ---- is spitting ---- ---- ---- ---- ----
pulse seems ---- ---- temp ---- ---- ---- ---- 22
visited by her daughters whom she recognised and was glad to see
they were told that she ---- ---- ---- ----

7th restless night some pain R.50 p.132 ---- in throat
later semicomatose ---- ---- ----
slept from 1.45 to 5pm 7.40 p.118 r.36 temp 100.8
fed twice with tube visited by daughters ---- ---- ----
not retained.

8th Slept better all night Eldest daughter remaining here
8.15 am P.124 resp. 44 simi comatose
11.am temp 102.1 resp 38. Tea at 11am
2.pm rose up in bed and turned over 7pm. P.96 r. 36
fed at 7.00 ---- at 10pm temp 103 p 126 r 46 ----
9th restless night a quiet day much expectoration
9.35pm r.34 p 110 t 100.8 skin moist and perspiring.

10th Restless night much ---- coughs continually and
---- easily ---- ---- ---- sometimes rusty and small white
lumps ---- in it like broken down ---- ---- physical
----
all over
t 99 p 90 resp 34 fed by tube 6.15pm p 106 t 99.6
r 32

June 11th
---- ---- ---- this morning is brighter
answering questions but refusing food skin cool no pain
temp 98.8 fed by tube at 11 am. Later drank a little beef tea.
5pm drank a little tea
7.45 fed with tube   p 94 t.99.4   C.M. Tuke

12th Weary night pain in right side and lower part of ---- t. 98.5
taking a little Brands essence. At 11 took from my hands
4 cups of food as prepared ½ tin of Brands essence.
Speaking a little and asking questions -   C.M. Tuke

      13th Considerable improvement
9.20   temp 97 which did not rise during the next 24 hours.
Taking some food ----   C.M. Tuke
---- ---- Clearer hardly any ---- ---- some bronchial
breathing heart action irregular ---- ---- ---- at
apex. ---- ---- ----(----) at ---- and all over
---- ----   C. M. Tuke
took food during the day.

14th Slept heavily. Refuses food ---- ----- ---- ---- ---- ----
will not be roused resists all attempts to feed her and spits out
anything put into her mouth. T.98   fed twice with tube.

                C. M. Tuke

Page 6
      16th is spitting very much today fed twice as before.
                C. M. Tuke

      19th Sitting up for some hours today answers questions in
a very low voice. Is quite conscious of all that goes on.
Fed by tube twice
                C.M. Tuke

   20th

22nd complained of pain last night refusing food.
                C.M. Tuke

   July 14th
      Mrs |Druitt has been in much the same condition she is
very quiet and can hardly be induced to speak and then only in
a whisper, ---- in weight evidently in strenth
is out in the garden daily for some hours in a bath
   chair.   Quiet at night is visited by her daughters.
                C.M. Tuke

July 22nd Requires feeding every few days much stronger, has
   Been walking in the garden lately.
                C. M. Tuke

      July 31st weight 5st 9 ¾ ozs Walked up to the ____ today
                C.M. Tuke

      Aug 30th left hand swollen and bruised this morning, not ---- ----
---- ---- a bandage applied.
                C.S.W. Cobbold

      31st Swelling less, bruising more evident. No cause for the injury

can be ascertained, so it was probably caused by the patient
herself during the night.

         C.S.W. Cobbolod

Sep 10th Hand practically well. Mrs D. takes food pretty
Freely now, appears ---- ---- ---- only replies to
Questions in monosyllables in a whisper. Takes no interest
In anything. Walks daily in the garden. Very depressed and full of delusions
Weight 5.10 ½

Page seven

Sep 16th urine examined, acid and cloudy with excess of
Lithates. No albumen. Mrs D. has to be fed
always by a nurse but she takes plenty of
food. Walked well in the garden this morning.

         C.S.W. Cobbold

Oct 20th Has had an attack of dioarreah which has
Resulted in a loss of strenth. There has been more
Restlessness but no complaints of pain being felt,
Some refusal of food on the 18th when it was
necessary to feed her with the stomach tube
Some ---- also lately, but this has now elapsed but
it was difficult to treat as Mrs Druitt ---- and spat
out all draughts. ---- very dirty will not speak
to anyone. visited by her daughters. Has not been
out lately but has sat up during the afternoons in
the sitting room.

         C.Molesworth Tuke

Oct 31st Has again had some diorreah

         T.S. Tuke

Nov 23rd Mrs Druitt has remained in much the same
Condition, obstinate, refusing food, taking nothing but liquid
and as a rule ----
There have been attacks of diorreah
lately and she is now rather sick. Her body weight
is certainly lighter. Gets up for a short time as a
rule, but is quiet in bed. Hides everything under her.
Has a slight cough ---- ----

Nov 26th Visited by her daughters. She
anxiety lately owing to her developing
disease: but there is ---- cough.

         T.S. Tuke

Dec 9th Mrs Druitt has not been so well, and occasionally
refuses food, which is entirely liquid now. She takes a
---- quantity as a rule. She has been sleeping lately
and has ------ slight cough, but there is no
sign of very serious ---- ---- breathing
shallow everywhere, ---- at night time. Breath

smells offensive, mutters to herself and coughs --- ---
of food taken. Evening temps 102 p 92 resp 28

Dec 13th Night T.101.7 p 4 R 26 restless at night and
attempting to get out of bed.
T. Seymour Tuke

Dec 14th Has not been so well today clenches her teeth
will take little food. ---- 101.7 p. 106 resp 38
congestion at left ----. Breathing very shallow. Has complained
of pain in ---- region. Hot ---- applied. Is getting
weaker, and her mind is wandering very much at
times. At other times she seems to know perfectly
what is going on.
T.S. Tuke

Page eight

Dec 15th. Wm ---- ---- Druitt saw her this
morning. Mrs Druitt has ---- a rather
restless night, and has become rather weaker ----
still able to take liquid food. Her breathing is
certainly worse but there is nothing to ----
immediate or impending danger. There is decided
congestion of the ---- and the heart sounds ----
---- ---- ---- ---- pulse temperature both
high (1 8 and 102.7 respectively). The Misses Druitt came
again in the afternoon and stayed till seven. Mrs Druitt
evidently very bad, but not worse than she had been all day.
Saw her again at 7.30. At 7.55 she evidently clutched
her nurse and fell back moribund. Death took
place at 8.5. Evidently from heart failure.

T.S. Tuke

Copy of notice sent to Coroner
Anne Druitt, female aged 60
Widow

Wimborne Dorset.
8.5.pm acute pneumonia and ----, melancholia --- ---
seven days
Dr T.S. Tuke. Dr Cobbold. Nurses Hancock and Knowles.

T. Seymour Tuke

Clearly then these notes indicate that Anne Druitt's physical condition had deteriorated since her son, Montague, had died even though her initial melancholia is documented from the summer of 1888. It is not known exactly when her psychotic delusions first appeared but, since Montague seems to have been in good physical health it may well have been this type of psychotic delusion which Montague had inherited.

The belief that one is lacking, or missing, one or more bodily organs is a quite common delusion among those suffering from severe, and extreme, forms of psychoses.

The symptoms, of Anne Druitts illness as described by Doctor Gasquet and subsequently elaborated upon by Doctor Tuke indicate a condition which contemporary textbooks described as Involutional Psychosis. Common in women it is a condition of agitated depression.

According to Biddle and VanSickel (Introduction to Psychiatry 1943.pp186) there are marked feelings of anxiety and apprehension with a strong tendency to self-mutilation and suicide. Delusions are self-condemnatory and normally based upon personal misdeeds of youth. Delusions of physical change are common. Patients suffering from this kind of mental illness may believe that they are being changed into some form of animal, or that they are dead, or that some vital organs are absent or not functioning. They often believe that they are being tortured, or that their families are being mistreated because of errors in their ways of living. Religious mania may also be apparent.

Since we know that Montague Druitt felt that he was '...becoming like mother', we can reasonably assume that he may have suffered from one, or maybe all of these symptoms. We must ask whether these symptoms might suggest a motive? - A 'desire to possess the missing organs'?

But for what purpose?

Trophy killing is a characteristic peculiar to serial killers. Often a serial killer will take clothing or personal possessions of his victim. John Christie, the Rillington Place murderer, collected pubic hair as a trophies. He kept his trophies in matchboxes. He also collected the bodies of his victims. The skeletons of two of his victims were discovered buried in his small back garden. Three more bodies were concealed behind a small partition wall in his kitchen, and, the body of his wife was concealed beneath the floorboards of his bedroom. These bodies however were not the trophies. The pubic hair, not all of it coming from his known victims was. The bodies were only kept because he had no other way of disposing of them. In 1953 Christie was convicted of his wifes murder and hanged. Christie was almost certainly guilty too of the murders of Beryl Evans and her baby daughter Geraldine in 1948 for which Timothy Evans, the husband and father of the victims was wrongfully convicted and hanged.

It is not often, however, that a serial killer will take the body parts of his victims as trophies although it does happen. One most notable example is that of Jeffery Dahmer. When, in 1991, two police officers called at Dahmers apartment, following up a complaint of assault they discovered a human head in his refrigerator. A thorough search later discovered human remains including three more heads and two more skulls. Several pairs of hands, and a penis, were found in a saucepan. a large quantities of human meat were found refrigerated In the Dahmer case there was some evidence which suggested, not only cannabilism but necrophilia. The heads had been used, post-mortem, for the purposes of Dahmers sexual gratification. In July 1992 Dahmer was convicted and sentenced to serve 15 life terms (957 years). Two years later, on November 28th 1994 at the Columbia Correctional Institute Jeffery Dahmer, and another inmate Jesse Anderson, were beaten to death by fellow inmate Christopher Scarver

An even more extreme example, however, is that of Ed Gein in 1957. Since the death of his beloved mother, 12 years earlier, Ed Gein had lived a solitary, and lonely existence, in an isolated farmhouse on a 160 acre farm seven miles from the town of Plainfield WisconsinGeins widowed mother had shielded Ed and his elder brother Henry from all women. They were to be avoided. Every night from childhood through manhood she had drummed the scriptural texts from revelations into their heads. However, according to Ed his mother viewed masturbation as a perfectly normal occupation. She encouraged such behaviour as preferable to any association with women.

After the death of their dominating and drunken father, in 1940, the farm ceased to be productive supported by Government grants paid to produce nothing. They supplemented the meagre grant by doing odd-jobs and farm labouring in and around the area.

Eds relationship with his mother grew disturbingly too close for brother Henrys comfort. Ed spent long periods of time closeted with his Mother in her bedroom. Henry, who was less impressed by his mothers semi-religious and moral ravings than was Ed, had had enough. Things came to a head when in May 1944 Henry chided, and teased his younger brother Eddie for what he considered a far too close a relationship with their mother. Henry, in fact, was disgusted at the overt sensual displays of attachment between them which he considered to be verging upon incest.

Eddie and Henry fought bitterly over this matter. The feud was still unresolved when, a few weeks later, Henry died, in very mysterious circumstances while assisting Ed to control a fire which Ed had set to clear an area of the farm.

Ed now had his mother all to himself. But not for long. A few days after Henrys funeral Augusta Gein suffered a severe stroke. Though now mostly bedridden she continued to dominate her doting son from her bed. Although Augusta recovered a little she died on December 29th the following year. Upon Julias death Ed sealed off his Mothers rooms from the rest of the house.

Ed was grief-stricken and lonely. Known locally as Little Ed (he stood only five feet tall) he was considered by most a hard worker, harmless, but a bit of a nut he knew that he could never form a relationship with another woman. By now his collection of books on Nazi atrocities, and his girlie magazines with their lurid and sexy pictures, were no longer enough for him. He needed the real thing or, at least as near as he could find.

. Over the next twelve years Ed Gein claimed that together with an accomplice, another weird loner, named Gus, systematically robbed graves of freshly interred elderly female corpses. They took the bodies to Geins barn where they were hung on hooks. The bodies were then butchered, eviscerated and skinned. Apart from grave robbing for his victims several young women, from the area around Plainfield, also mysteriously disappeared during this period.

Geins partnership with Gus ended when Gus was allegedly taken off to a lunatic asylum sometime around 1950. The identity of Gus, if indeed he ever existed has never been established.

When the three local cemeteries around Plainfield, the nearest town, ran out of fresh bodies Gein selected 51 years old divorcee Mary Hogan, from nearby Pine Grove. On the 8th December 1954 Gein shot and killed Mary Hogan and took her body to the barn. He later admitted to selecting Mary Hogan as a victim on the basis that she looked like his mother.

Ed used the skins of his victims to reupholster his chairs. He fashioned crude furniture and knick-knacks, such as soup bowls from the bones and skulls of his victims. Gein admitted that he also used the bodies for sexual purposes. He wore parts of their skin over his chest and genitals. Often, on warm evenings, he would wander around the fields and plains which surrounded his house. He admitted to performing sexual acts upon himself

while so attired. He admitted to covering his own penis with a vulva which he had preserved in salt. A large number of salted vaginas were found in a shoebox at his house. As well as sexual organs and breasts. Gein skinned the faces of his victims which he kept and wore as masks. He oiled the skins when they started to go stiff. Most of the rest of the bodies would be burned or boiled. Other body parts were found in the freezer, and, were clearly intended for Ed's consumption.

Gein was finally caught in 1957 after police, investigating the disappearance of another local shopkeeper, Bernice Worden, raided Geins dilapidated homestead. They found the missing womans freshly decapitated, and disembowelled body hanging by the heels in the barn.

Doctor Edward Kelleher, the chief of the Chicago Psychiatric Institute asserted, in a classic understatement, that Gein was obviously schizophrenic. He claimed that the condition was, among other things, an Oedipus complex created by a conflict set up by his mother. Ed Gein was declared insane and spent the rest of his life in a mental asylum. He died, still in psychiatric custody, in 1984. and was buried, secretly, and at night, next to his mother in the almost empty Plainfield cemetery

Ed Gein became the inspiration behind Alfred Hitchcocks movie 'bPsycho' in which motel owner Norman Bates (a play on the word masturbate) wore the skin of his mother and in such a way he became his own mother upon whom he, like his role model Ed Gein, had doted.

The decapitation, and disembowelment, of Geins victims, and the removal of the sexual organs, is remarkably similar to the injuries inflicted by Jack the Ripper. The differences are that Jack the Ripper did not possess a vehicle in which to transport his victims. Jack the Ripper had to secure the body parts he required in situ, and in a very short space of time. Jack the Ripper eviscerated his victims, and, in the cases of Polly Nichols, Annie Chapman and Catharine Eddowes, he made determined attempts at decapitation.

The desire, to possess the sexual organs, certainly appears to be the motive in the Jack the Ripper killings. But for what purpose ? Could the Whitechapel murderer, like Dahmer or Gein, have used these trophies for sexual purposes?

This horrible possibility may, at first, seem preposterous, but, it is precisely this kind of irrational association which often characterises this type of insanity.- and Montague John Druitt is, out of all of the known suspects, the only one against whom which there is some evidence of this type of insanity.

Druitts friends may have noticed his mental decline. We are told that he may have suffered from epileptic blackouts. MacNaghten describes Druitt as sexually insane. If we are to accept Montague's suicide note, then it must be reasonable to assume that he too felt that he was suffering from similar symptoms to those of his mother. Sometimes lucid, sometimes hopelessly insane, with bouts of depression and melancholia, delusions of missing organs, and, quite probably, like mother, sometimes violent.

The trigger, for Geins, repressed sexually insane behaviour was his mothers death. For Druitt the trigger was the certifying of his mother as insane. Anne Druitt had been certified insane in August 1888 just a few days before the slaying of Polly Nichols the first of the five, canonical victims of Jack the Ripper.

From Montague's note, ie: 'Since Friday...', (ie Friday 30th November) we may also assume that he had only just become aware of the implications of his own insanity. Montague's mental decline may have been noticed by his friend and boss, George Valentine - of the school at Blackheath where Montague had worked for the last eight years. He had sacked Montague for a 'serious offence'.

The nature of this 'serious offence' has caused some speculation that Montague may have been homosexual and that the 'serious offence', which, according to his brother William's evidence at the inquest, took place at the school, and for which Montague was dismissed, could have been of a homosexual nature.

Unfortunately no one has yet been unable to trace any kind of a record which casts any light upon the nature of Montague's 'serious offence'. Could it have been the 'serious offence' which caused Montague to realise that 'Since Friday...' he was becoming like mother?

If so, how could a homosexual offence make him feel that he was '...becoming like Mother?'

It may be reasonable to assume that, since Montague Druitts' mother was suicidal, he may have demonstrated his own suicidal tendencies. To attempt suicide was a serious offence punishable by imprisonment. If Druitt had attempted suicide, at the school, then Mr Valentine would surely have regarded this as a serious offence.

The serious offence may well have been sexual in nature. It might not have involved any other person. Druitt may simply have been caught masturbating. Not a criminal offence but possibly considered, by George Valentine, to be a sackable one.

Whatever the nature of the 'serious offence', though serious enough to warrant what appears to have been instant dismissal, it does not seem to have been serious enough to involve the police.

Could the serious offence have been the triggger to Montagues realisation that he was becoming like Mother? Or, Could Montagues realisation that he was becoming like Mother have triggered the serious offence? All that we do know is that both events appear to have taken place upon that fateful last Friday of November 1888.

The serious offence may well have been some manifestation of Druitts mental decline. Such as a fit or a blackout. But whatever it was it was clearly enough to suggest, at least to George Valentine, that Druitt was unfit, or unable, to continue his work at the school.

We do know, from the inquest report upon Montague Druitt, that the serious offence took place at the school. If the serious offence had been a suicide attempt then I feel sure that the principal of the school, George Valentine, would have been more sympathetic than to suddenly dismiss Druitt. Montague Druitt had worked for George Valentine for eight years. They were members of the same sporting clubs - they were friends. In such a case it might be thought that a period of sick-leave might have been a more appropriate sanction than instant dismissal. Whatever the offence was it was clearly George Valentines need to protect the reputation and integrity of his school which took priority over his long-standing friendship with Druitt.

The 'serious offence' may however have been nothing more than a contractural disagreement with George Valentine. Possibly a dereliction of his duty as an assistant schoolmaster. To support that possibility I offer the following for consideration.

A civil appeal case had been set down for hearing at the High Court in London for the end of November 1888. The case concerned a rating issue which had been heard by a reviving barrister at Christchurch Town Hall. The Christchurch solicitor for the appellant was William Druitt, Montagues brother. Montague thus held the brief for the appellant.

Montague duly appeared in court before The Lord Chief Justice Lord Coleridge and, arguing on a fine point of law he won the case, with costs. The following day the 30th November the press reported the story widely. And it was later that day that Druitt was summarily dismissed from his Job at Velentines school.

That was on Friday the 30th November. Without doubt this is the Friday referred to in Druitts suicide note. But instead of celebrating his legal victory he suddenly found himself homeless and unemployed. Less than one week later he was dead.

It is clear that when Montague Druitt left the Blackheath school that afternoon for the last time, George Valentine did not appear to anticipate Druitts suicide since he indicates that he was under the impression that Druitt was going abroad. Furthermore Valentine was obviously surprised to learn with some regret of Druitts death.

The instant dismissal of Druitt. His summary eviction from the school, and his apparent realisation that he was becoming like his mother, was all to much for Druitt. When he left Eliot Place for the last time he must have been holding on to whatever remnants of sanity remained. We are told that his friends entertained grave doubts as to his sanity, and Druitts own note tends to confirm that he too doubted his sanity. He may also have seen echoes of his own feelings in his recent defence of Powers the lunatic with the sodomy obsession?

Whom, among his friends could Montague turn to for help and advice? Who was best placed to help him?

We are only told that his funeral, at Wimborne, was attended by '...family and a few friends'. We can only speculate as to whom some of these friends might have been. The Hampshire Advertiser 12th Jan 1889 tells us that these friends included Montagues Uncle Mr J.T. Homer, a Wimborne prize pig-breeder and a Mr Wyke-Smith. Apart from family members no other mourners are mentioned.

Montague's working life, as a barrister, would have brought him into close contact with, for example, other members of his chambers. Situated as he was in Kings Bench Walk, he was surrounded by men who, interestingly enough, were all close friends of that other Jack the Ripper contender, Prince Albert Victor.

Just four doors away from Montague's chambers were the chambers of Harry Stephen, a brother of poet J.K. Stephen, who has himself been suggested as a suspect. Harry Wilson and John Lonsdale, both close friends of the Prince, had chambers nearby. Lonsdale himself lived at Eliot Cottages just a few yards from George Valentine's school in Eliot Place, Blackheath. Skinner and Howells observe that these men would have known each other well. They go further by suggesting that these men could have been part of a homosexual cartel into which Montague may have been drawn.

John Lonsdale appears to have almost shadowed the Druitt family. He lived just a few doors from Valentines school in Blackheath. He had chambers at Kings Bench Walk, a few doors from Druitts chambers in the Inner Temple, and in 1887 he was ordained and given the curacy of Wimborne Minster. He certainly knew Montagues elder Cousin Charles since, for a time, in 1887 they both shared the same house in Wimborne. This is confirmed by The Salisbury and Winchester Journal and General Advertiser which ran a story on 14th May 1887 in relation to the trial of some men who had robbed the house of JH Lonsdale and stolen certain items of his and Charles Druitts belongings.

Charles Druitt, the was Lonsdales immediate predecessor in the Curacy at Parkstone in Dorset. He was the Son of Montagues Uncle Robert. Charles was nine years older than Montague, deeply religious he was affectionately nicknamed 'Pope' by the Druitt family. He had vacated the post of Curate in early January but was known to be still living in the same house which he shared with the incoming Curate JH Lonsdale. Lonsdale eventually became Rector of nearby Fontwell Magna where he died in 1903 aged 47.

Other friends of Druitt might have included his cricket friends and clubmates, and members of the numerous and various sporting clubs to which he belonged. Such friends would have included Harry Goodhart, another close friend of Prince Albert Victor, and Evelyn Ruggles-Brise. Evelyn Ruggles-Brice had studied for his civil service entrance examination at exactly the same time as Druitt. They sat the exam together on the 14th January 1881 and eleven days later the announcement that both had passed was announced in the London Gazzette. Ruggles-Brise was also a cricketing contemporary of Druitt at Oxford. They had, in fact, played cricket together as early as 1876 when the two teenage opponents met in the Winchester v. Eton match of that year. There can be little doubt but that these two men were well known to each other and quite possibly good friends. Evelyn Ruggles-Brise was now the personal private secretary to no less than Henry Mathews, the Home Secretary.

Furthermore, Ruggles-Brise was the liaison man between the Home Secretary and the man who, at the time of the murders, was heading the secret Scotland Yard department overseeing the Ripper investigation - James Monro.

It is also worth noting that there was a marital connection between the Druitt family and Walter Boultbee, Private secretary, to Charles Warren, and successively to James Monro. In 1885 Walter Boultbee had married Ellen Baker a niece of Alfred Mayo. Alfred Mayo was himself a nephew of Jane Mayo Montagues Grandmother.

Harry Wilson mentioned above, lived at 'The Osiers', a tall thin house overlooking the River Thames at Chiswick.very close to the spot where Druitts body was found. Skinner and Howells have postulated that the fact that since Druitt's body was found nearby it, and his probable connection with 'the Eddy set' suggests that he may have been murdered by Harry Wilson and his homosexual friends after discovering Druitt's activities as the Whitechapel killer.

There is some evidence that Wilson's house, at Chiswick, was a popular meeting place for young men of a certain disposition. Prince Albert Victor was a frequent visitor. Several young Oxbridge undergraduates were listed as resident at Wilsons house. If any of these men were part of a homosexual ring then they could have seen Druitt as a danger to their own illegal activities. Furthermore, such a revelation would have seriously compromised the position of Prince Albert Victor, the Queen's grandson and heir apparent to the throne. When Albert Victor was eventually compromised in the Cleveland Street affair the matter was unreported in the British press.

But would Druitt have gone to any of these men? He is certain to have known them. He may even have been friendly with them. But he was not one of them. As an Oxford man he would not, and could not have been an integral part of their fraternity known as 'The Apostles'. But that would not exclude him from forming friendships, or even close relationships with any of them.

We cannot know if Montague Druitt was murdered or not. There was no post-mortem examination evidence given at the inquest apart from PC George Moulsom's assertion that there were no marks of injury. He did however add the comment that the body was rather decomposed. He implies that even if there had been any marks upon the body, then the advanced decomposition would have have rendered the detection of such marks, or injuries, impossible.

A body, which has been immersed in water for any length of time, will quickly turn black as it dries out. Bruising would have been very difficult to detect. Such bodies are also very difficult to handle after so long in the water.

There is no evidence that Montague Druitt was murdered. But the only evidence of his suicide is his note.

One may question why an athelete, such as Druitt, should choose drowning as a method of suicide. Druitt's instincts would make it a difficult task. No doubt this is why he weighted his clothing with stones.

I am told by the River Police, who deal with many suicides, that weighting oneself is a very unusual precaution for suicides to take. A weighted body will not travel too far. At first it will sink. Eventually, as the gases trapped within the body expand, the body will rise to the surface. Considering the ebb and flow of the River Thames at that point, a submerged and weighted body will not move significantly from the point of immersion. A floating body will move very slowly downstream. Druitt's body could not have been on the surface for more than a few hours since in those days the River was a very busy thoroughfare, and, overlooked by houses as it is, a floating body would quickly have been seen. It is possible therefore to conclude that Druitt, alive or dead, entered the river at, or about, the spot where his body was found three weeks later.

It was my good fortune to be born overlooking this particular stretch of the River Thames at Chiswick. In fact, I was born in the building adjacent to 'The Osiers', Harry Wilson's house. Coincidentally the house which stood adjacent to 'The Osiers' in 1888 was occupied by a Mrs Anderson. More interestingly however is that contemporary maps show that a foot-path directly behind 'The Osiers' led Northwest directly across open land linking it to the gates of the Manor House Asylum.

My own knowledge of the River Thames, at this point, is limited to my childhood, and to the frequent times that I found myself stuck in the mud while exploring the small island, known as Chiswick Eyot, before the tide came in. At low tide the shoreline extends quite a way into the river, so much so that one can walk practically across to the middle, where it is quite deep enough for one to drown. The point here is that Druitt must have waded for some distance through the icy water until he found a spot deep enough.

Alternatively he may have entered the deeper waters from a boat. Of course it is easy enough to drown in the shallow waters of the riverbank, but, as the tide receded, which it does twice a day, his weighted body would have been revealed long before the three weeks that it was said to have been in the water. Either way, Montague Druitt displayed a remarkable determination in ending his life in such a way.

Given Druitt's determination to end his life, why then did he buy a return ticket for his journey to Hammersmith?

This raises a doubt that suicide was the reason for his last journey. I don't accept that Druitt went to Chiswick just to commit suicide. I do believe he went there for help? If so from whom? Maybe a murderous cartel did await him at The Osiers. Or maybe he received a more sympathetic and discreet reception somewhere else in the area.

I had been struck by the coincidence of Montague Druitts body being discovered at Chiswick and his mothers eventual death in the same place two years later. There had to be more to this than a mere coincidence.

It is but a short walk, from Hammersmith railway station, towards the river at Chiswick to the spot where the body of Montague Druitt was found floating in the river.

With a few exceptions, the fashionable villa type houses overlooking the river along the Chiswick Mall are much the same now as they were in 1888. Brandenburgh House, where Caroline of Brunswick, the estranged and shunned wife of The Prince Regent established herself in exile, looks exactly the same today as it does in Regency prints.

Harry Wilson's house, 'The Osiers' is still there.

A little further westwards, along Chiswick Mall, is the intersection with Chiswick Lane, which runs northwards from the river where it joins the Chiswick High Road. Half-way along this lane is a small row of five terraced house fronted by depressing little gardens. On the north side of this terrace is a narrow alley. It is called Manor Alley and it marks what was the northern boundary of the once extensive grounds of the Manor House Asylum.

A large red-brick mansion with stone facings, the Manor House, demolished in 1929, was built in 1691 by Sir Stephen Fox, a faithful servant of Charles 11. It was Fox who had carried the news of Oliver Cromwells death to the future King. In his 77th year Fox had married 26 year old Frances Hope, being '..unwilling that so plentiful an estate should not go out of name' and '...being of a vegete and hale constitution.' That Sir Stephen Fox was of a 'hale constitution' should not be doubted since Frances subsequently bore him four children.

The house descended through the family until it was eventually acquired by Dublin born Edward Francis Tuke, who, with a partner, philantrophist Robert Bell, operated the house as a private mental asylum. But Edward was a gambler and he was finally forced to flee the country for debt. In his absence the asylum was carried on by his second wife Mary and their son Thomas Harrington Tuke.

The Tuke family were, like their unrelated namesakes from Yorkshire, pioneers into the humane treatment of the insane. The shackles and chains, previous hallmarks of the treatment of the insane, had been cast aside. The comfortable conditions of the new 'alienist' approach to mental illness meant that troublesome old relatives, as well as the genuinely mentally afflicted, could now be packed off to such institutions without fear of scandal, and with a considerable easing of the conscience in the knowledge that they would be well cared for.

The Manor House Asylum was one such establishment. It was well situated, within easy reach of central London and the suburbs, and just a short walk from the picturesque fishing village of Old Chiswick. The Manor House clearly enjoyed a good reputation for treatment, and discretion. The asylum was patronised by many from the arts. Dickens and Thackeray were both friends of Doctor Thomas Harrington Tuke. Among the illustrious to be treated at the Manor House were Edwin Landseer, Queen Victoria's favourite painter. Lady Harriet Mordaunt who was conveniently certified insane in 1870 after the notorious Mordaunt divorce scandal, which implicated the Prince of Wales, was a patient of Doctor Thomas Harrington Tuke for almost seven years. Tuke had given evidence of her insanity at her trial.

Interestingly enough there is a connection here with old Doctor Gull. A few days after Harriet Mordaunt was admitted to The Manor House Doctor Gull, together with Sir James Alderson, Doctor Boyd, Doctor Priestly and a Doctor Tweedie all examined Harriet Mordaunt, at the Manor House, before certifying her as insane. Harriet was placed under the care of Dr Andrew Wynter and although confined she lived in relative comfort at Chestnut Lodge in nearby Grove Park, until, in 1877, she was moved to Hayes Park Asylum in Hillingdon. She died in 1906.

In 1888 the Manor house was staffed by three doctors, Doctor Thomas Tuke, the son of Thomas Harrington Tuke, who had died in June of that year, was now the resident physician. His brother Doctor Charles Tuke assisted together with a locum. Thirty-nine ancillary staff were also employed at the establishment. Frederick Tuke, a brother of the two doctors, acted as administrator to the asylum. The forty or so patients were quite free to wander the extensive grounds, which boasted ornamental lawns and a bowling green. It was here, at the Manor House asylum, just a few hundred yards from where Montague Druitt's body was fished from the nearby River Thames, at the end of 1888, that his Mother Anne Druitt was to die two years later.

However desirable the facilities were it seemed to me very unlikely that Anne Druitt would have selected the Manor House for herself, even if lucid enough to do so, unless it was her deliberate purpose to be close to the spot where her son had died. It is possible that she was unaware of her location, although Dr Tuke does makes it clear, in his notes, that she knew '...perfectly well what was going on'. But, if she did not know where she was it demonstrates great insensitivity on the part of her eldest son William who, according to Doctor Gasquet, seems to have been the person responsible for arranging her move to the Manor House from the Brighton asylum.

So why was Anne Druitt sent to the Manor House Asylum? And was her presence there now connected with Montague's mysterious last journey to Chiswick eighteen months earlier?

The discovery of Montague's body in Chiswick and his mother's subsequent confinement in a private asylum just a few hundred yards from where her son's body had been found was too coincidental. Here perhaps was the key to unlock the answers to the questions - Why did Montague make that final journey to Chiswick? Why was Montague suspected of being the Whitechapel Killer? Could this asylum have been a source of the 'private information' which had ultimately so convinced MacNaghten and others that Druitt was the Whitechapel killer.

In order to answer these questions I needed to establish a connection between Montague Druitt and the Tuke family.

I am indebted to Sir David Tuke, grandson of Frederick William Tuke, for supplying me with a copy of his family history.

Thomas Harrington Tuke, had inherited the asylum from his Father Edward Francis, and had developed the use of non-restraint techniques in the treatment of the insane.

The 'alienist' approach to mental illness had been pioneered by his Father-in-law John Conally MD. FRCP. at his asylum at Hanwell. In 1852 Thomas Tuke married Connallys daughter Sophia. Sophias sister, Anne Caroline, was married to Doctor Henry Maudsley after whom the famous hospital is so named. Thomas Seymour Tuke, Charles Molesworth Tuke and Frederick William Tuke were the sons of Thomas and Sophia. A Daughter, Caroline, became a Deaconess and worked for many years with the Anglo Indian community in Madras.

It would appear that when not treating their illustrious patients, the Tuke brothers indulged themselves in their favourite pastime - the gentlemanly game of cricket. It was a game at which they excelled. They once raised a team to play against the great W.C. Grace and the MCC. Thomas Tuke and his elder brother Frederick had been playing cricket since their schooldays at St Pauls and Merchant -Taylors respectively. When they went up to Oxford University there is no reason to suppose that their enthusiasm for the game was diminished. In which case they would have almost certainly come into contact with the other leading lights of the Oxford University teams which included Evelyn Ruggles-Brise and the University team's opening bowler, their exact contemporary, Montague Druitt.

Thomas Tuke was also a lifelong member of the Oxford University Freemason Apollo lodge.

This link between Montague Druitt and the Tuke brothers may, at least, cast some light upon the final days of Montague Druitt.

AT THE BOTTOM OF THE THAMES

On Saturday 1st December 1888, Montague Druitt purchased a return railway ticket, from Charing Cross, and travelled to Hammersmith. He had been dismissed, for a serious offence just the day before, from his job at the Blackheath school where he had worked as an assistant master for the last eight years. Montague walked the short distance, along the river from Hammersmith to the Manor House at nearby Chiswick.

He might have visited the Tuke brothers often, we may never know, but on this day he must surely have been contemplating the reception he would get from his old friends. How was he going to tell them his dreadful secrets? He must have known that, if his secret were discovered, society would demand that he pay the ultimate price. What advice could the Tukes give him? Could they help him? Protect him? Would they want to? How much if anything could Montague confess to his friends?

Since the previous day he had started to '...feel like mother'. Clearly he was now becoming aware of his insanity.
Where better to seek help and advice than old friends, and brother masons, noted for discretion and whose speciality was just such illnesses. All that we can know is that at some point, over that weekend, while in Chiswick, Montague decided upon the course of action that he felt was '...best for all concerned' and he wrote his note to that effect.

To support the contention that the note was written at Chiswick, possibly at the Manor House asylum, consider the words 'Since Friday...' If Montague had written his note on Saturday 1st of December, the day he arrived at the Chiswick, he would have been much more likely to have used the phrase 'since yesterday'. Furthermore, since he had purchased a return ticket it is a compelling assumption that, at the time he purchased it, he had intended to return to Charing Cross. His decision to die, if indeed it was his decision, must have been made after he purchased his ticket and after he had used the outward portion of it.

His note therefore must have been found at the place where he had spent the last few days of his life - possibly at the Manor House Asylum or at The Osiers. But what supports this theory?

If we look again at the newspaper reports of Druitt's death and inquest, there are a number of curious discrepancies. One report appeared in the local weekly Chiswick paper, 'The Acton and Turnham Green Gazette', on the 5th January. This report, which I discovered in 1970, states that the deceased person's identity had already been established by 'papers found on the body' - yet, PC George Moulsom had told the inquest that, 'There were no papers or letters of any kind on the body'.

If the policeman's evidence was true, and it was he who had searched the 'badly decomposed' body when it was brought ashore, then how was the body identified so quickly?

Clearly the writer of the newspaper article must have been told that papers had been found. The press report lists, amongst other objects, two cheques, yet we had the policeman almost stressing, as if making a point, that no papers had been found on Montagues body. Furthermore any papers which had been immersed in water for three weeks would, in all probability have been completely unreadable.

The 'Middlesex Independent', published on the very day of the inquest, tells us that:

'From certain papers found friends have been telegraphed to. An inquest will be held today.'

Obviously papers had been found but, ...not on the body. The policeman did not commit perjury, he told the truth.

Describing the 'papers' as having been found '...on the body' neatly avoids any connection between Druitt and 'The Osiers chummery, and his 'friends' at the nearby Manor House asylum.

Some reports mention a letter written by Druitt and addressed to Mr Valentine, principal of the Blackheath school, in which Montague had alluded to suicide. This suggests that this letter might have been one of several which Montague had left.

Unfortunately we are not told where any of these papers, if any, were found other than at the place he had resided, possibly referring to his short stay in Chiswick. Furthermore, if Druitt had actually left a letter, for George Valentine, alluding to suicide, and left it at Valentines school, one should ask how Valentine had formed the opinion that Druitt had gone abroad.

On, or about, Tuesday 11th December, William Druitt had been informed that Montague had not been seen at his chambers for more than a week. We are told that Montague was last seen alive on Monday 3rd December, two days after he had made his journey to Hammersmith. But we are not told where, or by whom he had been seen. Upon learning this William had gone to London and had Montague's 'things searched where he (had) resided'.

We do not know where this residence was he had only just left Valentines school where he had been registered as resident. He may well have had other lodgings. But if Montague had left a suicide note at Valentines they must have been written before he left Charing Cross on Saturday 1st December.

Yet, if he left suicide notes at his 'lodgings' and then went off to commit suicide, why did he purchase a return railway ticket? These vexing discrepancies can be answered only if one accepts the probability that Druitt's final 'papers' were written and found at his final destination – The 'Osiers' or the Manor House asylum, both residences connected by a short footpath and that either of those 'dwellings' could have been the place where he had last resided albeit on a very temporary basis.

It has been suggested that Montague may have been a casual, almost informal, patient of the brothers Tuke. They may have been the friends who, according to MacNaghten, feared for his sanity. They may have been the ones who found Druitts 'since Friday' note and contacted William Druitt to tell him of his brother Montagues sudden disappearance. If this was the case then it is obvious that, by the end of December, William, and the brothers Tuke, must have known that Montague was dead and that it was just a question of time before the body would be discovered.

George Sims (Dagonet) certainly alludes to this possibility. He wrote:

'The homicidal maniac who shocked the world as Jack the Ripper had been once - I am not sure that it was not twice - in a lunatic asylum. At the time his dead body was found in the Thames, his friends, who were terrified at his disappearance from their midst, were endeavouring to have him found and placed under restraint again.'
And:

'After the maniacal murder in Miller's-court the doctor disappeared from the place in which he had been living, and his disappearance caused inquiries to be made concerning him by his friends (William) who had, there is reason to believe, their (his) own suspicions about him, and these inquiries were made through the proper authorities.'

If Montague's disappearance from the midst of his friends, possibly on the 3rd of December, when, as we are informed he was last seen alive, and the discovery of a suicide note had been reported to the local police, at Chiswick, before Montague's body was found, possibly at, or even before, the time of brother William's search for him during the middle of December, it would fully explain how the badly decomposed body of Montague Druitt was identified so quickly when it was eventually found.

Brother William had testified on oath at the inquest, that 'there were no other relatives'. This was a lie. There were two other brothers, and three sisters, and several aunts and cousins. William, a practising solicitor, must have been aware that his evidence was perjured. So, why should William Druitt, himself a Coroner in Dorset and a respectable solicitor, risk his entire professional standing as well as risk conviction and imprisonment for perjury?

It is not enough to suggest that William's peculiar and risky actions were to protect the reputation of his unmarried sisters, particularly as suicide carried a certain social stigma, since he quite freely volunteered the information to the Coroner that his mother, Anne, is a certified lunatic. He clearly made no reference to any of his alleged suspicions regarding Montague as suggested by Sims above.

But then he really had no choice in declaring his mother's insanity. The reference, in Montague's note, to his feelings of '...becoming like mother' had to be explained to the inquest. At least it guaranteed that the inquest did not become too searching. With the information of Druitts mother's insanity, Coroner Diplock closed the inquest with a verdict of suicide whilst of unsound mind.

Montague Druitts body was conveyed to Wimborne and buried in the family plot in Wimborne cemetery on the 10th January 1889. Six weeks later Montagues younger brother Edward married Christina Weld, daughter of Sir Frederick Weld of Chideock Manor. The, seemingly non-grieving, happy couple promptly emigrated to Australia.

MacNaghten tells us that he believed Druitt's own family believed him to be the Whitechapel murderer. Why should they hold such a belief without good reason? . More importantly, when did Druitt's family formulate such a belief? If the family had held such a belief before Montague's disappearance, Would they not have had him certified for his own protection? This could even have been the purpose for his appearance at the Manor House.
From what Sims has leaked to us it would seem that William confided his suspicions of Montague privately and through 'the proper authorities'.

It is entirely possible that a confession was made, possibly to a close relative. Let us consider the following press report which appeared in 1899:

'Western Mail
19 January 1899

WHITECHAPEL MURDERS
DID "JACK THE RIPPER" MAKE A CONFESSION?

We have received (says the Daily Mail) from a clergyman of the Church of England, now a North Country vicar, an interesting communication with reference to the great criminal mystery of our times - that enshrouding the perpetration of the series of crimes which have come to be known as the "Jack the Ripper" murders. The identity of the murderer is as unsolved as it was while the blood of the victims was yet wet upon the pavements. Certainly Major Arthur Griffiths, in his new work on "Mysteries of Police and Crime," suggests that the police believe the assassin to have been a doctor, bordering on insanity, whose body was found floating in the Thames soon after the last crime of the series; but as the major also mentions that this man was one of three known homicidal lunatics against whom the police "held very plausible and reasonable grounds of suspicion," that conjectural explanation does not appear to count for much by itself.

Our correspondent the vicar now writes:-

"I received information in professional confidence, with directions to publish the facts after ten years, and then with such alterations as might defeat identification.

The murderer was a man of good position and otherwise unblemished character, who suffered from epileptic mania, and is long since deceased.

I must ask you not to give my name, as it might lead to identification"

meaning the identification of the perpetrator of the crimes. We thought at first the vicar was at fault in believing that ten years had passed yet since the last murder of the series, for there were other somewhat similar crimes in 1889. But, on referring again to major Griffiths's book, we find he states that the last "Jack the Ripper" murder was that in Miller's Court on November 9, 1888 - a confirmation of the vicar's sources of information. The vicar enclosed a narrative, which he called "The Whitechapel Murders - Solution of a London Mystery." This he described as "substantial truth under fictitious form." "Proof for obvious reasons impossible - under seal of confession," he added in reply to an inquiry from us.

Failing to see how any good purpose could be served by publishing substantial truth in fictitious form, we sent a representative North to see the vicar, to endeavour to ascertain which parts of the narrative were actual facts. But the vicar was not to be persuaded, and all that our reporter could learn was that the rev. gentleman appears to know with certainty the identity of the most terrible figure in the criminal annals of our times, and that the vicar does not intend to let anyone else into the secret.

The murderer died, the vicar states, very shortly after committing the last murder. The vicar obtained his information from a brother clergyman, to whom a confession was made - by whom the vicar would not give even the most guarded hint. The only other item which a lengthy chat with the vicar could elicit was that the murderer was a man who at one time was engaged in rescue work among the depraved woman of the East End - eventually his victims; and that the assassin was at one time a surgeon.'

The Vicar is telling us that he was given this information by a fellow Clergyman. This may be one of the 'facts' which he had to change in order to disguise the idntity of the 'confessee'. It is quite possible that it was to this Vicar, who seemed anxious that his name should not be revealed lest it led to the identity of the 'confessee' to whom the confession had been made.

Could there be any truth in this story? Let us speculate here on what we are being told.

(1) The 'confesse' (the killer) was a man of good standing with an unblemished character.
(2) The man suffered from epilepsy.
(3) The man is dead.
(4) The man died shortly after the last murder
(5) The vicar obtained his information from a fellow clergyman to whom a confession had been made.
(6) The man was at one time *engaged in rescue work among the depraved women of the East-End.*
(7) That the assassin was at one time a surgeon.

Six of the seven fact listed fit Montague Druitt .who was not a surgeon That the killer was believed to have been a surgeon may account for this discrepancy (if it does refer to Druitt) It also presents some difficulty when considering the identity of the original vicar to whom the alleged conession was made.

Most telling, however, is the revelation that the killer had been engaged in rescue work among the prostitutes in the East End of London.

Montagues Cousin Charles Druitt a Vicar in Parkstone Dorset, not far from Wimborne, would have been unlikely to describe Montague as a surgeon. But, since we also know that the Vicar, who gave the story to the newspaper, had been tasked with distorting some facts in an attempt to disguise the identity, describing the confessee as a surgeon would achieve that objective. We should remember that the suggestion that the killer must have been a surgeon was quite consistent with the common belief at that time.

Another Cousin of Montague was Philip Druitt the Son of James Druitt (1816 – 1904). Philip, was born in 1865 one of eleven children. Philip graduated from Oxford in 1888 and enrolled at the Leeds Clergy School. He was ordained Deacon in 1891 and as a priest the following year. He served at Ripon, in Yorkshire and at St Bartholomews in Leeds. Philip might well have been described as a North Country vicar.

Solicitor Robert Druitt, the eldest son of Montagues Uncle Robert, and elder brother of The the Rev Charles, was married to Alice May Tupper the daughter of Martin Tupper the author of 'Proverbial Philosophy'.Tupper was employed in the Lord Chamberlains office at St James' Palace. As a member of the Royal Household he was thus was well placed to pass on private family information.

Yet another possibility exists. The original Vicar, to whom the confession was made could have been former barrister John Lonsdale, sometime roomate of Montagues Cousin Charles, and close friend of Harry Wilson of 'The Osiers' at Chiswick, and HRH Prince Eddy.

John Lonsdale, born in 1856, would have known Montague Druitt well. He had lived at Eliot Cottages in Blackheath just a few yards from George Valentines School where Druitt was based. He had chambers alongside Druitt at Kings Bench Walk in the Inner Temple. In 1887 Lonsdale was ordained as an Anglican Priest and became the immediate successor to Montagues cousin Charles Druitt as curate of Wimborne.

More interesting is the fact that in 1887 Charles Druitt and John Lonsdale had lived together for a time at the house in East Borough Wimborne. This is confirmed by the lengthy artcle in 'The Salisbury and Winchester Journal and General Advertiser' May 14th 1887 dealing with the burglary, which had taken place at their shared house. (see appendices for the full article).

Could John Lonsdale have been the priest to whom Druitt might have made a confession? Could Lonsdale have been staying with Harry Wilson at 'The Osiers', Wilsons House overlooking the River at Chiswick in early December 1888 when, and if Montague Druitt called upon them for help?

More to the point Could Montague have met Lonsdale at Wilsons house during that last weekend and confessed to Lonsdale before ending his life in the nearby river?
All of those questions can be answered as possibilities.

We are told that evidence, pointing to Druitt as Jack the Ripper, and 'of a factual nature' did at one time exist.

Skinner and Howells ('The Ripper Legacy') contacted Christopher Monro, the grandson of

Commissioner James Monro, who volunteered the information that his grandfather's views on the Whitechapel Murders had been set down in a highly private memorandum which he had subsequently passed to his eldest son Charles, Christohers uncle. Uncle Charles had discussed these papers with Christopher's father. The contents were described as a 'very hot potato'. So hot in fact that the papers had been kept secret even from James Monro's own wife. Christopher's father advised his brother Charlie to burn them and to forget the contents.

If this story is accurate then it is quite possible that these papers could have been, or at least contained, the Home Office report on Druitt's death. The fact that Monro appears to have kept the papers, and kept them highly private, and secret, suggests the reason why it was that so many police officers, including Littlechild and Abberline, never knew of the real conclusions of the Jack the Ripper investigations.

The official case papers, on the Whitechapel murders have, over the years, been plundered. Many of the most important documents appear to be missing. The Home Office files on the case have an enormous gap between the 23rd November 1888 and the 9th March 1889. The Scotland Yard files have a similar gap. Between the 10th of November 1888 and the 17th of July 1889 apart from Doctor Bonds post mortem report on Mary Kelly and George Hutchinsons statement, all documents which might have related to suspects, or the investigations have vanished..

The significance of the missing papers is that they would cover precisely the period during which, as we are told by Sims, the police were looking for Druitt. It would have been during the period, of the missing files, that the information regarding Druitt would have been brought to the notice of the police. The missing papers could have contained Montague Druitts confession, if indeed he ever made one, or documents containing the suspicions of his friends or family

These missing papers might well have been the very documents which Monro had kept in his possession. Such papers would certainly have been contained within the now empty spaces where papers are missing from both the Home Office and the Metropolitan police files. It is extremely likely that Monro discussed the contents, of the papers, with MacNaghten in the ensuing years, possibly at the time when MacNaghten was preparing his Memorandum.

James Monro's son, Christopher, might not have destroyed the papers. He might well have passed them on, or at least made them available, to his Fathers old friend Melville MacNaghten. If so then it could have been these papers which constituted as described by MacNaghten, 'the evidence of a factual nature' which according to MacNaghten did not come into his possession until some time after the killings.

But somewhere there seems to have been a leak. A full Three years beforeMacNaghten had penned his famous memo someone already seemed to have been onto Druitt.

The following story appeared in The Bristol Times and Mirror February 11th 1891:

' I give a curious story for what it is worth. There is a West of England member who in private declares he has solved the mystery of "Jack the Ripper." His theory – and he repeats it with so much emphasis that it might also be called his doctrine – is that "Jack the Ripper" committed suicide on the night of his last murder. I cant give details, for fear of a libel action, but the story is so circumstantial that a good many people believe it. He states that a man with blood stained clothes committed suicide on the night of the last murder and he asserts that he was the son of a surgeon who suffered from homicidal mania. I do not know what the police think of the story, but I believe that before long a clean breast will be made, and that the accusation will be sifted thoroughly.'

The same story, slightly edited, appeared in other papers of the same date, notably the Pall Mall Gazette published in London.

The identity of the West of England Member (of Parliament) slipped out a little over a year later when the Western Mail revealed him to be Henry Farquharson the MP for West Dorset from 1885 until his death in 1895.

Farquharson lived only nine miles from the Druitt family home in Wimborne. He was the son of the Lord of the Manor of Tarrant Gunville, and principal landowner, and would have known the family well, not just as neighbours but also as part of the high Tory gentry of West Dorset.

It is quite possible that Farquharson might have heard the story directly from a source in the Druitt family or through the Dorset grapevine. He might have heard it from MacNaghten himself or Farquharson might even have been the source of MacNaghtens own 'private info'.

Farquharson and MacNaghten were both contemporary old Etonians and would certainly have known each other well and had in common the fact that they had both owned or managed tea plantations in India or Ceylon. Despite the discrepancies between Farquharsons suspect and MacNaghtens favoured suspect there can be little doubt but that they refer to the same person.

Stephen Ryder - the man behind the very successful Jack the Ripper website WWW.casebook.org produced an interesting theory, originally published in The Ripperologist (no 37), regarding the possible origin of the Druitt familys concerns regarding Montague. The Perkins library, at Duke University, North Carolina appears to be the final resting place of some of the personal correspondence of Sir Robert Anderson. Altogether there are 680 items housed in three boxes. There are also a few photographs and sketches. Ryder has pointed out that there is almost nothing in the collection which deals with his period as head of the C.I.D He did, however, find one letter which actually mentions the Whitechapel Murders. It is undated and comprises of two sides of a single sheet.

It reads:

2 CAVENDISH SQUARE
W.

My dear Anderson,

I send you this line to ask you to see & hear the bearer, whose name is unknown to me. she has or thinks she has a knowledge of the author of the Whitechapel murders. The author is supposed to be nearly related to her, and she is in great fear lest any suspicions should attach to her & place her & her family in great peril.

I have advised her to place the whole story before you, without giving you any names, so that you may form an opinion as to its being worth while to investigate.

Very sincerely yours,
Crawford

From the address given it is clear that the writer was James Ludovic Lindsay, 26th Earl of Crawford. A friend. and correspondent of Sir Robert Anderson. Crawford was known to have a particularly keen interest in the Whitechapel murders. Indeed it is the same Lord Crawford who was the author of the article, on the murders, which Vittoria Cremers had found so interesting.

No clue is given, in Crawfords letter, as to the identity of the lady in question, and it is clear that she was unknown to him.

But Ryder makes some very reasonable assumptions. The phrase nearly related, can suggest a distant relation, such as a cousin or a niece or nephew. Ryder then makes an illuminating discovery by suggesting the possibility that the unnamed lady might have been Emily Druitt a daughter of MontaguesUncle Robert and a cousin of Montague.

A letter, dated September 1876, written by Montague to his Uncle Robert, preserved in the West Sussex Record Office(Druitt M8 12.f.27) describes how Emily, and her sister Kitty, were having such a dull time during their stay at Wimborne. The letter appears to be a report, from Montague to Uncle Robert on Emilys progress at translating Virgil and the problems thereof.

It would appear that Emily Druitt worked in collaboration with bookseller and publisher Bernard Quaritch (1819 - 1899). Quaritch was also a close personal family friend of the letter writer - the Earl of Crawford.

The letter itself is one of personal introduction since it asks Anderson to see and hear the bearer. Crawford himself must have been told the story and considered it credible enough to bring to Andersons attention. Since Crawford did not know the woman involved someone else must have told him the story. A future, and thorough search of the papers, of both Crawford, and Quatrich, may yet yield some interesting results.

It is, of course, as yet, speculation that Emily Druitt was the subject of Crawfords letter, and that she passed on the familys concerns regarding her cousin Montague to Anderson. But, according to MacNaghten, it is safe to assume that at least one of Montagues relatives had, at one time or another, denounced him as the killer.

Whoever the lady was Anderson must have interviewed her, and heard her story, otherwise he would not have had possession of Crawfords introductory letter which the lady would have presented in person.

If Emily Druitt was the person whose information led MacNaghten to his conclusion, that Druitts own family believed Montague to be the Whitechapel murderer, then the above chain of events could explain the vexed question as to why Montague was ever suspected in the first place. It would fit the known facts perfectly. Emily Druitts information would throw Montagues name into the frame possibly for the first time. .

It is to be regretted that Crawfords letter appears to be undated. Since this would have helped to place it into the time scale of events. Emilys information could have precipitated the report to be made on Montague Druitt, to which Abberline refers, and, since Abberline is clearly stating that he knew all about the report, which was on a drowned suspect, it can be reasonably speculated that Montague was already dead at the time of Emilys information.

The only alternative is that Montague was still alive at the time of Emilys information. If so then such information, could not have been ignored. It would have been thoroughly investigated thus, possibly, precipitating the hunt for Druitt which George Sims tells us was in progress at the time of Druitts death.

Emilys information may even have come at a much later date long after Montagues suicide.

If this was the case then it could easily account for MacNaghtens assertion, in his memorandum, that Druitts own family suspected him of being the Whitechapel murderer. It also makes sense of MacNaghtens revelation that his information came piecemeal. It could also have formed part of the later evidence of a factual nature which had not come into MacNaghtens possession until some years after he had become a detective officer.

It is, of course pure speculation that the lady, being introduced to Anderson, was Emily Druitt. Given Crawfords published beliefs that the killer was a black magician. It could just as easily have been someone such as Madame Blavatsky, or, one of Vittoria Cremers lady friends, They had shown great interest in Crawfords articles on the ripper as a black magician.

Vittoria Cremers claim, to have shared a house with D'Onston-Stephenson and Mabel Collins alleged infatuation with him, may well qualify these illustrious ladies as being nearly related him.

As Stephen Ryder points out - it is curious that Anderson chose to keep this one letter. It is the only one in Andersons' entire collection referring to the Whitechapel murders. Given Andersons subsequent belief that the killer was an insane Polish Jew it is clear that he, personally, did not pay much credence to the ladys information. Yet, as Ryder says it seems a reasonable assumption that this letter was of some importance

The Priests house museum, in Wimborne, holds another clue which strongly suggests that the Druitt family were concealing a family secret. Montagues Uncle, James Druitt, had, sometime in the late 1800s commenced writing a memoir. The memoir was dictated to his daughter Barbara. For some unknown reason the memoir breaks off in November 1888, between the last murder and Montagues death. It recommences again in 1894, with the following words – *'avoiding all mention of the defects which one hopes to conceal from ones neighbors.'* Whatever these defects might have been are, of course, pure speculation but clearly Uncle James was keeping it secret. Could James Druitt have received information possibly from his nephew Charles, or from Charles' friend J.H Lonsdale to whom Montague may have confessed?

James Druitts own son Philip, if he should prove to be the North Country vicar, may have got his information from either his Father, or from his sister Barbara, to whom the journal was dictated.

In 'My Life and a Few Yarns' (George Allen and Unwin, 1922) career naval officer H.L. Fleet made an interesting observation, as discovered by Paul Begg, which strongly suggests that rumours about Druitt may have been already in circulation as early as late 1888.

'On January 1st, 1895, my promotion to Captain was gazetted; another spell of half-pay! At Blackheath we found a lot of old friends, and one of my old C-in-C's Sir Walter Hunt-Grubbe, as Admiral at the college. The Heath itself had a bad reputation after dark. When we lived there formerly it was considered dangerous, *for the terrible series of crimes committed by 'Jack the Ripper' were then being perpetrated, and many people believed that he lived in Blackheath*. His victims were invariably women of the unfortunate class, and it was evident that he was a homicidal maniac with a grudge against such people. He was never caught, although it was sometimes stated that he had been and was confined in Broadmoor.'

The rumour that Jack the Ripper had lived in Blackheath could not have originated with the MacNaghten memo since the memo, an unpublished and highly confidential document, makes no mention of Blackheath. Furthermore Captain Fleet appears to be describing, in January 1895, a rumour which was known in the area when he had formerly lived there *at the time of the killings* in late 1888. If this is the case then Captain Fleets' rumour predates the Macnaghten memo by six years. . This makes it even more likely that the rumour originated locally in Blackheath, and quite possibly from Mr Valentines school at, or about the time of Montague Druitts death.

. In 1987 a package was received at Scotland Yard. The sender did not identify his, or her, self. The anonymous package contained several documents, and photographs, which had, many years earlier, been removed from the Scotland Yard files on the Whitechapel murders. This package contained, among other things, the original Dear Boss letter, Doctor Bonds' post-mortem report on Catharine Eddowes, and, a previously unknown photograph of Mary Kellys corpse. It is generally thought that these papers had been removed from the files some years ago by a senior officer, and, were now being returned by his descendants. These papers had been taken from the files at Scotland Yard as souvenirs and are clearly not the papers referred to by the Monro family as a 'very hot potato'. Though they made have formed part of the original file.

We are told that Monro had taken personal control over the hot potato papers. Surely he would not have had any interest in the papers unless they really were a hot potato and contained important material.

In 1995 Monro's grandson, Christopher Monro, apparently disclosed that Monro had been convinced that Montague Druitt had been Jack the Ripper but was prevented from saying so. William Druitt, brother of Montague, had, according to Christophers understanding, threatened that if his brother was named, he would reveal that there were homosexuals in high positions in Parliament, the Bar, the Army and the Church. Christopher Monro claims that he was told this by his father Douglas Monro, who had examined Monro's papers after his death.

If this story is true it may well explain why it was that so much of what we know about Druitt, his activities, his dismissal from Valentines school, his final journey to Chiswick, his death, and perjured inquest, has been blurred and distorted and possibly even concealed.

Even so could such papers alone constitute the evidence of a factual nature which according to MacNaghten, 'did not come into my possession until some years after I became a Detective officer'? What value could be placed in Druitt's confession, if indeed there ever was one, unless it contained information known only to the killer? Apart from the possibility of Emily Druitts information, What other 'evidence of a factual nature' could have existed?

MacNaghten tells us, in an article published in the 'Daily Mail' in 1913, that he would never reveal what he knew. He writes:

'I have destroyed all my documents and there is now no record of the secret information which came into my possession at one time or another.'

That does appear to have been the case. All that remains of the evidence which did 'at one time exist' are the ensuing conclusions which are contained within MacNaghten's various memorandum. The fact that MacNaghten tells us that the information came at '...one time or another' suggests that his conclusions were not based solely on one single piece of information but piecemeal over a period of time.

However, it is quite clear that whatever it was, that MacNaghten had learned in the seventeen years since he penned his famous memo, it appears only to have strengthened his belief that Montague Druitt was the Whitechapel murderer.

There must have been something which led to the high-placed belief that Montague Druitt was Jack the Ripper. The killings did stop at his death, and only three weeks after Montagues body was found, in the river Thames, the manhunt for Jack the Ripper was called off.

The questions are legion and may never be answered, but we should not let the absence of firm evidence deter us from investigation. Neither should we be deterred from using reasoned speculation, as well as lateral thinking, in our search for a solution as long as any such speculation is supported by the facts. As each piece of the puzzle is assembled so it is the shape of the missing pieces which become clearer.

Montague Druitt appears to have been abandoned, by most researchers, as a suspect. But this was, without little doubt, precisely the intention of those who sought not only to conceal his identity, as the Whitechapel murderer, but to distort or destroy any and every piece of evidence against him. They appear to have been successful in this endeavour.

The reasons, for not publicly naming Druitt, as the killer may, as was intended, never be known. Druitts own fairly well-placed family in society.The marital relationship between Druitt and Walter Boultbee secretary to Police Commissioners Warren and Monro successively.Druitts probable relationships with so many highly placed persons such as Ruggles-Brise, Private Secretart to Henry Mathews the Home Secretary. The professional reputations of his family and friends in both the medical and legal professions His link to the Royal Household, and his distant, yet established marital connection with the MacNaghten family may all provide good enough reasons for a cover-up.

Contemporary press reports of Druitts inquest would seem to suggest that some of the evidence given was not only perjured but contradictory and does not appear to have been particularly searching despite Doctor Diplocks vast experience as a Coroner. It is worth mentioning that Doctor Diplock had trained at St Georges Hospital at the same time as Montagues Uncle, Robert, was the Medical Officer for Health at the same hospital. It is inconceivable that Doctor Diplock would have not heard of the Druitt name. I find it difficult to resist the temptation to draw any inference from that fact.

Monro could never have revealed that Jack the Ripper was a cousin of his own secretary. The Monro family would have aptly described such a revelation as a 'hot potato-'.Even more so if we accept that, according to the Monro family, William Druit had threatened to expose homosexuals in high places if Montague was identified as Jack the Ripper.

The case against Druitt, which I have tried to set out here is, of course, speculative. But much less so than the case against Tumblety, or Maybrick, or Walter Sickert, or Prince Albert Victor, or even poor Kosminski and the many other Jack the Ripper suspects.

I have attempted to answer some of the many questions posed by those who dismiss Druitt as a serious suspect, and in doing so I hope that I have shed a little more light into this darkened and abandoned corner of the investigation. I believe that in doing so I have found enough to justify my own gut-feelings regarding Druitt.

It remains, therefore, my contention that unless and until, evidence is discovered which positively exonerates Druitt from the Whitechapel murders, he must remain, so far, still the most plausible of all of the known suspects.

Yet all that we can ever hope to discover about Montague Druitt are the reasons why he was ever suspected. There is still, as yet, just as there is with every other suspect, not one scintilla of evidence to connect him to any of the killings. But that is no less than we might expect of Jack the Ripper.

In life Montague John Druitt remains an enigma. In death he became a mystery. His inquest permeates intrigue. Even his final internment begs questions.

Anyone who has a mind to visit Wimborne cemetery will find the Druitt family plot laid out next to the path which runs between the two chapels. His grave is just a few yards from that of his boyhood here Nicholas Wanstrocht.

As I stared at Montague's grave it did not occur to me that there was anything odd or unusual about it. Ken Richmond, now retired, used to be the Cemetery Superintendent. He had noticed something very odd about the entry for Montague Druitt in the internment ledger. He told me:

'If you look in the book, at all of the other entries for those years, you can see that the average cost recorded for a burial is about eight shillings. The unusual thing about this one (Montague Druitt) is that it cost five pounds eleven shillings.'

This is thirteen times the average cost. !!

It has been suggested that the additional amount could have been an inducement to bury a suicide. But this would not be necessary since the cemetery is partly non-conformist.

Secondly, such an inducement would not have been recorded in the internment ledger. The sole purpose of the ledger is to record the name of the deceased, the date of burial, and the burial plot number. The fee recorded is for the preparation of the grave and its filling-in after the burial service. Any tips, to the gravediggers etc, would have been given directly and would not have been recorded in any ledger.

Why then should this particular grave have cost so much more to prepare and fill-in?

It is only a suggestion but it is worth considering that - when the American gangster John Dillinger was buried, his family insisted upon having several tons of concrete poured into the grave, on top of the coffin, so that future souvenir hunters would be deterred from disturbing the grave. Could the Druitt family have felt that some kind of similar precaution was necessary? In view of the fact that we are told that they believed their recently deceased relative was the notorious Jack the Ripper, it is just possible.

I have, however, searched the official archived burial records for Druitt but from them I am unable to substantiate the claim made by Ken Richmond. As yet though I have been unable to get sight of any records kept at the cemetery. But if, indeed, the Druitt family plot, in Wimborne, does conceal the mortal remains of the the hunted killer then it is perhaps with some considerable irony that the hunters own mortal remains are not far away. In the nearby Wimborne Road cemetery, in an unmarked grave no: Z259N, repose the mortal remains of Inspector Frederick George Abberline.
He died, in Holdenhurst Road Bournemouth, in 1929.

LIKE MOTHER

Montagues Mother Anne Druitt was admitted to the Manor House Asylum on the 31st May 1890. In the letter to Doctor Tuke, Dr Gasquet, of the Brighton Asylum where Anne had been treated, writes that:
'...the patient had been suffering from a melancholic stupor. She imagined herself to be having electric shocks'. Gasquet indicates that she has recovered a little, and has had frequent leaves of absence. He notes, interestingly, that the treatment which suited her best was the occasional use of Indian Hemp ' (cannabis)...for a week or two'.

Gasquet's letter also suggests that at the time of the Jack the Ripper killings, Anne Druitt was not incarcerated. If her leave of absence, from the Brooke house asylum, at Clapton, granted in July 1888, a few weeks before the first Jack the Ripper murder, had 'inadvertantly' run out 'at the beginning of 1889' she must have been on leave for some months beforehand - precisely at the time when Jack the Ripper was reaping his bloody harvest.

If we accept that the Druitt family believed Montague to have been Jack the Ripper, one wonders how much Anne might have known of what was happening. After all if her late son Montague had been Jack the Ripper then it was she who, according to Montague himself, was the very inspiration behind his murderous insanity. But even if she had known, or had even suspected, the effects of the Indian Hemp (Cannabis), together with the secure umbrella of the discreet Tukes, who themselves may have been made privy to the secret, her silence was guaranteed.

Once at the Manor House Asylum, and close to the scene of her son's death, Anne Druitts health seems to have deteriorated rapidly, but not through lack of care. Her case notes describe an unhappy woman who has lost all will to live. On the afternoon of December 15th 1890, Ann Druitt was visited by two of her daughters. Her condition on that day is described as '...evidently not worse than she has been, but still very weak'. Later, that evening, at 7.55, she suddenly clutched at her nurse and fell back 'moribund'. She died of heart failure ten minutes later.

Doctor Thomas Tuke has recorded, in Anne Druitt's medical notes, the facts that the patient's mother had committed suicide, and also that the patient's sister had attempted suicide. These facts are, without any doubt, important facts in ascertaining Anne Druitt's own mental condition at that time. It is astonishing therefore that absolutely no mention is made of the fact that the patients own son had also committed suicide only eighteen months earlier, and. more to the point, he had done so practically on the very doorstep of Dr Tuke's own Asylum
How eloquent such an ommision.

I had spent some considerable time decyphering Doctor Tukes handwriting. I had concentrated on the body of the document which is written in a daily diary form. Consequently it was not for many months before I realised something of a personal significance. Two nurses were present when Anne Druitt died. Their names appear on the case notes as witnesses to her death. Their names were Knowles and Hancock. The significance to me was that my next door neighbour, old Charlie, who had claimed to have met Jack the Ripper was surnamed Hancock. I do not know what age old Charlie was when he died in the 1960's My guess would be that he was in his Eighties. That would have made him aged about 10 at the time that Anne Druitt died at the Manor House Asylum. He could have been a son of nurse Hancock who worked at the asylum and was present at Ann Druitts death. If so it is altogether possible that he was allowed to play in the extensive grounds of the asylum. Old Charlie Hancock may never have met Montague, but he may well have heard local rumours that there was a connection between the asylum and Jack the Ripper.

It is also interesting to note that the other nurse, Nurse Knowles, who was also present at Ann Druitts death, shares the same surname as Dan Farsons elusive informant.

In 1894 the Tuke brothers vacated the Manor House and it was sadly, after a fire, demolished for redevelopment into the five 3-storey terraced houses, which stand there today. The Tuke brothers moved, together with their illustrious patients to the more spatial surroundings of nearby Chiswick House, the sometime summer retreat of the young sons of the Prince of Wales, Edward Albert Victor (Prince Eddy) and his younger brother Georgie (later King George the Fifth). Charles Tuke continued to treat the mentally ill at Chiswick House until he retired in 1925.

In 1894 Frederick Tuke married Mabel Sich, a daughter of the local brewer and owner of the Lamp Tap public house in which Montague Druitt's hurried inquest had been held. Thomas Tuke lived with his patients at Chiswick House. He continued to indulge his passion for cricket and was responsible for the laying-out of the excellent cricket field at Chiswick House. It is still much used and appreciated by the residents of the area and those who visit the house and grounds. Thomas Tuke died in February 1917. His obituary praises his work among the mentally ill and recalls his dedication to Freemasonry. He is buried in St. Nicholas Churchyard in Chiswick. Just yards fom the spot where Druitts body had been found twenty-nine years earlier.

Charles Tuke bought a large house in nearby Hartington Road. In later years he was to have two illustrious neighbours, for just a few yards behind his house stood number 15 Bolton Road. It was to this house that Ex Commissioner of Police, and head of the Home Office secret department which had inestigated the Ripper killings, James Monro finally retired. He died there, aged 82 in 1920. Dr Thomas Diplock the Coroner who had presided at Druitts inquest lived just seven houses down from Monro.

Yet another ironic coincidence? - That James Monro, the man who had headed up the hunt for Jack the Ripper, should end up as a neighbour of Charles Tuke, one of the men who not only nursed the prime suspect's mother in her final, and assuredly silent days, but was also, in all probability, a friend, and possible confidante of the prime suspect himself.

The Tuke family have all gone from Chiswick now. Even so many of the older residents still refer to the house and grounds of Chiswick House as Tukes'.Some even remember the rumour that at one time the Tukes had looked after the most dangerous man in the land.

Life-long Chiswick resident Rhoda Bickerdike was in her 90s when I interviewed her in 1988. Her comfortable terraced cottage in Paxton Road backed on to the grounds of Chiswick House. We sipped tea and ate cake. Unaware of the true purpose of my visit, she told me of her life as a child in Chiswick. I asked about the Tuke family. The old lady clearly remembered being taken, as a young girl, to dance with the inmates at garden parties which the Tukes frequently held in the grounds of Chiswick House. She showed me faded photographs and party programmes. Her old eyes danced and sparkled as she recalled her youth. I asked Rhoda if she had ever heard the rumour of the dangerous inmate cared for by the Tukes. She told me that as a child it had been a well-known local story, with which grown-ups had teased her and her friends about. Indeed, as a little girl, feeling slightly apprehensive about the possibility of dancing with the most dangerous man in the country at Dr Tukes parties, she had sought some personal reassurance from her host. Doctor Tuke had

told her that the story was true. He had, however, told her that she should not worry about it since it had been before her time. She said:
'There was something odd about that rumour, all of the locals knew it - and, as small children do we teased each other. We all believed the dangerous patient was Jack the Ripper'.

END

Appendices

The MacNaghten memorandum

Contemporary Press reports

Extracted writings of George Sims

Further Reading

The MacNaghten Memorandum

The case referred to in the sensational story told in The Sun in its issue of 13th inst, & following dates, is that of Thomas Cutbush who was arraigned at the London County Sessions in April 1891 on a charge of maliciously wounding Florence Grace Johnson, and attempting to wound Isabella Fraser Anderson in Kennington. He was found to be insane, and sentenced to be detained during Her Majesty's Pleasure.

This Cutbush, who lived with his mother and aunt at 14 Albert Street, Kennington, escaped from the Lambeth Infirmary, (after he had been detained only a few hours, as a lunatic) at noon on 5th March 1891. He was rearrested on 9th idem. A few weeks before this, several cases of stabbing, or jabbing, from behind had occurred in the vicinity, and a man named Colicott was arrested, but subsequently discharged owing to faulty identification. The cuts in the girls dresses made by Colicott were quite different to the cut(s) made by Cutbush (when he wounded Miss Johnson) who was no doubt influenced by a wild desire of morbid imitation. Cutbushs antecedents were enquired into by C.Insp (now Supt.) Chris by Inspector Hale, and by P.S. McCarthy C.I.D.- (the last named officer had been specially employed in Whitechapel at the time of the murders there,) -- and it was ascertained that he was born, and had lived, in Kennington all his life. His father died when he was quite young and he was always a spoilt child. He had been employed as a clerk and traveller in the Tea trade at the Minories, and subsequently cavassed for a Directory in the East End, during which time he bore a good character. He apparently contracted syphilis about 1888, and, -- since that time, -- led an idle and useless life. His brain seems to have become affected, and he believed that people were trying to poison him. He wrote to Lord Grimthorpe, and others, -- and also to the Treasury, -- complaining of Dr Brooks, of Westminster Bridge Road, whom he threatened to shoot for having supplied him with bad medicines. He is said to have studied medical books by day, and to have rambled about at night, returning frequently with his clothes covered with mud; but little reliance could be placed on the statements made by his mother or his aunt, who both appear to have been of a very excitable disposition. It was found impossible to ascertain his movements on the nights of the Whitechapel murders. The knife found on him was bought in Houndsditch about a week before he was detained in the Infirmary. Cutbush was the nephew of the late Supt. Executive.

Now the Whitechapel murderer had 5 victims -- & 5 victims only, -- his murders were

(1)   31st August, 88. Mary Ann Nichols-at Bucks Row-who was found with her throat cut -- & with (slight) stomach mutilation.

(2)   8th Sept. 88 Annie Chapman-Hanbury St.; -- throat cut-stomach & private parts badly mutilated & some of the entrails placed round the neck.

(3)   30th Sept. 88. Elizabeth Stride-Berners Street-throat cut, but nothing in shape of mutilation attempted, & on same date.

Catherine Eddowes-Mitre Square, throat cut & very bad mutilation, both of face and stomach. 9th November. Mary Jane Kelly-Millers Court, throat cut, and the whole of the body mutilated in the most ghastly manner-

The last murder is the only one that took place in a room, and the murderer must have been at least 2 hours engaged. A photo was taken of the woman, as she was found lying on the bed, withot seeing which it is impossible to imagine the awful mutilation.

With regard to the double murder which took place on 30th September, there is no doubt but that the man was disturbed by some Jews who drove up to a Club, (close to which the body of Elizabeth Stride was found) and that he then, mordum satiatus, went in search of a further victim who he found at Mitre Square.

It will be noted that the fury of the mutilations increased in each case, and, seemingly, the appetite only became sharpened by indulgence. It seems, then, highly improbable that the murderer would have suddenly stopped in November 88, and been content to recommence operations by merely prodding a girl behind some 2 years and 4 months afterwards. A much more rational theory is that the murderers brain gave way altogether after his awful glut in Millers Court, and that he immediately committed suicide, or, as a possible alternative, was found to be so hopelessly mad by his relations, that he was by them confined in some asylum. No one ever saw the Whitechapel murderer; many homicidal maniacs were suspected, but no shadow of proof could be thrown on any one. I may mention the cases of 3 men, any one of whom would have been more likely than Cutbush to have committed this series of murders:

(1)   A Mr M. J. Druitt, said to be a doctor & of good family-who disappeared at the time of the Millers Court murder, & whose body (which was said to have been upwards of a month in the water) was found in the Thames on 31st December -- or about 7 weeks after that murder. He was sexually insane and from private information I have little doubt but that his own family believed him to have been the murderer.

(2)   Kosminski-a Polish Jew -- & resident in Whitechapel. This man became insane owing to many years indulgence in solitary vices. He had a great hatred of women, specially of the prostitute class, & had strong homicidal tendencies: he was removed to a lunatic asylum about March 1889. There were many circumstances connected with this man which made him a strong suspect.

(3)   Michael Ostrog, a Russian doctor, and a convict, who was subsequently detained in a lunatic asylum as a homicidal maniac. This mans antecedents were of the worst possible type, and his whereabouts at the time of the murders could never be ascertained.

And now with regard to a few of the other inaccuracies and misleading statements made by The Sun. In its issue of 14th February, it is stated that the writer has in his possession a facsimile of the knife with which the murders were committed. This knife (which for some unexplained reason has, for the last 3 years, been kept by Inspector Hale, instead of being sent to Prisoners Property Store) was traced, and it was found to have been purchased in Houndsditch in February 91 or 2 years and 3 months after the Whitechapel murders ceased! The statement, too, that Cutbush spent a portion of the day in making rough drawings of the bodies of women, and of their mutilations is based solely on the fact that 2 (scribble) drawings of women in indecent postures were found torn up in Cutbushs room. The head and body of one of these had been cut from some fashion plate, and legs were added to shew a womans naked thighs and pink stockings.

In the issue of 15th inst. it is said that a light overcoat was among the things found in Cutbushs house, and that a man in a light overcoat was seen talking to a woman at Backchurch Lane whose body with arms attached was found in Pinchin Street. This is hopelessly incorrect! On 10th Sept. 89 the naked body, with arms, of a woman was found wrapped in some sacking under a Railway arch in Pinchin Street: the head and legs were never found nor was the woman ever identified. She had been killed at least 24 hours before the remains which had seemingly been brought from a distance, were discovered. The stomach was split up by a cut, and the head and legs had been severed in a manner identical with that of the woman whose remains were discovered in the Thames, in Battersea Park, and on the Chelsea Embankment on the 4th June of the same year; and these murders had no connection whatever with the Whitechapel horrors. The Rainham mystery in 1887 and the Whitehall mystery (when portions of a womans body were found under what is now New Scotland Yard) in 1888 were of a similar type to the Thames and Pinchin Street crimes.

It is perfectly untrue to say that Cutbush stabbed 6 girls behind. This is confounding his case with that of Colicott. The theory that the Whitechapel murderer was left-handed, or, at any rate, ambidexter, had its origin

in the remark made by a doctor who examined the corpse of one of the earliest victims; other doctors did not agree with him.

With regard to the additional murders ascribed by the writer in the Sun to the Whitechapel fiend

(1)   The body of Martha Tabram, a prostitute was found on a common staircase in George

Yard buildings on 7th August 1888; the body had been repeatedly pierced, probably with a bayonet. This woman had, with a fellow prostitute, been in company of 2 soldiers in the early part of the evening: these men were arrested, but the second prostitute failed, or refused, to identify, and the soldiers were eventually discharged.

(2)   Alice McKenzie was found with her throat cut (or rather stabbed in Castle Alley on 17th July 1889; no evidence was forthcoming and no arrest were made in connection with this case. The stab in the throat was of the same nature as in the case of the murder of

(3)   Frances Coles in Swallow Gardens, on 13th February 1891 -- for which Thomas Sadler, a fireman, was arrested, and, after several remands, discharged. It was ascertained at the time that Saddler had sailed for the Baltic on 19th July 89 and was in Whitechapel on the nights of 17th idem. He was a man of ungovernable temper and entirely addicted to drink, and the company of the lowest prostitutes.

(4)   The case of the unidentified woman whose trunk was found in Pinchin Street: on 10th September 1889 -- which has already been dealt with.

M.S. Macnaghten
23rd February 1894

Contemporary press reports

The Times August 24th 1888
Martha Turner Murder

The Times September 1st 1888
Polly Nicholls Murder

The Times September 3rd 1888
Polly Nicholls Inquest

Illustrated Police News September 8th 1888
Polly Nicholls Murder

The Times September 11th 1888
Pizer/Piggot Arrests
Annie Chapman Inquest

The Times September 15th 1888
Investigation and arrest of vagrant.

The Times November 10th 1888
The murder of Mary Kelly

The Salisbury and Winchester Journal and General Advertiser May 14th 1887

THE MURDER IN WHITECHAPEL

Yesterday afternoon Mr. G. Collier, Deputy Coroner for the South-Eastern Division of Middlesex, opened an inquiry at the Working LadsInstitute, Whitechapel-road, respecting the death of the woman who was found on Tuesday last, with 39 stabs on her body, at George-yard-buildings, Whitechapel.

Detective-Inspector Reid, H Division, watched the case on behalf of the Criminal Investigation Department.

Alfred George Crow, cabdriver, 35, George-yard-buildings, deposed that he got home at half-past 3 on Tuesday morning. As he was passing the first-floor landing he saw a body lying on the ground. He took no notice, as he was accustomed to seeing people lying about there. He did not then know whether the person was alive or dead. He got up at half past 9, and when he went down the staircase the body was not there. Witness heard no noise while he was in bed. John S. Reeves, of 37, George-yard-buildings, a waterside labourer, said that on Tuesday morning he left home at a quarter to 5 to seek for work. When he reached the first-floor landing he found the deceased lying on her back in a pool of blood. He was frightened, and did not examine her, but at once gave information to the police. He did not know the deceased. The deceaseds clothes were disarranged, as though she had had a struggle with some one. Witness saw no footmarks on the staircase, nor did he find a knife or other weapon. Police-constable Thomas Barrett, 226 H, said that the last witness called his attention to the body of the deceased. He sent for a doctor, who pronounced life extinct. Dr. T.R. Killeen, of 68, Brick-lane, said that he was called to the deceased, and found her dead. She had 39 stabs on the body. She had been dead some three hours. Her age was about 36, and the body was very well nourished. Witness had since made a post mortem examination of the body. The left lung was penetrated in five places, and the right lung was penetrated in two places. The heart, which was rather fatty, was penetrated in one place, and that would be sufficient to cause death. The liver was healthy, but was penetrated in five places, the spleen was penetrated in two places, and the stomach, which was perfectly healthy, was penetrated in six places. The witness did not think all the wounds were inflicted with the same instrument. The wounds generally might have been inflicted with a knife, but such an instrument could not have inflicted one of the wounds, which went through the chest-bone. His opinion was that one of the wounds was inflicted by some kind of dagger, and that all of them had been caused during life. The CORONER said he was in hopes that the body would be identified, but three women had identified it under three different names. He therefore proposed to leave the question open until the next occasion. The case would be left in the hands of Detective-Inspector Reid, who would endeavour to discover the perpetrator of this (illegible) murder. It was one of the most dreadful murders any one could imagine. The man must have been a perfect savage to inflict such a number of wounds on a defenceless woman in such a way. The inquiry would be adjourned for a fortnight.

The Times. August 24 1888

Inquests

Yesterday afternoon Mr. George Collier, the Deputy Coroner for the South-Eastern Division of Middlesex, resumed his inquiry at the Working Lads Institute, Whitechapel Road, respecting the death of the woman who was found dead at George-yard-buildings, on the early morning of Tuesday, the 7th inst., with no less than 39 wounds on various parts of her body. The body has been identified as that of MARTHA TABRAN, aged 39 or 40 years, the wife of a foreman packer at a furniture warehouse. Henry Samuel Tabran, 6, River-terrace, East Greenwich, husband of the deceased woman, said he last saw her alive about 18 months ago, in the Whitechapel Road. They had been separated for 13 years, owing to her drinking habits. She obtained a warrent against him. For some part of the time witness allowed her 12s. a week, but in consequence of her annoyance he stopped this allowance ten years ago, since which time he had made it half-a-crown a week, as he found she was living with a man. Henry Turner, a carpenter, staying at the Working Mens Home, Commercial Street, Spitalfields, stated that he had been living with the woman Tabran as his wife for about nine years. Two or three weeks previously to this occurance he ceased to do so. He had left her on two or three occasions in consequence of her drinking habits, but they had come together again.

He last saw her alive on Saturday, the 4th inst:, in Leadenhall-street. He then gave her 1s. 6d. to get some stock. When she had money she spent it in drink. While living with witness deceaseds usual time for coming home was about 11 oclock. As far as he knew she had no regular companion and he did not know that she walked the streets. As a rule he was, he said, a man of sober habits, and when the deceased was sober they usually got on well together. Inspector Reid At times the deceased had stopped out all night. After those occasions she told him she had been taken in a fit and was removed to the police-station or somewhere else. The Coroner He knew she suffered from fits, but they were brought on by drink. Mrs. Mary Bousfield, wife of a wood cutter, residing at 4, Star-place, Commercial Road, knew the deceased by the name of Turner. She was formerly a lodger in her house with the man Turner. Deceased would rather have a glass of ale than a cup of tea, but she was not a woman who got continually drunk, and she never brought home any companions with her. She left without giving notice, and owed two weeks rent. Mrs. Ann Morris, a widow, of 23, Lisbon Street, E., said she last saw the deceased, who was her sister-in-law, at about 11 oclock on Bank Holiday night in the Whitechapel Road. She was then about to enter a publichouse. Mary Ann Connolly, who at the suggestion of Inspector Reid was cautioned in the usual manner before being sworn, stated she had been for the last two nights living at a lodging house in Dorset Street, Spitalfields. Witness was a single woman. She had known the woman Tabran for about four or five months. She knew her by the name of Emma. She last saw her alive on Bank Holiday night, when witness was with her about three quarters of an hour, and they separated

at a quarter to 12. Witness was with Tabran and two soldiers^one private and one corporal. She did not know what regiment they belonged to, but they had white bands around their caps. After they separated, Tabran went away with the private, and witness accompanied the corporal up Angel Alley. There was no quarrelling between any of them. Witness had been to the barracks to identify the soldiers, and the two men she picked out were, to the best of her belief, the men she and Tabran were with.

The men at the Wellington Barracks were paraded before the witness. One of the men picked out by witness turned out not to be a corporal, but he had stripes on his arm. By Inspector Reid.^Witness heard of the murder on the Tuesday. Since the occurrance witness had threaten to drown herself, but she only said it was for a lark. She stayed away two days and two nights, and she only said that when asked where she was going. She knew the police were looking after her, but she did not let them know her whereabouts.

A Juryman. The woman Tabran was not drunk. They were, however, drinking at different houses for about an hour and three-quarters. They had ale and rum. Detective-Inspector Reid made a statement of the efforts made by the police to discover the perpetrator of the murder.

149

Several persons had stated that they saw the deceased woman on the previous Sunday with a corporal, but when all the corporals and privates at the Tower and Wellington Barracks were paraded before them they failed to identify the man. The military authorities afforded every facility to the police. Pearly Poll picked out two men belonging to the Coldstream Guards at the Wellington Barracks. One of those men had three good conduct stripes, and he was proved beyond doubt to have been with his wife from 8 oclock on the Monday night until 6 oclock the following morning. The other man was also proved to have been in barracks at five minutes past 10 on Bank Holiday night. The police would be pleased if anyone would give them information of having seen anyone with the deceased on the night of Bank Holiday. The Coroner having summed up, the jury returned a verdict to the effect that the deceased had been murdered by some person or persons unknown.

Report as Printed in the London Times September 1, 1888
ANOTHER WHITECHAPEL MURDER

Another murder of the foulest kind was committed in the neighbourhood of Whitechapel in the early hours of yesterday morning, but by whom and with what motive is at present a complete mystery.

At a quarter to 4 oclock Police constable Neill, 97J, when in Bucks Row, Whitechapel, came upon the body of a woman lying on a part of the footway, and on stooping to raise her up in the belief that she was drunk he discovered that her throat was cut almost from ear to ear. She was dead but still warm. He procured assistance and at once sent to the station and for a doctor.

Dr. Llewellyn, of Whitechapel Road, whose surgery is not above 300 yards from the spot where the woman lay, was aroused, and, at the solicitation of a constable, dressed and went at once to the scene. He inspected the body at the place where it was found and pronounced the woman dead. He made a hasty examination and then discovered that, besides the gash across the throat, the woman had terrible wounds in the abdomen. The police ambulance from the Bethnal-green Station having arrived, the body was removed there. A further examination showed the horrible nature of the crime, there being other fearful cuts and gashes, and one of which was sufficient to cause death apart from the wounds across the throat.

After the body was removed to the mortuary of the parish, in Old Montague Street, Whitechapel, steps were taken to secure, if possible, identification, but at first with little prospect of success. The clothing was of a common description, but the skirt of one petticoat and the band of another article bore the stencil stamp of Lambeth Workhouse.

The only articles in the pockets were a comb and a piece of a looking glass. The latter led the police to conclude that the murdered woman was an inhabitant of the numerous lodging-houses of the neighbourhood, and officers were despatched to make inquiries about, as well as other officers to Lambeth to get the matron of the workhouse to view the body with a view to identification. The latter, however, could not identify, and said that the clothing might have been issued any time during the past two or three years. As the news of the murder spread, however, first one woman and then another came forward to view the body, and at length it was found that a woman answering the description of the murdered woman had lodged in a common lodging-house, 18, Thrawl-street, Spitalfields.

Women from that place were fetched and they identified the deceased as Polly, who had shared a room with three other women in the place on the usual terms of such houses^nightly payment of 4d. each, each woman having a separate bed. It was gathered that the deceased had led the life of an unfortunate while lodging in the house, which was only for about three weeks past. Nothing more was known of her by them but that when she presented herself for her lodging on Thursday night she was turned away by the deputy because she had not the money.

She was then the worse for drink, but not drunk, and turned away laughing, saying, I'll soon get my doss money; see what a jolly bonnet Ive got now. She was wearing a bonnet which she had not been seen with before, and left the lodging house door. A woman of the neighbourhood saw her later, she told the police even as late as 2:30 on Friday morningin Whitechapel Road, opposite the church and at the corner of Osborne-street, and at a quarter to 4 she was found within 500 yards of the spot, murdered. The people of the lodging-house knew her as Polly, but at about half-past 7 last evening a woman named Mary Ann Monk, at present an inmate of Lambeth Workhouse, was taken to the mortuary and identified the body as that of Mary Ann Nicholls, also called Polly Nicholls.

She knew her, she said, as they were inmates of the Lambeth Workhouse together in April and May last, the deceased having been passed there from another workhouse. On the 12th of May, according to Monk, Nicholls left the workhouse to take a situation as servant at Ingleside, Wandsworth Common. It afterwards became known that Nicholls betrayed her trust as domestic servant, by stealing L3 from her employer and absconding. From that time she had been wandering about. Monk met her, she said, about six weeks ago when herself out of the workhouse and drank with her. She was sure the deceased was Polly Nicholls, and, having twice viewed the features as the body lay in the shell, maintained her opinion.

So far the police have satisfied themselves, but as to getting a clue to her murderer they express little hope. The matter is being investigated by Detective Inspector Abberline, of Scotland Yard, and Inspector Helson, J Division. The latter states that he walked carefully over the ground soon after 8 oclock in the morning, and beyond and the discolourations ordinarily found on pavements there was no sign of stains.

Viewing the spot where the body was found, however, it seemed difficult to believe that the woman recieved her death wounds there. The police have no theory with respect to the matter, except that a gang of ruffians exists in the neighborhood, which, blackmailing women of the unfortunate class, takes vengeance on those who do not find money for them. They base that surmise on the fact that within 12 months two other women have been murdered in the district by almost similar meansone as recently as the 6th of August lastand left in the gutter of the street in the early hours of the morning.

If the woman was murdered on the spot where the body was found, it is impossible to believe she would not have aroused the neighborhood by her screams, Bucks Row being a street tenanted all down one side by a respectable class of people, superior to many of the surrounding streets, the other side having a blank wall bounding a warehouse. Dr. Llewellyn has called the attention of the police to the smallness of the quantity of blood on the spot where he saw the body, and yet the gashes in the abdomen laid the body right open.

The weapon used would scarcely have been a sailors jack knife, but a pointed weapon with a stout backsuch as a cork-cutters or shoemakers knife. In his opinion it was not an exceptionally long-bladed weapon. He does not believe that the woman was seized from behind and her throat cut, but thinks that a hand was held across her mouth and the knife then used, possibly by a left-handed man, as the bruising on the face of the deceased is such as would result from the mouth being covered with the right hand. He made a second examination of the body in the mortuary, and on that based his conclusion, but will make no actual post mortem until he receives the Coroners orders. The inquest is fixed for to-day.

Report as Printed in the London Times September 3, 1888
THE WHITECHAPEL MURDER

Up to a late hour last evening the police had obtained no clue to the perpetrator of the latest of the three murders which have so recently taken place in Whitechapel, and there is, it must be acknowledged, after their exhaustive investigation of the facts, no ground for blaming the officers in charge should they fail in unravelling the mystery surrounding the crime.

The murder, in the early hours of Friday morning last, of the woman now known as Mary Ann Nicholls, has so many points of similarity with the murder of two other women in the same neighbourhoodone Martha Tabram, as recently as August 7, and the other less than 12 months previously that the police admit their belief that the three crimes are the work of one individual. All three women were of the class called unfortunates, each so very poor, that robbery could have formed no motive for the crime, and each was murdered in such a similar fashion, that doubt as to the crime being the work of one and the same villain almost vanishes, particularly when it is remembered that all three murders were committed within a distance of 300 yards from each other.

These facts have led the police to almost abandon the idea of a gang being abroad to wreak vengeance on women of this class for not supplying them with money. Detective Inspectors Abberline, of the Criminal Investigation Department, and Detective Inspector Helson, J Division, are both of opinion that only one person, and that a man, had a hand in the latest murder. It is understood that the investigation into the George-yard mystery is proceeding hand-in-hand with that of Bucks Row. It is considered unlikely that the woman could have entered a house, been murdered, and removed to Bucks Row within a period of one hour and a quarter.

The woman who last saw her alive, and whose name is Nelly Holland, was a fellow-lodger with the deceased in Thrawl Street, and is positive as to the time being 2:30. Police constable Neil, 79 J, who found the body, reports the time as 3:45. Bucks Row is a secluded place, from having tenements on one side only. The constable has been severely questioned as to his working of his beat on that night, and states that he was last on the spot where he found the body not more than half an hour previously—that is to say, at 3:15.

The beat is a very short one, and quickly walked over would not occupy more than 12 minutes. He neither heard a cry nor saw any one. Moreover, there are three watchmen on duty at night close to the spot, and neither one heard a cry to cause alarm. It is not true, says Constable Neil, who is a man of nearly 20 years service, that he was called to the body by two men. He came upon it as he walked, and flashing his lantern to examine it, he was answered by the lights from two other constables at either end of the street. These officers had seen no man leaving the spot to attract attention, and the mystery is most complete. The utmost efforts are being used, a number of plainclothes men being out making inquiries in the neighbourhood, and Sergeants Enright and Godley have interviewed many persons who might, it was thought, assist in giving a clue.

On Saturday afternoon Mr. Wynne E. Baxter, coroner for the South-Eastern Division of Middlesex, opened his inquiry at the Working Lads Institute, Whitechapel Road, respecting the death of MARY ANN NICHOLS, whose dead body was found on the pavement in Bucks-row, Whitechapel, on Friday morning.

Detective Inspectors Abberline and Helston and Sergeants Enright and Godley watched the case on behalf of the Criminal Investigation Department.

The jury having been sworn and having viewed the body of the dead woman, which was lying in a shell in the Whitechapel Mortuary.

Edward Walker, of 16 Maidswood-road, Camberwell, deposed that he was now of no occupation, but had formerly been a smith. He had seen the body in the mortuary, and to the best of his belief it was that of his daughter, whom he had not seen for two years. He recognized the body by its general appearance and by some of the front teeth being missing. Deceased also had a scar on the forehead which was caused by a fall when she was young. There was a scar on the body of the woman then lying in the mortuary.

His daughters name was Mary Ann Nichols, and she had been married quite 22 years. Her husbands name was William Nichols, a printers machinist, and he was still alive. They had been living apart for seven or eight years. Deceased was about 42 years of age. The last time witness heard of the deceased was about Easter, when she wrote him a letter. He produced the letter, which was in the handwriting of the deceased. It spoke of a situation she was in, and which, she said, she liked very much. He answered that letter, but had not since heard from the deceased.

The last time he saw deceased was in June, 1886, when she was respectably dressed. That was at the funeral of his son, who was burnt to death through the explosion of a paraffin lamp. Some three or four years previous to that the deceased lived with witness; but he was unable to say what she had since been doing.

Deceased was not a particularly sober woman, and that was the reason why they could not agree. He did not think she was fast with men, and she was not in the habit of staying out late at night while she was living with him. He had no idea what deceased had been doing since she left him. He did not turn the deceased out of doors. They simply had a few a words, and the following morning she left home.

The reason deceased parted from her husband was that he went and lived with the woman who nursed his wife during her confinement. Witness knew nothing of his daughters acquaintances, or what she had been doing for a living. Deceased was not 5ft. 4in. in height. She had five children, the eldest of whom was 21 years of age and the youngest eight or nine. She left her husband when the youngest child was only one or two years of age. The eldest was now lodging with witness.

He was unable to say if deceased had recently been living with any one; but some three or four years ago he heard she was living with a man named Drew, who was a house smith by trade and had a shop of his own in York Street, Walworth. Witness believed he was still living there. The husband of the deceased had been summoned for the keep of the children, but the charge was dismissed owing to the fact that she was then living with another man. Deceased was in the Lambeth Workhouse in April last, when she left to go to a situation. Her husband was still living at Coburg-road, Old Kent Road, but witness was not aware if he was aquainted with his wifes death. Witness did not think the deceased had any enemies, as she was too good for that.

Police constable John Neil, 97 J, deposed that on Friday morning he was passing down Bucks Row, Whitechapel, and going in the direction of Brady Street, and he did not notice any one about. He had been round the same place some half an hour previous to that and did not see any one. He was walking along the right-hand side of the street when he noticed a figure lying in the street. It was dark at the time, although a street lamp was shining at the end of the row. He walked across and found the deceased lying outside a gateway, which was about 9ft. or 10ft. in height and led to some stables, was closed. Houses ran eastward from the gateway, while the Board school was westward of the spot. On the other side of the road was the Essex Wharf. The deceased was lying lengthways, and her left hand touched the gate. With the aid of his lamp he examined the body and saw blood oozing from a wound in the throat. Deceased was lying upon her back with her clothes disarranged. Witness felt her arm, which was quite warm from the joints upwards, while her eyes were wide open.

Her bonnet was off her head and was lying by her right side, close by the left hand. Witness then heard a constable passing Brady Street, and he called to him. Witness said to him, Run at once for Dr. Llewellyn. Seeing another constable in Bakers Row, witness despatched him for the ambulance. Dr. Llewellyn arrived in a very short time. In the meantime witness had rung the bell of Essex Wharf and inquired if any disturbance had been heard. He was told No. Sergeant Kerby then came, and he knocked.

The doctor, having looked at the woman, said: Move the woman to the mortuary; she is dead. I will make a further examination of her. They then placed deceased on the ambulance and removed her to the mortuary. Inspector Spratley came to the mortuary, and while taking a description of deceased lifted up her clothes and discovered she was disembowelled. That had not been noticed before. On the deceased was found a piece of comb and a bit of looking glass, but no money was found. In the pocket an unmarked white pocket handkerchief was found. There was a pool of blood where the neck of deceased was lying in Bucks Row.

He had not heard any disturbance that night. The farthest he had been that night was up Bakers Row to the Whitechapel Road, and was never far away from the spot. The Whitechapel-road was a busy thoroughfare in the early morning, and he saw a number of women in that road, apparently on their way home. At that time any one could have got away. Witness examined the ground while the doctor was being sent for. In answer to a juryman, the witness said he did not see any trap in the road. He examined the road, but could not see any marks of wheels.

The first persons who arrived on the spot after he discovered the body were two men who worked at a slaughterhouse opposite. They stated that they knew nothing of the affair, nor had they heard any screams. Witness had previously seen the men at work. That would be a quarter past 3, or half an hour before he found the body.

Mr. Henry Llewellyn, sugeon, of 152, Whitechapel Road, stated that at 4 oclock on Friday morning he was called by the last witness to Bucks Row. The officer told him what he was wanted for. On reaching Buck Row he found deceased lying flat on her back on the pathway, her legs being extended. Deceased was quite dead, and she had severe injuries to her throat. Her hands and wrists were cold, but the lower extremeties were quite warm. Witness examined her chest and felt the heart.

It was dark at the time. He should say the deceased had not been dead more than half an hour. He was certain that the injuries to the neck were not self-inflicted. There was very little blood round the neck, and there were no marks of any struggle, or of blood as though the body had been dragged. Witness gave the police directions to take the body to the mortuary, where he would make another examination. About an hour afterwards he was sent for by the inspector to see the other injuries he had discovered on the body. Witness went, and saw that the abdomen was cut very extensively. That morning he made a post mortem examination of the body.

It was that of a female of about 40 or 45 years. Five of the teeth were missing, and there was a slight laceration of the tongue. There was a bruise running along the lower part of the jaw on the right side of the face. That might have been caused by a blow from a fist or pressure from a thumb. There was a circular bruise on the left side of the face, which also might have been inflicted by the pressure of the fingers. On the left side of the neck, about 1in. below the jaw, there was an incision about 4in. in length, and ran from a point immediately below the ear. On the same side, but an inch below, and commencing about 1in. in front of it, was a circular incision, which terminated in a point about 3in. below the right jaw. That incision completely severed all the tissues down to the vertebrae. The large vessels of the neck on both sides were severed. The incision was about 8in. in length. The cuts must have been caused by a long-bladed knife, moderately sharp, and used with great violence.

No blood was found on the breast, either of the body or clothes. There were no injuries about the body until just below the lower part of the abdomen. Two or three inches from the left side was a wound running in a jagged manner. The wound was a very deep one, and the tissues were cut through. There were several incisions running across the abdomen. There were also three or four similar cuts, running downwards, on the right side, all of which had been caused by a knife which had been used violently and downwards. The injuries were from left to right, and might have been done by a left-handed person. All the injuries had been caused by the same instrument.

At this stage Mr. Wynne Baxter adjourned the inquiry until this morning.

Report as Printed in the Illustrated Police News Sept. 8, 1888

THE MURDER IN WHITECHAPEL

AT a quarter to four on Friday morning Police-constable Neil was on his beat in Bucks-row, Thomas-street, Whitechapel, when his attention was attracted to the body of a woman lying on the pavement close to the door of the stable-yard in connection with Essex Wharf. Bucks-row, like many other miser thoroughfares in this and similar neighbourhoods, is not overburdened with gas lamps, and in the dim light the constable at first thought that the woman had fallen down in a drunken stupor and was sleeping off the effects of a night debauch. With the aid of the light from his bullseye lantern Neil at once perceived that the woman had been the victim of some horrible outrage. Her livid face was stained with blood and her throat cut from ear to ear. The constable at once alarmed the people living in the house next to the stable-yard, occupied by a carter named Green and his family, and also knocked up Mr. Walter Perkins, the resident manager of the Essex Wharf, on the opposite side of the road, which is very narrow at this point. Neither Mr. Perkins nor any of the Green family, although the latter were sleeping within a few yards of where the body was discovered, had heard any sound of a struggle.

Dr. Llewellyn, who lives only a short distance away in Whitechapel-road, was at once sent for an promptly arrived on the scene. He found the body lying on its back across the gateway, and the briefest possible examination was sufficient to prove that life was extinct. Death had not long ensured, because the extremities were still warm.

With the assistance of Police-sergeant Kirby and Police-constable Thane, the body was removed to the Whitechapel-road mortuary, and it was not until the unfortunate womans clothes were removed that the horrible nature of the attack which had been made upon her transpired. It was then discovered that in addition to the gash in her throat, which had nearly severed the head from the body, the lower part of the abdomen had been ripped up, and the bowels were protruding. The abdominal wall, the whole length of the body, had been cut open, and on either side were two incised wounds almost as severe as the centre one. This reached from the lower part of the abdomen to the breast-bone. The instrument with which the wounds were inflicted must have been not only of the sharpness of a razor, but used with considerable ferocity. The murdered woman is about forty-five years of age, and 5ft. 2in. in height. She had a dark complexion, brown eyes, and brown hair, turning grey. At the time of her death she was wearing a brown ulster fastened with seven large metal buttons with the figure of a horse and a man standing by its side stamped thereon. She had a brown linsey frock and a grey woollen petticoat with a flannel underclothing, close-ribbed brown stays, black woollen stockings, side-spring boots, balck straw bonnet trimmed with black velvet. The mark Lambeth Workhouse P.R. was found stamped on the petticoat bands, and a hope is entertained that by this deceaseds identity may be discovered. A photograph of the body has been taken, and this will be circulated amongst the workhouse officials.

CORONERS INQUEST

On Saturday Mr. Wynne E. Baxter, the coroner for South-East Middlesex, opened an inquiry at the Working Lads Institute, Whitechapel-road. Inspector Helston, who has the case in hand, attended, with other officers, on behalf of the Criminal Investigation Department. Edward Walker was the first witness called. He said: I live at 15, Maldwell Street, Albany Road, Camberwell, and have no occupation. I was a smith when I was at work, but I am not now. I have seen the body in the mortuary, and to the best of my belief it is my daughter, but I have not seen her for three years. I recognise her by her general appearance and by a little mark she had on her forehead when a child. She also has either one or two teeth out, the same as teh woman I have just seen. My daughters name was Mary Ann Nicholls, and she had been married twenty-two years. Her husbands name was Williams Nicholls, and he is alive. He is a machinist. They have been living apart for some length of time, about seven or eight years. I last heard of her before Easter. She was forty-two years of age. The Coroner: How did you see her? Witness: She wrote to me. The Coroner: Is this letter in her handwriting? Witness: Yes, that is her writing.

The letter, which was dated April 17th, 1888, was read by the coroner, and referred to a place which the deceased had gone to at Wandsworth.

The Coroner: When did you last see her alive? Witness: Two years ago last June. The Coroner: Was she then in a good situation? Witness: I dont know. I was not on speaking terms with her. She had been living with me three or four years previously, but thought she could better herself, so I let her go.

The Coroner: What did she do after she left you?

Witness: I dont know.

The Coroner: This letter seems to suggest that she was in a decent situation. Witness: She had only just gone there.

The Coroner: Was she a sober woman?

Witness: Well, at time she drank, and that was why we did not agree.

The Coroner: Was she fast?

Witness: No; I never heard anything of that sort. She used to go with some young women and men that she new, but I never heard of anything improper.

The Coroner: Have you any idea of what she has been doing lately?

Witness: I have not the slightest idea.

The Coroner: She must have drank heavily for you to turn her out of doors?

Witness: I never turned her out. She had no need to be like this while I had a home for her.

The Coroner: How is it that she and her husband were not living together?

Witness: When she was confined her husband took on with the young woman who came to nurse her, and they parted, he living with the nurse, by whom he has another family.

The Coroner: Have you any reasonable doubt that this is your daughter.

Witness: No, I have not. I know nothing about her acquaintances, or what she had been doing for a living. I had no idea she was over here in this part of the town. She has had five children, the eldest being twenty-one years old and the youngest eight or nine years. One of them lives with me, and the other four are with their father.

The Coroner: Has she ever lived with anybody since she left her husband?

Witness: I believe she was once stopping with a man in York Street, Walworth. His name was Drew, and he was a smith by trade. He is living there now, I believe. The parish of Lambeth summoned her husband for the keep of the children, but the summons was dismissed, as it was proved that she was then living with another man. I dont know who that man was.
The Coroner: Was she ever in the workhouse?
Witness: Yes, sir; Lambeth Workhouse, in April last, and went from there to a situation in Wandsworth.
By the Jury: The husband resides at Coburg Road, Old Kent Road. I dont know if he knows of her death.
Coroner: Is there anything you know of likely to throw any light upon this affair?
Witness: No; I dont think she had any enemies, she was too good for that.
John Neil, police-constable 97 J, said: On Friday morning I was preceeding down Bucks Row, Whitechapel, going towards Brady Street. There was not a soul about. I had been round there half an hour previously, and I saw no one then. I was on the right hand side of the street when I noticed a figure lying in the street. It was dark at the time, though there was a street lamp shining at the end of the row. I went across and found deceased lying outside a gateway, her head towards the east.
The gateway was closed. It was about nine or ten feet high, and led to some stables. There were houses from teh gateway eastward, and the School Board school occupies the westward. On the opposite side of the road is Essex Wharf. Deceased was lying lengthways along the street, her left hand touching the gate. I examined the body by the aid of my lantern, and noticed blood oozing from a wound in the throat. She was lying on her back, with her clothes disarranged. I felt her arm, which was quite warm, from the joints upwards. Her eyes were wide open. Her bonnet was off and lying at her side, close to the left hand. I heard a constable passing Brady-street, so I called him. I did not whistle. I said to him, Run at once for Dr. Llewellyn, and seeing another constable in Bakers-row, I sent him for the ambulance. The doctor arrived in a very short time. I had, in the meantime, rung the bell at Essex Whard, and asked if any disturbance had been heard. The reply was No. Sergeant Kirby came after and he knocked. The doctor looked at the woman and then said, Move the woman to the mortuary. She is dead, and I will make a further examination of her. We then placed her on the ambulance, and moved her there. Inspector Spratley came to the mortuary, and while taking a description of the deceased turned up her clothes, and found that she was disembowelled. This had not been noticed by any of them before. On the body was found a piece of comb and a bit of looking-glass. No money was found, but an unmarked white handkerchief was found in her pocket.
The Coroner: Did you notice any blood where she was found?
Witness: There was a pool of blood just where her neck was lying. The blood was then running from the wound in her neck
The Coroner: Did you hear any noise that night?
Witness: No; I heard nothing. The farthest I had been that night was just through the Whitechapel-road and up Bakers Row. I was never far away from the spot.
The Coroner: Whitechapel-road is busy in the early morning, I believe.
Could anybody have escaped that way?
Witness: Oh, yes, sir. I saw a number of women in the main road going home. At that time anyone could have got away.
The Coroner: Someone searched the ground, I believe?
Witness: Yes; I examined it while the doctor was being sent for.
Inspector Spratley: I examined the road, sir, in daylight.
A Juryman (to witness): Did you see a trap in the road at all?
Witness: No.
A Juryman: Knowing that the body was warm, did it not strike you that it might just have been laid there, and that the woman was killed elsewhere?
Witness: I examined the road, but did not see the mark of wheels. The first to arrive on the scene after I had discovered the body were two men who worked at a slaughter house opposite. They said they knew nothing of the affair, and that they had not heard any screams.

I had previously seen the men at work. That would be about a quarter-past three, or half an hour before I found the body.

Henry Llewellyn, surgeon, said: On Friday morning I was called to Bucks Row at about four oclock. The constable told me what I was wanted for. On reaching Bucks Row I found the deceased woman lying flat on her back in the pathway, her legs extended. I found she was dead, and that she had severe injuries to her throat. Her hands and wrists were cold, but the body and lower extremities were warm. I examined her chest and felt the heart. It was dark at the time. I believe she had not been dead more than half an hour. I am quite certain that the injuries to her neck were not self-inflicted. There was very little blood round the neck. There were no marks of any struggle or of blood, as if the body had been dragged. I told the police to take her to the mortuary, and I would make another examination. About an hour later I was sent for by the inspector to see the injuries he had discovered on the body. I went, and saw that the abdomen was cut very extensively. I have this morning made a postmortem examination of the body. I found it to be that of a female about forty or forty-five years. Five of the teeth are missing, and there is a slight laceration of the tongue. On the right side of the face there is a bruise running along the lower part of the jaw. It might have been caused by a blow with the fist or pressure by the thumb. On the left side of the face there was a circular bruise, which also might have been done by the pressure of the fingers. On the left side of the neck, about an inch below the jaw, there was an incision about four inches long and running from a point immediately below the ear. An inch below on the same side and commencing about an inch in front of it was a circular incision terminating at a point three inches below the right jaw. This incision completely severs all the tissues down to the vertabrae. The large vessels of the neck on both sides were severed. The incision is about eight inches long. These cuts must have been caused with a long-bladed knife, moderately sharp, and used with great violence. No blood at all was found on the breast, either of the body or clothes. There were no injuries about the body till just about the lower part of the abdomen. Two or three inches from the left side was a wound running in a jagged manner. It was a very deep wound, and the tissues were cut through. There were several incisions running across the abdomen. On the right side there were also three or four similar cuts running downwards. All these had been caused by a knife, which had been used violently and been used downwards. The injuries were from left to right, and might have been done by a left-handed person. All the injuries had been done by the same instrument.

The inquiry was adjourned. On Monday the inquest was resumed. Inspector John Spratling, of the J Division, was the first witness called. He stated that he first heard of the murder about half-past four on Friday morning, while in Hackney-road. Proceeded to Bucks Row, he saw Police constable Thain there, and the constable pointed out the spot where the deceased had been found. Witness noticed a slight stain of blood on the footpath. Witness, continuing, stated that he returned to the mortuary about noon on Friday. He then found the body stripped, and the clothes lying in a heap in the yard. The clothes consisted of a reddish brown ulster, with seven large brass buttons. It was apparently an old garment, but a brown linsey dress looked new. There was a grey woollen petticoat and a flannel one belonging to the workhouse. Some pieces bearing the words Lambeth Workhouse, P.R. (Princes Road), had been cut out by inspector Helson with the object of identifying th edeceased. Among the clothes there was also a pair of stays in fairly good condition, though they had been repaired, but he did not notice how they fastened.

Henry Tompkins, of Coventry-street, Bethnal-green, stated that he was a horse slaughterer in the employ of Mr. Barber. He was at work in teh slaughterhouse, Winthrop street, adjoining Bucks Row, from eight oclock on Thursday night till twenty minutes past four oclock on Friday morning. He generally went home after leaving work, but that morning he had a walk. A police constable passed the slaughterhouse about a quarter-past four, and told the men there that a woman had been murdered in Bucks Row. They then went to see the dead woman. Besides witness two other men, named James Mumford and Charles Britten, worked in the slaughterhouse. Witness and Britten had been out of the slaughterhouse previously that night, namely, from twenty minutes past twelve till one oclock, but not afterwards till they went to see the body. It was not a great distance from the slaughterhouse to the spot where the deceased was found. The work at the slaughterhouse was very quiet work.

The Coroner: Was all quiet, say after two oclock on Friday morning?

Witness: Yes, quite quiet. The gates were open, and we heard no cry.

The Coroner asked if anybody came to the slaughterhouse that morning.

Witness stated that nobody passed except the policeman.

The Coroner: Were there any women about?

Witness: Oh, I dont know anything about them. I dont like them.

(Laughter.)

The Coroner: Never mind whether you like them or not. Were there any about that night?

Witness replied that in Whitechapel Road there were all sorts and sizes.

(Laughter.) He could tell them that it was a rough neighbourhood.

The Coroner: Had anybody called for assistance from the spot where the deceased was found would you have heard it in the slaughterhouse?

Witness thought not, as it was too far away. When he arrived in Bucks Row with the intention of seeing the murdered woman he found the doctor and three or four policemen there, and he believed that two other men whom he did not know were also there. He heard no statement as to how the deceased came into Bucks Row. About a dozen people came up before the body was taken away. He did not see anyone from one oclock on Friday morning till a quarter-past four, when the policeman passed the slaughterhouse.

A Juror: Did you hear any vehicle pass the slaughterhouse?

Witness: No, sir. If one had passed I should have heard it.

A Juror: Where did you go when you went out between twenty minutes past twelve and one oclock?

Witness: My mate and I went to the front of the road.

A Juror: Is not your usual time of quitting work six in the morning?

Witness: No; it is according to what we have to do.

A Juror: Why did the constable call to tell you about the murder?

Witness: He called to get his cape.

Detective-inspector Joseph Helson said that he received information about the discovery of the body at a quarter to seven oclock on Friday morning, and between eight and nine oclock he saw the body, with the clothing still on it, at the mortuary. He noticed that the dress was fastened in front with the exception of two or three buttons, and the stays were also fastened. They were fastened with clasps, and were fairly tight but short. There was blood in the hair and about the collars of the dress and ulster, but he saw none at the back of the skirts. He found no marks on the arms such as would indicate a struggle and no cuts in the clothing. All the wounds could, in my opinion, have been inflicted without the removal of the clothing. The only suspicious mark about the place where the body was found was one spot in Brady Street. It might have been blood.

Witness: No, I should say that the offence was committed on the spot.

Police Constable Mizen deposed that at about a quarter to four oclock on Friday morning, while he was at the corner of Hanbury Street and Bakers Row, a carman passing by, in company with another man, said, You are wanted in Bucks Row by a policeman. A woman is lying there. The witness then went to Bucks Row, and Police constable Neil sent him for the ambulance. Nobody but Neil was with the body at that time. In reply to a juryman, witness said that when the carman spoke to him he was engaged in knocking people up, and he finished knocking at the one place where he was at the time, giving two or three knocks, and then went directly to Bucks-row, not wanting to knock up anyone else.

Charles A. Cross, a carman, said that he was in the employment of Messrs. Pickford and Co. He left home about half-past three oclock on Friday morning to go to work, and in passing through Bucks Row he saw on the opposite side something lying against a gateway. He could not tell in the dark what it was at first. It looked like a tarpaulin sheet, but, stepping into the middle of the road, he saw that it was the body of a woman. At this time he heard a

man^about forty yards offapproaching from the direction that witness had himself come from. He waited for the man, who started on one side, as if afraid that witness meant to knock him

159

down. Witness said, Come and look over here. Theres a woman. They then went over to the body. Witness took hold of teh hands of the woman, and the other man stooped over her head to look at her. Feeling the hands cold and limp witness said, I believe shes dead. Then he touched her face, which felt warm. The other man put his head on her heart saying, I think shes breathing, but it is very little if she is. The man suggested that they should shift her, meaning to set her upright. Witness answered, I am not going to touch her. The other man tried to pull her clothes down to cover her legs, but they did not seem as if they would come down. Her bonnet was off, but close to her head. Witness did not notice that her throat was cut. The night was very dark. Witness and the other man left the woman, and in Bakers Row they saw Police-constable Mizen. They told him that a woman was lying in Bucks Row, witness adding, She looks to me to be either dead or drunk. The other man observed, I think shes dead. The policeman replied, All right. The other man, who appeared to be a carman, left witness soon afterwards. Witness did not see Constable Neil. He saw no one except the man that overtook him, the constable in Bakers Row whom he spoke to, and the deceased. In reply to further questions, the witness said the deceased looked to him at the time as if she had been outraged, and had gone off in a swoon. He had then no idea that she was so seriously injured. The other man merely said that he would have fetched a policeman, but he was behind time. Witness was behind time himself. He did not tell constable Mizen that another policeman wanted him in Bucks Row.

William Nicholls, a printers machinist, living in Coburg Road, Old Kent Road, said that the deceased woman was his wife. They did not live together, but had lived apart for eight years last Easter. He last saw her alive about three years ago. He had not heard from her since. He did not know what she had been doing during the last three years.

A Juror: It is said that you were summoned by the Lambeth Union for her maintenance, and that you pleaded that she was living with another man. Did that refer to the blacksmith that she had lived with?

Witness: No, to another man or men. I had her watched. That was seven years ago.

The Juror: Did you leave her or did she leave you?

Witness: She left me. She had no occasion for leaving me. The witness further stated that but for the drink his wife would have been all right. It was not true that he took up with a nurse eight years ago when his wife left him.

Emily Holland stated that she was a married woman, and lived at Thrawl Street, Spitalfields, in a common lodging house. Deceased had lived there about six weeks, but was not there during the last ten days. AT about half-past two oclock on Friday morning witness saw the deceased going down Osborne-street into Whitechapel Road. She was staggering along drunk and was alone. She told witness that where she had been living recently they would not let her in because she could not pay. Witness tried to persuade her to go home with her. The deceased refused, saying, I have had my lodging money three times today, and have spent it. The deceased then went along Whitechapel-road, stating that she was going to get some money to pay for her lodgings. Witness did not know what deceased did for a living, or whether she stayed out late at night. She was a quiet woman, and kept herself to herself. Witness did not know whether she had any male acquaintance or not. She had never seen the deceased quarrel with anybody. When deceased left witness at the corner of Osborne-street and Whitechapel-road she said that she would not be long before she was back.

Mary Ann Monk deposed that she last saw the deceased about seven weeks ago in a public-house in New Kent-road. She had previously seen her in the Lambeth Workhouse, but she had no knowledge of the acquaintance of the deceased.

As this was all the evidence the police were prepared to offer at present, the inquest was then adjourned until the 17th inst., and it was arranged that the jury should inspect the clothes of the deceased at the mortuary instead of in the room where the inquiry was held.

Notwithstanding every effort the police engaged in investigating the murder of Mary Ann Nicholls have to confess themselves baffled, their numerous inquiries having yielded no positive clue to the perpetrator of the crime. At the conclusion of the inquest Detective-inspector Abberline and Detective-inspector Helson were busily engaged in the matter, but have not elicited any new facts of importance. A large number of constables are engaged upon the case. Crowds of spectators continue to visit the scene of the murder in Bucks Row.

Report as Printed in the London Times Sept. 15, 1888
THE WHITECHAPEL MURDERS

The police at the Commercial Street station have made another arrest on suspicion in connection with the recent murders. It appears that among the numerous statements and descriptions of suspected persons are several tallying with that of the man in custody, but beyond this the police know nothing at present against him. His apprehension was of a singular character. Throughout yesterday his movements are stated to have created suspicion among various persons, and last night he was handed over to a uniform constable doing duty in the neighbourhood of Flower and Dean Street on suspicion in connection with the crime. On his arrival at the police station in Commercial Street the detective officers and Mr. Abberline were communicated with, and an inquiry concerning him was at once opened. On being searched perhaps one of the most extraordinary accumulation of articles were

discovered^a heap of rags, comprising pieces of dress fabrics, old and dirty linen, two purses of a kind usually used by women, two or three pocket handkerchiefs, one a comparatively clean white one, and a white one with a red spotted border; two small tin boxes, a small cardboard box, a small leather strap, which might serve the purpose of a garterstring, and one spring onion.

The person to whom this curious assortment belongs is slightly built, about 5ft. 7in. or 5ft. 8in. in height, and dressed shabbily. He has a very careworn look. Covering a head of hair, inclined somewhat to be sandy, with beard and moustache to match, was a cloth skull cap, which did not improve his appearance. Suspicion is the sole motive for his temporary detention, for the police, although making every possible inquiry about him, do not believe his appehension to be of any importance.

Regarding the man Pigott, who was captured at Gravesend, nothing whatever has been discovered by the detectives in the course of their inquiries which can in any way connect him with the crimes, and his release, at all events, from the custody of the police is expected shortly.

In connexion with the arrest of a lunatic at Holloway, it appears that he has been missing from his friends for some time now. The detectives have been very active in prosecuting their inquiries concerning him, and it is believed the result, so far, increases their suspicion. He is at present confined in the asylum at Grove Road, Bow.

All inquiries have failed to elicit anything as to the whereabouts of the missing pensioner who is wanted in connexion with the recent murder.

On the question as to the time when the crime was committed, concerning which there was a difference between the evidence of the man Richardson and the opinion of Dr. Phillips, a correspondent yesterday elicited that Mr. Cadoche, who lives in the next house to No. 29, Hanbury Street, where the murder was committed, went to the back of the premises at half-past 5 a.m. As he passed the wooden partition he heard a woman say No, no. On returning he heard a scuffle and then someone fell heavily against the fence. He heard no cry for help, and so he went into his house. Some surprise is felt that this statement was not made in evidence at the inquest. There is a very strong feeling in the district and large numbers of persons continue to visit the locality.

Annie Chapman, the victim of the crime, was buried early yesterday morning at Manor Park Cemetery. Some of her relatives attended the funeral.

Report as Printed in the London Times September 11, 1888
THE WHITECHAPEL MURDERS

Two arrests were made yesterday, but it is very doubtful whether the murderer is in the hands of the police. The members of the Criminal Investigation Department are assisting the divisional police at the East-end in their endeavours to elucidate the mystery in which these crimes are involved. Yesterday morning Detective Sergeant Thicke, of the H Division, who has been indefatigable in his inquiries respecting the murder of Annie Chapman at 29, Hanbury Street, Spitalfields, on Saturday morning, succeeded in capturing a man whom he believed to be Leather Apron. It will be recollected that this person obtained an evil notoriety during the inquiries respecting this and the recent murders committed in Whitechapel, owing to the startling reports that had been freely circulated by many of the women living in the district as to outrages alleged to have been committed by him. Sergeant Thicke, who has had much experience of the thieves and their haunts in this portion of the metropolis, has, since he has been engaged in the present inquiry, been repeatedly assured by some of the most well-known characters of their abhorrence of the fiendishness of the crime, and they have further stated that if they could only lay hands on the murderer they would hand him over to justice. These and other circumstances convinced the officer and those associated with him that the deed was in no way traceable to any of the regular thieves or desperadoes at the East-end. At the same time a sharp look-out was kept on the common lodginghouses, not only in this district, but in other portions of the metropolis. Several persons bearing a resemblance to the description of the person in question have been arrested, but, being able to render a satisfactory account of themselves, were allowed to go away. Shortly after 8 oclock yesterday morning Sergeant Thicke, accompanied by two or three other officers, proceeded to 22, Mulberry Street and knocked at the door. It was opened by a Polish Jew named Pizer, supposed to be Leather Apron. Thicke at once took hold of the man, saying, You are just the man I want. He then charged Pizer with being concerned in the murder of the woman Chapman, and to this he made no reply. The accused man, who is a boot finisher by trade, was then handed over to other officers and the house was searched. Thicke took possession of five sharp long-bladed knives^which, however, are used by men in Pizers trade^and also several old hats. With reference to the latter, several women who stated they were acquainted with the prisoner, alleged he has been in the habit of wearing different hats. Pizer, who is about 33, was then quietly removed to the Leman Street Police station, his friends protesting that he knew nothing of the affair, that he had not been out of the house since Thursday night, and is of a very delicate constitution. The friends of the man were subjected to a close questioning by the police. It was still uncertain, late last night, whether this man remained in custody or had been liberated. He strongly denies that he is known by the name of Leather Apron.

The following official notice has been circulated throughout the metropolitan police district and all police stations throughout the country: -- Description of a man who entered a passage of the house at which the murder was committed of a prostitute at 2 a.m. on the 8th.^Age 37; height, 5ft. 7in.; rather dark beard and moustache. Dress-shirt, dark vest and trousers, black scarf, and black felt hat. Spoke with a foreign accent.

Great excitement was caused in the neighbourhood of Commercial Street Police station during the afternoon on account of the arrival from Gravesend of a suspect whose appearance resembled in some respects that of Leather Apron. This man, whose name is William Henry Pigott, was taken into custody on Sunday night at the Popes Head publichouse, Gravesend. Attention was first attracted to Pigott because he had some bloodstains on his clothes. Superintendent Berry, the chief of the local police, was communicated with, and a sergeant was sent to the Popes Head to investigate the case. On approaching the man, who seemed in a somewhat dazed condition, the sergeant saw that one of his hands bore several recently-made wounds.

Being interrogated as to the cause of this Pigott made a somewhat rambling statement to the effect that while going down Brick Lane, Whitechapel, at half-past 4 on Saturday morning he saw a woman fall in a fit. He stooped to pick her up, and she bit his hand. Exasperated at this he struck her, but seeing two policemen coming up he then ran away. The sergeant, deeming the explanation unsatisfactory, took Pigott to the police-station, where his clothing was carefully examined by Dr. Whitcombe, the divisional surgeon.

The result of the scrutiny was an announcement that two shirts which Pigott carried in a bundle were stained with blood, and also that blood appeared to have been recently wiped off his boots. After the usual caution the prisoner made a further statement to the effect that the woman who bit him was in the street at the back of a lodging-house when seized with the fit. He added that he slept at a lodging-house in Osborne Street on Thursday night, but on Friday was walking the streets of Whitechapel all night. He tramped from London to Gravesend on Saturday. He gave his age as 52, and stated he was a native of Gravesend, his father having some years ago had a position there in connexion with the Royal Liver Society.

Subsequently Pigott told the police that he had been keeping several publichouses in London. As the prisoners description tallied in some respects with that furnished by headquarters of the man wanted, Superintendent Berry decided to detain him until the morning. In response to a telegram apprising him of the arrest Inspector Abberline proceeded to Gravesend yesterday morning, and after hearing the circumstances of the case decided to bring the prisoner at once to Whitechapel, so that he could be confronted with the women who had furnished the description of Leather Apron.

A large crowd had gathered at Gravesend railway station to witness the departure of the detective and his prisoner, but his arrival at London-bridge was almost unnoticed, the only persons apprised beforehand of the journey being the police, a small party of whom in plain clothes were in attendance. Inspector Abberline and Pigott went off in a four-wheeled cab to Commercial Street where from early morning groups of idlers had hung about in anticipation of an arrest.

The news of Pigotts arrival, which took place at 12 48, at once spread, and in a few seconds the police-station was surrounded by an excited crowd anxious to get a glimpse of the supposed murderer. Finding that no opportunity was likely to occur of seeing the prisoner, the mob after a time melted away, but the police had trouble for some hours in keeping the thoroughfare free for traffic. Pigott arrived at Commercial Street in much the same condition as he was when taken into custody. He wore no vest, had on a battered felt hat, and appeared to be in a state of high nervous excitement.

Mrs. Fiddymont, who is responsible for the statement respecting a man resembling Leather Apron being at the Prince Albert publichouse on Saturday, was sent for, as were also other witnesses likely to be able to identify the prisoner; but after a very brief scrutiny it was the unanimous opinion that Pigott was not Leather Apron. Nevertheless, looking to his condition of mind and body, it was decided to detain him until he could give a somewhat more satisfactory explanation of himself and his movements. After an interval of a couple of hours, the mans manner becoming more strange and his speech more incoherent, the divisional surgeon was called in, and he gave it as his opinion that the prisoners mind was unhinged. A medical certificate to this effect was made out, and Pigott will, for the present, remain in custody.

Intelligent observers who have visited the locality express the upmost astonishment that the murderer could have reached a hiding place after committing such a crime. He must have left the yard in Hanbury Street reeking with blood, and yet, if the theory that the murder took place between 5 and 6 be accepted, he must have walked in almost broad daylight along streets comparatively well frequented, even at that early hour, without his startling appearance attracting the slightest attention.

Consideration of this point has led many to the conclusion that the murderer came not from the wretched class from which the inmates of common lodging-houses are drawn. More probably, it is argued, he is a man lodging in a comparatively decent house in the district, to which he would be able to retire quickly, and in which, once it was reached, he would be able at his leisure to remove from his person all traces of his hideous crime. It is at any rate practically certain that the murderer would not have ventured to return to a common lodging-house smeared with blood as he must have been. The police are\ therefore exhorted not to confine their investigations, as they are accused of doing, to common lodging-houses and other resorts of the criminal and outcast, but to extend their inquiries to the class of householders, exceedingly numerous in the East-end of London, who are in the habit of letting furnished lodgings without particular inquiry into the character or antecedents of those who apply for them.

A visit to Dorset Street, which runs parellel with Spitalfields Market from Commercial Street, reveals the fact that nearly every house in the street is a common lodging-house, in which wretched human beings are, at certain seasons of the year, crammed from cellar to roof. The streets leading into Dorset Street, where the woman was last seen alive, are also occupied by lodging-houses. In Hanbury-street, Deal Street, Great Garden Street, and several smaller thoroughfares houses of the same sort are located and are frequented by the poorest class of the casual community.

Some of these places have been searched and inquiries made as to their recent inhabitants, but so far nothing has been discovered to lead to the supposition that any regular frequenter of these establishments committed the murder. The woman Chapman was known by appearance to the policemen on the night beats in the neighbourhood, but none of those who were on duty between 12 and 6 on Saturday morning recollect having seen her. It is ascertained that several men left their lodgings after midnight with the expressed intention of returning who have not returned. Some men went to their lodgings after 3 oclock, and left again before 6 in the morning, which is not an unfrequent occurrence in those houses.

None of the deputies or watchmen at the houses have any have any memory of any person stained with blood entering their premises, but at that hour of the morning little or no notice is taken of persons inquiring for beds. They are simply asked for the money, and shown up dark stairways with a bad light to their rooms. When they leave early, they are seldom noticed in their egress. It is then considered quite probable that the murderer may have found a refuge for a few hours in one of these places, and even washed away the signs of his guilt. The men in these houses use a common washing place, and water once used is thrown down the sink by the lodger using it. All this might happen in a common lodging-house in the early morning without the bloodstained murderer being noticed particularly. The conviction is growing even, that taking for granted that one man committed all the recent murders of women in the Whitechapel district, he might in this fashion, by changing his common lodging-house, evade detection for a considerable time. Whoever the man may be, if the same person committed the last three murders, he must on each occasion have been bespattered profusely with bloodstains. He could not well get rid of them in any ordinary dwelling-house or public place. Therefore it is supposed he must have done so in the lodging-houses.

The murderer must have known the neighbourhood, which is provided with no fewer than four police stations, and is well watched nightly, on account of the character of many of the inhabitants. On Saturday morning, between half past 4 oclock and 6, several carts must have passed through Hanbury-street, and at 5 oclock, on the opening of the Spitalfields Market, the end of which the murder occurred was blocked with market vehicles, and the market attendents were busy regulating the traffic. In the midst of the bustle it is admitted that two persons might have passed through the hall of 29, Hanbury-street, and in consequence of the noise of passing vehicles, any slight altercation might have occurred without being overheard. Although at first, from the contiguity of Bucks Row to a slaughter-house and the neighbourhood of the Aldgate Shambles, suspicion fell on the butchers employed in those establishments during the night, the suspicion is disappearing, inasmuch as the names and addresses and the movements of all those engaged in the occupation are known.

A meeting of the chief local tradesmen was held yesterday, at which an influential committee was appointed, consisting of 16 well-known gentlemen, with Mr. J. Aarons as the secretary. The committee issued last evening a notice stating that they will give a substantial reward for the capture of the murderer or for information leading thereto. The movement has been warmly taken up by the inhabitants, and it is thought certain that a large sum will be subscribed within the next few days.

The proposal to form district vigilance committees also meets with great popular favour and is assuming practical form. Meetings were held at the various working mens clubs and other organizations, political and social, in the districts, at most of which the proposed scheme was heartily approved.

From inquiries which have been made in Windsor, it seems that the deceased was the widow of a coachman in service at Clewer. While the deceased lived at Clewer she was in custody for drunkenness, but had not been charged before the magistrates.

The Inquest

Yesterday morning Mr. Wynne E. Baxter, the Coroner for the North-Eastern Division of Middlesex, who was accompanied by Mr. George Collier, the Deputy Coroner, opened his inquiry in the Alexandra room of the Working Lads Institute, Whitechapel Road, respecting the death of Annie Chapman, who was found murdered in the back yard of 29, Hanbury Street, Spitalfields, on Saturday morning.

Detective Inspectors Abberline (Scotland Yard), Helson, and Chandler, and Detective Sergeants Thicke and Leach watched the case on behalf of the Criminal Investigation Department and Commissioners of Police.

The court room was crowded, and, owing to the number of persons assembled outside the building, the approaches had to be guarded by a number of police constables.

The jury having been impanelled, proceeded to the mortuary to view the body of the deceased, which was lying in the same shell as that occupied a short time since by the unfortunate Mary Ann Nichols.

John Davis, a carman, of 29, Hanbury Street, Spitalfields, deposed that he occupied the front room, which was shared by his wife and three sons. About 8 oclock on Friday night he went to bed, and his sons came in at different times. The last one arrived home about a quarter to 11. Witness was awake from 3 to about 5 oclock, when he fell off to sleep for about half an hour. He got up about a quarter to 6. Soon afterwards he went across the yard.

The front portion of the house faced Hanbury Street. On the ground floor there was a front door, with a passage running through to the back yard. He was certain of the time, because he heard the bell of Spitalfields Church strike. The front door and the one leading into the yard were never locked, and at times were left open at nights. Since he had lived in the house witness had never known the doors to be locked; and when the doors were shut any person could open them and pass into the yard. When he went into the yard on Saturday morning the back door was shut; but he was unable to say whether it was latched. The front door was wide open, and he was not surprised at finding it so, as it was frequently left open all night. Between the yard of 29, Hanbury-street, and the next house there was a fence about 5ft. high. When witness went down the steps he saw the deceased woman lying flat on her back.

The coroner here observed that in similar inquiries in the country the police always assisted him by preparing a plan of the locality which happened to be the subject of investigation. He thought the present case was one of sufficient importance for the production of such a plan, and he hoped that in future a plan would be laid before him.

Inspector Chandler told the Coroner a plan would be prepared.

The coroner replied it might then be too late to be of any service.

Witness, continuing, said the deceased was lying between the steps and the fence, with her head towards the house. He could see that her clothes were disarranged. Witness did not go further into the yard, but at once called two men, who worked for Mr. Bailey, a packingcase maker, of Hanbury Street, whose place was three doors off. These men entered the passage and looked at the woman, but did not go into the yard. He was unable to give the names of these two men, but knew them well by sight. Witness had not since seen the men, who went away to fetch the police. Witness also left the house with them.

In answer to the Coroner, Inspector Chandler said these men were not known to the police.

The coroner remarked that they would have to be found, either by the police or by his own officer.

Witness further stated that on leaving the house he went direct to the Commercial Street Police station, and reported what he had seen. Previous to that he had not informed any one living in the house of the discovery. After that he went back to Hanbury Street, but did not enter his house. He had never previously seen the deceased.

In cross-examination, the witness said he was not the first person down that morning, as a man, named Thompson, who also lived in the house, was called about half-past 3. He had never seen women who did not live in the house in the passage since he had lived there, which was only a fortnight. He did not hear any strange noises before getting up on Saturday morning.

Amelia Farmer stated that she lived at a common lodginghouse at 30, Dorset Street, Spitalfields, and had lived there for the past four years. She had identified the body of the deceased in the mortuary, and was sure it was that of Annie Chapman. The deceased formerly lived at Windsor, and was the widow of Frederick Chapman, a veterinary surgeon, who died about 18 months ago. For four years, or more, the deceased had lived apart from her husband, and during that period had principally resided in common lodginghouses in the neighbourhoods of Whitechapel and Spitalfields.

About two years since the deceased lived at 30, Dorset Street, and was then living with a man who made iron sieves. She was then recieving an allowance of 10s. a week from her husband. Some 18 months since the payments stopped, and it was then that she found her husband was dead. That fact was also ascertained from a relative of the deceased, who used to live in Oxford Street, Whitechapel. The deceased went by the name of Sievey, on account of the man with whom she had cohabited being a sieve maker. This man left her some time ago. During the past week witness had seen the deceased some two or three times.

On Monday, in Dorset Street, she complained of feeling unwell. At that time she had a bruise on one of her temples. Witness inquiring how she got it, the deceased told her to look at her breast, which was also bruised. The deceased said, You know the woman, and she mentioned a name which witness did not remember. Both the deceased and the woman referred to were acquainted with a man called Harry the Hawker. In giving an account of the bruises, the deceased told witness that on the 1st inst. she went into a publichouse with a young man named Ted Stanley in Commercial Street. Harry the Hawker and the other woman were also there. The former, who was drunk, put down a florin, which was picked up by the latter, who replaced it with a penny. Some words passed between the deceased and the woman, and in the evening the latter struck her and inflicted the bruises. Witness again saw the deceased on Tuesday by the side of Spitalfields Church.

The deceased again complained of feeling unwell, and said she thought she would go into the casual ward for day or two. She mentioned that she had had nothing to eat or drink that day, not even a cup of tea. Witness gave deceased twopence saying, Here is twopence to have a cup of tea, but dont have rum. She knew that deceased was given to drinking that spirit. The deceased, who frequently got the worse for drink, used at times to earn money by doing crochet work, and at others by selling flowers.

Witness believed she was not very particular what she did to earn a living and at times used to remain out very late at night. She was in the habit of going to Stratford. Witness did not again see the deceased until Friday afternoon, and about 5 oclock on that day she met her in Dorset Street.

The deceased, who was sober, in answer to a question from witness as to whether she was going to Stratford, said she felt too ill to do anything. A few minutes afterwards witness again saw the deceased, who had not moved, and she said, Its no use my giving way. I must pull myself together and go out and get some money, or I shall have no lodgings. That was the last time witness saw her. She mentioned that she had been an inmate of the casual ward.

Deceased was generally an industrial woman, and witness considered her clever. For the last five years she had been living an irregular life, more especially since her husband died. She had two children, and on the death of her husband they were sent away to school. The deceased had a sister and mother, but witness believed they were not on friendly terms.

Timothy Donovan stated he was the deputy of a common lodginghouse at 35, Dorset Street, Spitalfields. He had seen the body in the mortuary, and identified it as that of a woman who had lodged at his place. She had been living there for about four months, but was not there any day last week until Friday. About 7 oclock that day she came to the lodginghouse and asked him to allow her to go down into the kitchen. He asked where she had been all the week, and she replied, In the infirmary. He then allowed her to go down into the kitchen. She remained there until shortly before 2 oclock the next morning. When she went out she said, I have not any money now, but dont let the bed; I will be back soon.

At that time there was a vacant bed, and it was the one she generally occupied. She then left the house, but witness did not see which way she turned. She had had enough to drink when he last saw her, but she was well able to walk straight. The deceased generally got the worse for drink on Saturdays, but not not on the other days of the week. He told her that she could find money for drink but not for her bed, and she replied that she had only been to the top of the street as far as the Ringers publichouse. He did not see her with any one that night. On Saturday night deceased used to stay at the lodginghouse with a man of military appearance, and witness had heard he was a pensioner.

She had brought other men to the lodginghouse. On the 2d inst. deceased paid 8d. a night for her bed. The pensioner was about 45 years of age and about 5ft. 8in. in height. At times he had the appearance of something better. Witness had never had any trouble with the deceased, who was always very friendly with the other lodgers.

John Evans, night watchman at the lodginghouse, also identified the body of deceased. He saw her leave the house at about a quarter to 2 on Saturday morning. Just before he had asked her whether she had not sufficient, and then told the last witness she would not be long before she got it. Witness saw her enter a court called Paternoster Row and walk in the direction of Brushfield Street.

Witness should say she was the worse for drink. She told him she had that night been to see one of her sisters who lived at Vauxhall. Before he spoke to her about her lodging money she had been out for a pint of beer. He knew that she had been living a rough life, but only knew one man with whom she associated. That man used to come and see her on Saturdays. He called about half-past 2 on Saturday afternoon to make inquiries about the deceased. He said he had heard of her death. Witness did not know his name or address. After hearing an account of the death of the deceased he went out without saying a word. Witness had never heard any person threaten the deceased, and she had never stated she was afraid of any one. He did not see the deceased leave the lodginghouse with the pensioner on Sunday week.

On Thursday the deceased and a woman called Eliza had a fight in the kitchen, during which she got a blow on the chest and a black eye.

The coroner here intimated that that was as far as he proposed to carry the inquiry at present, and it was adjourned until tomorrow afternoon.

Extracted writings of George Sims (Dagonet)

Sept. 9, 1888.

The Whitechapel murders, which have come to the relief of newspaper editors in search of a sensation, are not the kind of murders which pay best. The element of romance is altogether lacking, and they are crimes of the coarsest and most vulgar brutality - not the sort of murders that can be discussed in the drawing-room and the nursery with any amount of pleasure. The best element in the cases for newspaper purposes is that they are similar to a murder which was committed near the same spot some time previously, and this enables the talented journalist to start the idea that the four crimes are by the same hand. Given this idea, and "the maniac who lures women into lonely spots and cuts them up" speedily assumes a definite shape. If only the women had belonged to another class, or been in more comfortable circumstances, there might, with skillful manipulation, have been worked up an excitement almost equal to the Marr and Williamson sensation.

The murder of the Marrs created such a widespread panic that it led to a great reform in the police administration of the metropolis. The old Charley was voted an anachronism, and he gave way to a corps of civilian guards, who have since developed into our helmeted Roberts. The Whitechapel murder looks like causing the question of inadequate police protection to be trotted out again. As a matter of fact the London police force is utterly inadequate to the growing needs of the rapidly increasing metropolis. The wonder is, not that so many attacks on life and property are made with impunity, but that there are so few. If the criminal classes had anything like organisation, London would be at their mercy.

The police up to the moment of writing are still at sea as to the series of Whitechapel murders - a series with such a strong family likeness as to point conclusively to one assassin or firm of assassins. The detective force is singularly lacking in the smartness and variety of resource which the most ordinary detective displays in the shilling shocker. As a rule, your modern detective waits for "information," instead of making a clue for himself by joining together the links of circumstantial evidence. In the Whitechapel cases the theory is that there is either a maniac at the bottom of them, or that they are the work of a "High Rip" gang. That theory should be followed up until it is proved to be a false one. The decoy system might very well be tried. Decoys could be sent out all over the neighbourhood, and the chances are the bird would be caught by one of them. If a number of old gentlemen had been knocked down and robbed of their gold chains in a certain neighbourhood, the best thing would be to dress up a police agent as an old gentleman, give him a chain, and tell him to expose himself to danger. Directly the thief came he could give the signal, and his confederates in the force would close in, and the thief would be caught. Scotland-yard ought to be able to put temptation in the way of the Whitechapel ruffian (if he is a habitual woman murderer) to make him walk into the trap.

Sept.16, 1888.
Room for Leather Apron! Stand aside, all you other celebrities, and hide your diminished heads. Mr. Gladstone might take a walk abroad, and make a speech from every doorstep that he came to; Mr. Parnell might commence an action against the Times in every town in the three kingdoms; Mrs. Mona Caird might suggest polygamy on the three years' system; Professor Baldwin might go up into the sky attached to a halfpenny kite, and cut its tail off, and come down after attaining an altitude of a hundred miles; the Queen of Servia might knock King Milan's hat off on a public promenade; General Boulanger might fight a duel with M. Chevreuil, and get the worst of it; Bismarck might come over here and chalk a rude name on Sir Morell Mackenzie's front door; the great Donnelly himself might discover a cryptogram which proved that the Rev. Mr. Spurgeon was the author of all Rider Haggard's books; little Josef Hofmann might favour the Daily Telegraph with his views on the marriage question; "Mr. Manton" might adopt the stage as a profession; and appear as Juliet to little Mr. Penley's Romeo; and General Booth might turn the Grecian Theatre into a Music Hall Company (Limited) - and still Leather Apron would remain the hero of the hour.

It is only the careful observer, the close student of our insular everyday life, the professional expert, who can thoroughly gauge the extent to which Leather Apron has impressed himself upon the public mind. Up to a few days ago the mere mention of Leather Apron's name was sufficient to cause a panic. All England was murmuring his name with bated breath. In one instance, which is duly recorded in the police reports, a man merely went into a public-house and said that he knew Leather Apron, and the customers, leaving their drinks unfinished, fled en masse, while the landlady, speechless with terror, bolted out of a back door and ran to the police-station, leaving the grim humorist in sole possession of the establishment, till and all. Never since the days of Burke and Hare has a name borne such fearful significance.

The joke - if joke there can be in connection with a tale which puts all the vampire stories of fiction to bed and tucks them up for the rest of their natural lives - which has been considered the most excruciating by the larky young men of the period has been to call each other Leather Apron in places of public resort. A wag the other day, finding a steamer on which he was about to take a journey inconveniently crowded, just stepped up to the man at the wheel and said, "I am Leather Apron," and in two seconds he had the steamer to himself, the captain and the man at the wheel being among the first to leap ashore.

Now that the first wild excitement has died down, and common sense is having a peep in, most people are beginning to see that Leather Apron has probably as much to do with the Whitechapel murders as the Archbishop of Canterbury or the Baroness Burdett-Coutts. It is astonishing how eagerly the Press seized upon the mere mention of a person with this ordinary nickname, and worked it up into a blood-curdling sensation. The name of Leather Apron has been flashed from pole to pole. It is to-day as much a byword on Greenland's icy

168

mountains and on India's coral strand as it is in Whitechapel and Scotland-yard. And why? Primarily because there was something in the sound which suggested a big catch-on. It is possible that the harmless individual who was arrested as Leather Apron; and discharged because there wasn't enough evidence against him to convict a bluebottle of buzzing, may not lose his celebrity for a generation. He has been written up with such a vengeance that he will be a famous man to the end of his days.

The booming of Leather Apron in connection with the Whitechapel murders illustrates the bungling way in which the business is being conducted by the police. It is a million to one that when (O that all-important when!) the bona-fide murderer (bona-fide murderer is good!) is arrested he will be found to be someone who never heard of a leather apron in his life. The police may be playing a game of spoof, but the fact remains that in no suggestion made by the authorities up to the present is the slightest technical knowledge of the "specialty" of the Whitechapel atrocities shown.

When the doctor who was called in to see the body publicly requests the coroner not to ask him to go into particulars, as they are too horrible, the purveyors of news for the Press may well hesitate before they turn on their extra-realistic young men. One enterprising journal has trotted out for the benefit of its readers the Marquis de Sade - probably the most infamous person in the entire history of infamy - and the young lady of fifteen, when she has finished the free love discussion in the Telegraph, turns to her ma and says, "Mamma, dear, who was the Marquis de Sade that they are talking about in connection with these Whitechapel murders?" Mamma probably asks papa, and papa is quite possibly as ignorant as the police; but inquiry begets inquiry, and a great moral pestilence once more sweeps over the surface of society, and leaves its traces upon this generation.

Lest I should be accused of doing myself that which I blame in others, let me come to my point, which is that we are in very grave danger of an epidemic of butchery. The minute details given by the papers of the hideous mutilation of the last Whitechapel victim only repel a certain class - a very much larger class is fascinated by them. The public mind becomes familiarised with the details of outrage, and is literally saturated with blood. We shall begin to expect too much from our murderers by-and-by, and an ordinary crime will pass without recognition. On the whole, there is good reason to look upon the Whitechapel horrors as national misfortunes, coming as they do in the middle of the silly season, when the papers are glad to fill up with anything - blood for choice. Better a whole year of the Failure of Marriage than a week of the Success of Murder and Mutilation.

Thank goodness! There is a little bit of blue sky visible at last. "The police believe that they are now on the track of the murderer." Bless them! it would be cruel to undeceive them or to shatter their childlike and innocent faith in themselves. Let them go on believing that they are on the track of the murderer. Where ignorance is bliss, 'tis folly to be wise.

ON THE TRACK

The summer had come in September at last,
And the pantomime season was coming on fast,
When a score of detectives arrived from the Yard
To untangle a skein which was not very hard.
They looked very wise, and they started a clue;
They twiddled their thumbs as the best thing to do.
They said, "By this murder we're taken aback,
But we're now, we believe, on the murderer's track."
They scattered themselves o'er the face of the land -
A gallant, devoted, intelligent band -
They arrested their suspects north, east, south, and west;
From inspector to sergeant each man did his best.
They took up a bishop, they took up a Bung,
They arrested the old, they arrested the young;
They ran in Bill, Thomas, and Harry and Jack,
Yet still they remained on the murderer's track.

The years passed away and the century waned,
A mystery still the big murder remained.
It puzzled the Bar and it puzzled the Bench,
It puzzled policemen, Dutch, German, and French;
But 'twas clear as a pikestaff to all London 'tecs,
Who to see through a wall didn't want to wear specs.
In reply to the sneer and the snarl and the snack
They exclaimed, "We are still on the murderer's track."
They remained on his track till they died of old age,
And the story was blotted from history's page;
But they died like detectives convinced that the crime
They'd have traced to its source if they'd only had time.
They made a good end, and they turned to the wall
To answer the Great First Commissioner's call;
And they sighed as their breathing grew suddenly slack -
"We believe we are now on the murderer's track."
Leather Apron has suddenly had to take a back seat. Harry the Hawker and Ted Stanley have come to the front instead.
There is not the slightest truth in the rumour that the police are of opinion that the murder of Major Barttelot in Central Africa is also the work of the Whitechapel miscreant. On inquiry at Scotland-yard this morning, our reporter was informed that the Stanley mentioned in the telegram which brings the news of the gallant major's untimely fate is not the Ted Stanley referred to at the Whitechapel inquest.
HUSH!
There isn't much to talk about -
We live in dullish times;
The only things the newsboys shout
Are these Whitechapel crimes.
The Tories one and all agree
The fiend who'd make Hyde blush,
And does the deeds is Mr.--
There's someone listening - hush!
Some time ago a merry dame,
Who'd worn two wedding-rings,
Desired once more at love's bright flame
To singe her ample wings.
To shyly wed a lad she chose,
Society to "rush,"
She was the Duchess of--
There's someone listening - hush!
The duke has had his willful whim,
And Wimbledon must go;
Our Volunteers now, thanks to him,
Have had a smashing blow.
He's thrown the splendid movement back,
In spite of all his gush;
I think ought to have the --
There's someone listening - hush!
Of all the papers published now,
In all the kingdoms three,
There is not one but has to bow
Before the --
Of all the writers, you can bet
(I see his pale face flush),
The nicest one is --

There's someone listening hush!

Sept.23, 1888.

The police are still on the track of the Whitechapel lady-killer, and several really remarkable clues have been obtained and followed up. The wrong man has not been arrested this week quite so frequently as he was last, and there are undoubted signs that "a clue" has at last rewarded the efforts of the police authorities. In fact, there is rather an embarrass de richesses in the matter of clues, as the reader will readily imagine when he peruses the following, which are carefully selected from the published list as per the daily morning and evening Press.

THE WHITECHAPEL MURDERS. -SOME IMPORTANT CLUES.

Some ten years ago it has transpired that a man in Scotch attire used to stand outside a tobacconist's shop in the Whitechapel-road. He was generally to be seen in the act of taking a pinch of snuff The police have had their attention called to the fact that this Scotchman has mysteriously disappeared, and they are making inquiries with regard to him, as they consider it quite possible that he may be the Whitechapel murderer.

A man was seen on Monday evening last in High-street, Camden Town, evidently in a state of considerable excitement. A lady who was passing at the time thinks she saw a knife up his sleeve, but she is not sure. The police are following up this clue to the Whitechapel murderer with the greatest caution, and from their reticence it is evident that they attach considerable importance to the facts brought to light.

A boy of twelve years old, living at Slush-in-the-Marsh, has, it is stated, told his grandmother that one of the boys at the national school told him that he believed that the schoolmaster, who had recently given him a severe whipping, was the Whitechapel murderer. The grandmother at once communicated with the local police, and the local inspector left at once for Scotland-yard. After a long and earnest consultation with the heads of departments, several Scotland-yard detectives returned with the local inspector to Slush-in-the-Marsh, where they are prosecuting the most rigid inquiries. It is believed that a genuine clue to the Whitechapel murders has at last been obtained.

A well-known dramatic author has, it is understood, been placed under close police surveillance, although the fact is not generally known. It has transpired that one evening last week he was heard at the club to remark that the Whitechapel murders wouldn't make a good play. "It's not the sort of murder that goes," he said. "I've often done murders of that sort, but I've never found them answer. When I kill a woman I do it better than that - more effectually." The police are not inclined to give any information to our reporter; but from certain facts which have transpired, it is evident that they have now a definite clue to the mystery which has for so long a time enshrouded the metropolis in gloom.

Should any new clues arrive before we go to press we shall not fail to place them at the disposal of the public. The statement that the police believe the Whitechapel murders to have been committed by a baboon which recently escaped from a ship in the East India Docks is authoritatively denied, but Sir Charles Warren is understood to have said that it wanted Edgar Allan Poe at the yard to give them something to work on.

A great many letter writers in the daily papers are pointing the lesson of the Whitechapel horrors, and endeavouring to attract public attention to the conditions under which the East-end poor live. Under any civilised conditions it would have been impossible for these monstrous crimes to have been committed one after the other in the heart of a densely-populated neighbourhood. In a series of articles which I wrote some years ago, I described these back yards and the lawless scenes which went on in them night after night, and I explained why the inhabitants took no notice and in no way resented the intrusion of bad characters of both sexes upon their premises. I called attention then to the evil which would certainly result to children reared amid scenes of violence and vice, and familiarised with everything that was loathsome and criminal from their earliest infancy. In "How the Poor Live," these murders which are now horrifying London were clearly foreshadowed. I have no wish to dwell on the subject, and I only refer to it now as others have taken it up as though it were quite new, and as it will probably be the means of starting a fresh nine days' crusade against the plague spots of "Horrible London."

Oct. 7, 1888.

JACK THE RIPPER is the hero of the hour. A gruesome wag, a grim practical joker, has succeeded in getting an enormous amount of fun out of a postcard which he sent to the Central News. The fun is all his own, and nobody shares in it, but he must be gloating demonically at the present moment at the state of perturbation in which he has flung the public mind. Grave journals have reproduced the sorry jest, and have attempted to seriously argue that the awful Whitechapel fiend is the idle and mischievous idiot who sends blood-stained postcards to the news agency. Of course the whole business is a farce. The postcard is an elaborately-prepared hoax. To imagine a man deliberately murdering and mutilating women, and then confessing the deed on a postcard, is to turn Mr. W. S. Gilbert loose upon the Whitechapel murders at once.

Everybody has a private theory of his own with regard to these crimes, and naturally I have mine. In all probability mine is as idiotic as the coroner's. But this is such an unpleasant subject - it is becoming such a dangerous subject - that I will spare the public my private views upon the matter, and try and get to something more cheerful as speedily as possible. Bloodshed always has an immense fascination for ordinary mortals. Murders and battles are the things to hurl the circulation of a newspaper sky high, and the Whitechapel lady-killer's essays in lightning surgery have become as a boon and a blessing to men of the Press, who were weary of concocting in the office letters on various subjects of domestic interest, and trying to make them look like genuine outside contributions.

I have said that this series of murders is a dangerous subject to discuss, and I honestly think so. The enormous publicity and the sensational turn given to these atrocities are bound to effect the public mind, and give ill-balanced brains an inclination towards bloodshed. There will be for some time an epidemic of savage butchery, and the unfortunate women who have furnished the lightning anatomist with his subjects will be especially liable to murderous attack.

Jack the Ripper - now that Leather Apron has retired Jack is the hero of the situation - has already fired the imagination of a vast number of idiots and ruffians. Men with knives in their hands, threatening to "rip" a lady, are to be heard of all over the country already. In the police reports such cases, especially in the provinces, are as thick as blackberries on a September hedgerow. Or should it be October, and are the blackberries in my neighbourhood specially backward? I have been waiting for a blackberry pudding for weeks, and can't get one. If you never tried a blackberry pudding do so at once. Put a little apple in it, mind - that brings the flavour of the blackberries out. Blackberry jelly is also worth living for. The mulberries in my garden are as backward as the blackberries on my hedges. I am passionately fond of mulberries - in fact, I was mark - Dear me, dear me, how my pen does run away with me!- as if anybody cared about these little personal details. It is all my vanity. I don't think so myself, but that is what I have heard. I cannot, however, leave the question of mulberries without asking you if you ever tasted mulberry gin. If you have not, you should at once repair the error of your youth. I will tell you how to make it at the very first opportunity. I have kept Jack the Ripper waiting for a long time now, and that is not polite. I like to be polite to everyone, even to Jack.

Not only has Ripperism been put extensively into practice, but vast numbers have yielded to its fascinations in theory. The newspapers, ever ready to take occasion by the hand and make the bounds of fooldom wider yet, have allowed Colney Hatch, Hanwell, and Earlswood to empty the vials of idiocy upon the head of the general reader. Every crackpot in the kingdom who has a whim, a fad, a monomania, a crotchet, or a bee in his bonnet is allowed to inflict it upon the public under the heading of "The East-end Horrors." It is impossible to read the puerile twaddle, the utterly inconsequent nonsense which is served up in a mixed heap for our breakfast every morning in the D.T. without feeling that England is indeed in danger. Any country inhabited by a race which could write such letters and make such suggestions as those which appear in the Telegraph would be in danger. The School Board has much to answer for. Many people foresaw a danger in placing the pen within the reach of everyone. It was felt that the indiscriminate use of a weapon far more dangerous than the revolver, far more murderous than Jack the Ripper's knife, would lead to much discomfort and confusion; but the greatest pessimist among the anti-educationists never imagined that the great newspaper Press of the country would make itself a dustbin for the reception of the waste scribble of irresponsible frivolity and bumptious ignorance.

One point in connection with the murders, and the revelations of life in the common lodging-houses and the courts and alleys of the slums, which has been of strong personal interest to me, is the way in which the Continental Press, in commenting upon the murders, have quoted from "How the Poor Live" and "Life Dramas of the London Poor." I had no idea that these articles had circulated much beyond the English-speaking countries. I was, therefore, somewhat surprised when the Press Cutting Agency forwarded me many leading articles from French, German, Italian, and Belgian papers, in each of which long extracts were given from my articles. The Journal des Debats, in fact, devotes a special article to "How the Poor Live" itself - which will, no doubt, send up the sale of the French translation tremendously. As there is not only a French, but also a German and Italian, translation in existence, the ill wind of Whitechapel would have blown me some good had the foreign publishers recognised my rights - which, alas! they have not done. By the cruel irony of fate, the murders, while sending up my book, have knocked down a play in which I am interested. "The Golden Ladder" at the Pavilion did pantomime business for a fortnight. Then came the Saturday night double butchery, and on Monday Mr. Isaac Cohen felt "worried" as he missed the usual rush at the extra door. There were plenty of men, but hardly a single female. The ladies were one and all panic-stricken, and didn't relish the idea of having to be out after dark. The Spring-Heeled Jack scare of the good old times had been suddenly revived. However, by Wednesday the scare had somewhat subsided, and the ladies of the East flocked out once more, under the protecting wing of husband, brother, and sweetheart, to see "The Golden Ladder."

More "personal journalism," I hear the carping critic cry - more self-advertisement. To tell the honest truth, the hero of the hour is such a remarkably unpleasant person that I feel inclined to think that I myself "Moi-meme," may be a relief. It is possible that there may be human beings so depraved in their tastes that they would rather read about Jack the Ripper than DAGONET; but, even if such there be, I do not think that I am bound to cater specially for them.

The fact that the self-postcard-proclaimed assassin sent his imitation blood-besmeared communication to the Central News people opens up a wide field for theory. How many among you, my dear readers, would have hit upon the idea of "the Central News" as a receptacle for your confidence? You might have sent your joke to the Telegraph, the Times, any morning or any evening paper, but I will lay long odds that it would never have occurred to communicate with a Press agency. Curious, is it not, that this maniac makes his communication to an agency which serves the entire Press? It is an idea which might occur to a Pressman perhaps; and even then it would probably only occur to someone connected with the editorial department of a newspaper, someone who knew what the Central News was, and the place it filled in the business of news supply. This proceeding on Jack's part betrays an inner knowledge of the newspaper world which is certainly surprising. Everything therefore points to the fact that the jokist is professionally connected with the Press. And if he is telling the truth and not fooling us, then we are brought face to face with the fact that the Whitechapel murders have been committed by a practical journalist - perhaps by a real live editor! Which is absurd, and at that I think I will leave it.

There is no getting away from the aroma of the knife. I put in a day at Kempton Park on Friday just to study the subject of horse-racing and betting, to which the Church Congress has this week drawn attention. Received with charming and gracious hospitality by Mr, George Everitt, smiled upon by Judge Lawley, and welcomed back to the turf with open arms by the merry metallicians, I strolled about the enclosure and the paddock, enjoyed the excellent music and the glorious sunshine, let the pure breezes play upon my pallid cheeks, and forgot that I was on a racecourse until a fiend in human guise came up and whispered in my ear, "There's a real good thing for the last race - back Assassin."

Assassin! An Assassin at Kempton Park. I shuddered audibly, and replied, "I suppose that's the Whitechapel tip." "Well," replied my friendly counsellor, who was a well-known M. P., "I don't know about Whitechapel, but this Assassin is a Ripper." And he was, for he won in ripping style, "Squire" Abington up; and as the gay and aristocratic company filed off the course, under a lowering sky, everywhere one heard, "Assassin! Assassin! Good old Assassin!"

THE BLOODHOUNDS. - (BY A LUNATIC LAUREATE)

The brow of Sir Charles it was gloomy and sad,
He was slapped by the Tory and kicked by the Rad.;
His inspectors were all of them down in the dumps,
And his staff of detectives were clean off their chumps.
The populace clamoured without in the yard
For Matthews, Home Sec., to be feathered and tarred;
When Matthews peeped out of a window hard by,
And grinned at the mob with a leer in his eye.
"Do something - do something!" Lord Salisbury cried
"We've done all we can!" Worried Warren replied;
"We keep on arresting as fast as we can,
And we hope soon or late we shall get the right man."
Then, goaded by taunts to the depths of despair,
The poor First Commissioner tore at his hair,
And fell upon Matthews's breast with a sob -
But the Whitechapel Vampire was still on the job.
At last when the city was maddened with fears,
And the Force had dissolved into impotent tears,
A sweet little boy who had dog stories read
Put the bloodhound idea in C.W.'s head.
They brought of him bloodhounds the best to be found,
And the "tecs" and the dogs sought the murderer's ground;
Then the bow-wows were loosed, and with noses to earth
They trotted away 'mid the bystanders' mirth.
The bloodhounds ran east, and the bloodhounds ran west,
Enjoying the sport with an infinite zest;
The bloodhounds ran north, and the bloodhounds ran south,
While Matthews looked on with a wide-open mouth.
"Good heavens!" he cried, "are you dotty, Sir Charles?"
As a hound smelt his calf with two ominous snarls.
"Is it possible you, with your stern common sense,
Believe in this melodramatic pretence?"
But he followed the bloodhounds - he'd sworn that he would
While Sir Charles ran beside them as well as he could;
And so Warren and Matthews, though both out of breath,
Ran about with the hounds to be in at the death.
They followed to Clapham, they followed to Kew;
Away through the streets of Whitechapel they flew.
They dodged in and out of the slums of St. Giles,
And they followed the hounds for some hundreds of miles.
They followed in 'buses, they followed in trams;
Our Charles was all groans, and our Matthews all "damns."
They dodged into houses, they popped into shops,
They jumped over hedges, and damaged the crops.
The bloodhounds grew gay with the fun of the chase,
And they ran like two thoroughbreds running a race;
They leaped o'er the wall, and they swam o'er the stream,

Their tongues lolling out and their eyeballs agleam.
But Warren and Matthews kept up with them still
They followed through valley, they followed o'er hill;
Then darkness came down, and afar in the haze
Hounds, Warren, and Matthews were lost to our gaze.
And never since then, though they're much overdue,
Have those hounds or officials returned to our view;
But a legend relates that in lands far away
They are still running on in pursuit of their prey.
And at eve, when the citizens gather to drink,
They speak of the lost ones, and say, with a wink,
"'Twas an excellent thing to put hounds on the track,
Since it took off two men who are not wanted back."

This (Saturday) morning the Daily Telegraph solves the great mystery. It publishes a portrait of the Duke of Portland as that of the man who was seen hanging around Whitechapel and talking to a lady on the night of the murder. His grace will doubtless feel flattered at the delicate attention. The other portrait, said to be of the same man, is not the duke, but Albert Edward. This guesswork portraiture of murderers is rather dangerous. The portrait is bound to be like somebody, and the somebody it is like will have a bad time. What with bloodhounds and fancy portraits and facsimile postcards and female charms and legs and arms lying about in the country in picturesque confusion, things are getting a bit mixed in the old country, and the emigration returns ought to go up rapidly.

Everybody is on the private detective lay now. In the railway, on the tram, in the omnibus, at the restaurant, in the street, everybody looks at everybody else, and wonders if the other man is the Blanca Cappella Assassino. Several people have looked at me lately in a way I don't like, and the other evening, in Oxford-street, a bloodhound, followed by Sir Charles Warren and Mr. Matthews, came and walked around me, and growled, and evidently had doubts about my moral character. However, as the police seem to be doing their arresting in a systematic manner, by taking up everybody in turn and then letting them go again, nobody will be very much astonished if the next gentleman locked up on suspicion of being Leather Apron, Jack the Ripper, Alaska the Malay, the American-German-English medical student, slaughterman, baker, Texan Ranger, ship's cook, religious enthusiast, specimen collector for a medical work, pigsticker, and lady killer, is DAGONET.

Oct. 21, 1888.

It is a relief to turn from this spectacle of German and English doctors playing at king of the castle on the body of the dead Kaiser to the more wholesome atmosphere of Whitechapel. Last Saturday night, having a holiday, I spent it there, in the hope that I should be able to work up a nice picturesque article, entitled "A Night with Jack the Ripper," and to wind up with the announcement that I had caught him and handed him over to justice. I have all along had the idea that it would be a magnificent advertisement for me to run "the Terror" to earth. Imagine the sensation which would be created when Monday's contents-bill displayed in huge letters, "The Whitechapel Murderer Captured by DAGONET. Fearful Struggle. Heroic Conduct of the Captor. Message from the Queen."

I cannot tell you exactly when this idea came into my mind, but I know that when it did get there it hung up its hat behind the door as though it meant to stay. It was ever present by day, and by night it haunted my dreams. A secret voice seemed to whisper to me, "Go to Whitechapel. Who knows but that you really may succeed in catching Jack!" The presentiment that I was to be the means of laying Jack by the heels and earning the gratitude of the police and the public grew so strong upon me that last Saturday night, having ascertained that Jack had sent a postcard to the authorities, informing them that he meant to do two more murders, I determined to turn amateur detective and go upon the war-path. And with this explanation of how I came to spend last Saturday night in Whitechapel, I must ask the reader to accept my assurance that every word which now follows is strictly true. It is no exaggeration - no effort of the imagination. It is a solid and sober statement of facts.

I left home at nine in the evening, dressed as a ship's engineer, accompanied by Albert Edward, who was made up as a foreign sailor. It was nearly ten when we arrived in Whitechapel, and we had no sooner turned into the murder district than we found things remarkably lively. Once or twice, as we walked along, we spotted the private detectives and amateur policemen, who were out on the same job as ourselves. Most of them eyed Albert Edward rather suspiciously, and I must confess they had reason, for a more villainous-looking foreign sailor I never saw in my life. He looked capable of all the murders that have ever been committed and a good many that haven't been thought of yet.

We had not been surveying the busy scene many minutes - what a scene Whitechapel-road is on Saturday night! - before we heard a cry, and instantly there was a rush towards a gateway. It was only two ladies quarrelling; but as we hurried up a small boy saluted us with a grin and exclaimed, "'Ere ye har, guv'nor! This way to the murder! Triple murder up this court!" There was a roar of laughter, and, the true state of the case being ascertained, the crowd dispersed. The border line between the horrible and the grotesque has grown very fine in Whitechapel of late. There has probably been a revulsion of feeling, and the inhabitants have relieved their overstrained nerves by laughing. Certainly last Saturday night, although another murder was confidently expected, the general body of sightseers and pedestrians were making light of the matter. Along the pavement, which for many a mile is hedged with shooting-galleries and various arrangements based upon the six-throws-a-penny principle, plenty of hoarse-voiced ruffians were selling a penny puzzle in which the puzzle was to find Jack the Ripper. Jack was upon every tongue, male and female, last Saturday night. The costermonger hawking his goods dragged him in; the quack doctor assured the crowd that his marvellous medicine would cure even Jack of his evil propensities; and at the penny shows, outside which the most ghastly pictures of "the seven victims," all gashes and crimson drops were exhibited, the proprietors made many a facetious reference to the local Terror.

Just past the Pavilion Theatre we came on a gentleman who was standing in the roadway and banging on an empty bloater-box with a big stick. As soon as he had obtained an audience he delivered himself as follows:- Tennybrooze! Tennybrooze! If there's any gent as was here when I give Tennybrooze for the Seesirwitch I'd be werry much obliged if he'd come forward. I give everyone as bought my enverlope Tennybrooze when he was 20 to 1, and now I've got another enverlope 'ere what's got the winner of the Cambridge. If there's anyone as 'ears my voice ternite as was here when I give it, he'll p'raps say so. I haint Duglis 'All, and I haint Jack Dickinson, but my brother's the 'ead jockey in a big racin' stable, and my infermation's the best as money can buy, though I sell it in Whitechapel for a penny. I belong to Whitechapel, and I like to do my neighbours a good turn. I hain't Johnny the Ripper. I'm Johnny the Tipper. (Roars of laughter in the crowd.) Yus; Johnny the Tipper, what give yer Tennybrooze; and here I've got the winner of the Cambridge at 20 to 1, and it's one penny.

Johnny the Tipper then went round with his envelopes, but evidently he hadn't a racing audience, for the sale was slack, and, cursing his "blooming luck," Johnny put his hands in his pockets and took the certain winner of "the Cambridge" off with him to another pitch. I'm afraid he hadn't backed his Cesarewitch tip for himself, as he was in the last state of raggedness, and as he turned away I heard him mutter that he'd been out six hours and hadn't earned his "doss" yet.

As soon as the humours of Whitechapel had begun to pall we left the main thoroughfare, and plunged into the back streets and labyrinthine network of courts and alleys. We visited the spots where the murders were committed, and about midnight we had Buck's-row entirely to ourselves. How on earth a murder was committed here without attracting the slightest attention is a great mystery. The houses are so close to the spot - there are so many chances against a secret crime being committed - the place was such an unlikely one for a deliberate assassin to select! Albert Edward and I tried to work the murder out and get a theory, but we failed utterly. We, however, attracted attention. When we next visited Buck's-row there was not a soul in sight. We had not stopped by the gate where the murder was committed two seconds before a dozen people were about us as if by magic. Two policemen came up, goodness knows where from, and flashed their lanterns on us, and the rest of the company, who were evidently amateur watchmen, eyed us suspiciously. A few words to the constables satisfied them as to the nature of our business, and we were allowed to pass; but everywhere we went that night in the hope of dropping on Jack the Ripper we found that the police were on the alert, and that plenty of amateur detectives were hiding round the corners. From personal observation, I should say that there was not a corner of Whitechapel, no matter how obscure, that was left unwatched last Saturday night. All night long the police were about, and we saw them come again and again, and enter dark passages, and turn their bull's-eyes on to dark corners. If Jack had tried another experiment last Saturday, it would have been almost impossible for him to get away. Probably he knew it; at any rate, he didn't come near enough for any of us to put the salt upon his tail with which we were all provided.

Soon after midnight the principal thoroughfares in Whitechapel began to clear rapidly. The stalls packed up, the shops closed, and the people went to their homes. The ladies, I noticed, who were out late walked in twos and threes. At midnight we were outside a public-house not far from Mitre-square, and we noticed the men as they came out got together and walked towards home in company. One lady's pal lingered behind to talk to another lady. Her lady friend, who was waiting, called out, "Come on, Sylviar - I'm frightened! Let's git 'ome!" Sylvia replied, "All right, Liz, I'll see as Jack don't have yer." And then Sylvia came along, and, with a passing compliment to Albert Edward, joined her friend and went off. She was not at all the sort of lady whose name you would guess to be Sylvia.

We stayed in Whitechapel till three in the morning. We crept into back yards, and we hid ourselves down side streets; we adventured ourselves into some of the most lonely and desolate-looking spots it has ever been my lot to witness; but we never remained long in undisputed possession. A policeman was on to us directly. I can bear personal testimony to the marvellous vigilance exercised by Sir Charles Warren's merry men on that Saturday night at least. At three o'clock in the morning we agreed that there was no chance of getting Jack that night, and, after a little friendly converse with a policeman or two, we turned our weary steps towards home. I must confess that I was disappointed. I had quite made up my mind that Albert Edward and myself were to be heroes by Sunday morning. I had arranged it all. The moment we saw Jack, Albert Edward was to spring on him and hold him, while I went off for a policeman. I had my notebook and a freshly-sharpened lead pencil all ready to do a special there and then for Sunday's Referee. And, instead of waking up the following morning a hero, I woke up with a dreadful headache, and a fixed determination not to play at being an amateur detective again. There are too many of them about just now for the game to pay.

The papers are lively reading again. What with the Bye-bye Boss gentleman who is giving the Vigilance Committee beans - kidney beans - and the doctors who are dissecting the Emperor Frederick over and over again on our breakfast-tables, there is a rare healthy atmosphere around Press literature. A good, thorough, go-ahead non-compromising Dare-Devil Dick or Sixteen-String Jack or Sweeney Todd feuilleton is alone wanting to complete the picture. Apropos to pictures, something like a shudder ran through society when the D.T. began to give illustrations of the late Kaiser's inside. It was felt that we were standing with trembling feet on the frontier of an unknown territory. Once let anatomical illustrations be accepted by the public as part of its breakfast-table literature, and there is no knowing to what empyrean heights or infernal depths the genius of popular journalism might not wing its flight. For days after that awful picture spoiled my breakfast, and sent me to the chemist's, I opened my D.T. with fear and trembling. I had an idea that I might come suddenly upon the "remains" of Whitehall, or fragments of Buck's-row and Mitre-square. Thank goodness, there has been no repetition of the anatomical illustration, and I understand that there is not likely to be. For which let us all be devoutly thankful.

Nov.18, 1888.

The resignation of Sir Charles Warren has given rise to a good deal of discussion which is about as wide of the mark as it could well be. The incident is in no way connected with the question of Sir Charles's fitness or unfitness for his post. It has been brought about not by a difference of opinion between Sir Charles and the public, but by a difference of opinion between Sir Charles and Mr. Matthews on a question of professional etiquette. Sir Charles has retired from the office of Chief Commissioner because Mr. Matthews wrote him a rude letter because he disapproved of Sir Charles writing articles in a monthly magazine. That is Murray's guide to the situation, and you have it in a nutshell.

Personally, I thought at the time Sir Charles was appointed that he was too good a soldier to be a good policeman. He had, in my opinion, certain strong characteristics which would handicap him in his new office. Refereaders will not need to be reminded that I freely expressed my views on the subject both at the time he was summoned home from the Soudan and subsequently. When the Trafalgar-square troubles commenced, and a certain school of politicians (the word covers a multitude of sins) tried to set the mob against the police, I felt that it would be assisting the agitation if I helped to swell the chorus of Sir Charles's detractors. In dealing with the grave danger which threatened London the soldierly qualities of the Chief Commissioner's were invaluable. It was a soldier that was wanted, for something like civil war had passed the confines of the possible and was entering the territory of the probable. Now that Sir Charles has resigned his office, I am not inclined to join in the chorus of jubilation which his enemies are uttering over his retirement. I content myself with expressing a hope that the new Chief Commissioner may possess all Sir Charles's good qualities, and be in addition a practical policeman.

Mr. Matthews, the official who has succeeded in unseating Sir Charles, is probably the most exasperating person who ever reigned at the Home Office. His very description is a misnomer, for he is a Secretary who is never at home on any question, but always very much abroad. In the art of rubbing the public up the wrong way he never had an equal. He enjoys the unenviable distinction of being cordially detested by all political parties, and the supporters of the Government to which he belongs are quite as disgusted with him as are the supporters of the Opposition. Why Lord Salisbury still retains him is a mystery, unless it be that the generally astute marquis is anxious to let him have every inch of the rope with which he has for so long a time past been making experiments in self-strangulation.

We have not many days set apart as public festivals and periods of national rejoicing, but the happy day on which Mr. Matthews is dismissed or resigns should certainly be one of them. Sinbad, relieved of the Old Man of the Sea, whose cruel legs were wound about his neck, executed, according to the original text of "The Arabian Nights," the wildest sailor's hornpipe of delight that the world had ever witnessed. John Bull, with Matthews off his back, ought to do a dance that will live for ever in the annals of saltatory prowess.

A PARADOX.
Sir Charles at last throws up the sponge,
He yields to Matthews' latest lunge;
The latter says, with angry spite,
Sir Charles did wrong when he did write.

I have seen a courteous letter from the Lord Mayor, in which his lordship states that his speech at the lighting-up dinner has been misquoted. He did not use the words attributed to him with regard to "consulting the Almighty," and he is anxious that it should be known that he did not. I have much pleasure in making the correction, and in wishing his lordship a happy and prosperous mayoralty.

The evidence in the latest Whitechapel atrocity is worth more than passing study, especially to the few innocent people still inhabiting the earth who read history and believe it, or who accept as strongly impregnated with fact the foreign intelligence as served up by the Press. Mary Jane Kelly was well known to her neighbours. Some of them who knew her, and were in the habit of talking to her, were called at the inquest to certify as to her movements on the night of the crime. It is beyond doubt that the woman was murdered during the night, but witnesses who knew her were found to come forward and swear that they spoke to her and had detailed conversations with her several hours after she had been murdered and mutilated. At least half-a-dozen stories, all diametrically opposed to each other, were told of her movements on the preceding evening, and the man who was seen to accompany her home was, according to the evidence collected by the police, a tall, sandy-whiskered man of rough appearance; a short man of German appearance; a gentleman with a black bag and moustache; a foreign-looking man with a brown paper parcel under his arm; a swell, with spats on his boots, a gold watch-chain, and an astrachan collar to his overcoat; a blotchy-faced fellow, who looked like a labourer; and an elderly, respectable-looking man with the appearance of a clergyman.

With this wide field of contradictory statements to contend with in a matter which was practically under the witnesses' own noses, how can we ever believe a millionth part of the statements with regard to events and occurrences which come to us from far away or from a distant date? To get at the actual facts of anything nowadays seems to be as hopeless a task as discovering the exact whereabouts of the North Pole.

With every fresh outburst of horror caused by a fresh murder, the theorists rush to the front to air their remarkable theories. Some of the most remarkable go to the police and never reach the columns of the ever-enterprising Press. If the letters which the police have received come to be published, they would at once lead to an earnest public discussion as to the advisability of building a few hundred extra lunatic asylums, and of insisting upon the contractors working on at night by the aid of the electric light in order to have them completed as soon as possible. Many well-known persons have been named to the police by gratuitous informers as the real original Jack the Ripper. One earnest citizen is convinced that a nobleman whose name he mentions in committing these crimes because his wife ran away with a paramour; another gives the name of a well-known Social Purity advocate in confidence, and declares that there are blood-stains still on his doorstep. But perhaps the most remarkable piece of evidence is that of a laundress, who forwards a pair of cuffs, and says:- "Sir Charles Warren. - Sir, - These cuffs come in the washin from Mr. ~ (name and address given). "There is a stain on them which looks like blood. He is a queer-looking man, my dorter says, as she has seen him when calling for the bill, and is wife is a inverlid. If he is not the Whitechapel murderer, please return, as I do not want to be mix up in the affair. P.S. - If the rewarde is pade, I hope I shall have my rites."

Everyone has, of course, by this time heard the absurd and utterly idiotic idea that the unhappy Matthews is really Jack, and that is why he refused to offer a reward. This is only a fair specimen of the utter twaddle which the murders have given rise to. Up to the present the Archbishop of Canterbury has not been mentioned, but there is no knowing what the latest rumour, that a suspicious-looking clergyman has been seen about Dorset-square, may give rise to. My own opinion (perhaps as mad as those I have ridiculed) is that when - if ever - the culprit is arrested, he will be found to be a man who resides in the locality, or whose business brings him there, that his calling is one which has familiarised him with the sight of blood, and that most probably he has had frequent opportunity of witnessing the dissection of human bodies. He is a man who lives either in lodgings or in one of the numerous flats in the neighbourhood by himself, and is enabled to let himself in at any hour without attracting attention. The neighbourhood of his crimes has not been selected hap-hazard, but because he has been familiar with it for some years, and he is thoroughly acquainted with the habits and haunts of his victims.

The probabilities are that the monster known as Jack the Ripper is at the present moment living in the calm and peaceable enjoyment of his quiet lodging or flat, within one mile of the scene of his exploits. He is not a man who uses common lodging-houses; he is not a sailor who has to go on board his ship to sleep; he does not apply for a bed at coffee-houses, and he does not have to take a long walk to disappear after his work is done. In either of these cases the chances are a million to one that he would have been spotted by someone and connected with the crimes in consequence of the peculiarity of his conduct or of his appearance. He is probably a man of the type of the Alton murderer, who, after butchering a little girl in the most awful manner, entered in his diary against the date, "Killed a little girl - nice and warm." This form of mania takes a fierce delight in the sight of blood, and is a form that is well known to experts in criminal cases. Such a man, for example, was Dr. Tardieu, of Paris. The man's face would betray him to an expert. The features in most of these bloodthirsty maniacs are peculiar - especially the mouth, the chin, and the eyes. If you look at a collection of the photographs of criminals of the Alton type (I had such a collection myself for years, and it only got scattered by friends borrowing one or two and forgetting to return them), you will see at once what I mean.

If a thorough and searching inquiry were made among the unfortunate women of the neighbourhood of the murders, it would be found that many of them know a man of this type (let the police show them a photograph or two of the Alton kind), and it will be found that many of them have seen him lately, and probably been spoken to by him. It was a man of exactly this type, I gather from the slight description (peculiar looking), who spoke to the Kennedys on the night of the last murder. Once fix this point and the police can narrow their search, for they will know the description and type of man for whom they must look.

The man who is wanted has a mouth, a chin, and a pair of eyes which are characteristic of nearly all "blood maniacs" - the expression will do for lack of a better. This fact once understood and appreciated by the police and the unfortunates who are likely to furnish Jack the Ripper with his next victim, the chances of his discovery are increased a thousand-fold. If the Continental system of regulation was pursued, such a series of butcheries would have been impossible - the whole body of unfortunates would have been a huge vigilance committee, under police direction, on the look-out for the monster directly his first murder had been committed.

As it is, it is to the unfortunate class that the police should look for the capture. The difficulty is to get them together to give them the little lesson in physiognomy which will enable them to detect Jack the Ripper at once, and lure him into the arms of the police.

This man is a murderer not for a reason, but by instinct. And an instinct of this sort is always shown in the features. Jack murders and mutilates exactly as another man goes to the theatre or the music-hall, pour so distraire.

Endeavouring to escape from the suicidal mania engendered by Thursday's weather, I rushed to divert my thoughts at a railway bookstall. The first thing which attracted my attention was a book on the white cover of which was the smear of a bloody hand. I discovered afterwards that it was a Christmas annual. Poor old Christmas! We shall have the proprietors of an illustrated paper presenting a portrait of Jack the Ripper with their Christmas supplement by-and-by.

Dec. 2, 1888.

MONRO is not a good name for the jokists or the comic poets. Henderson rather bothered these gentry, and it must have been after an enormous expenditure of thought which might have been devoted to a better cause that one burst out:-

"For beer she wished to send her son,
The pubs were closed by Henderson."

When Colonel Henderson was rioted out of office, and Sir Charles Warren came from the Soudan to take his place, a few feeble attempts were made to say that his appointment was Warren-ted by the circumstances, and slanting allusions were made to the home of the rabbit; but as a peg on which to hang the jocund jape Sir Charles was as dismal a failure as his predecessor

Now comes Mr. Monro, and again the would-be wag receives a facer. Very late on the night of the appointment a Conservative member who had dined well remarked to another, "We Mon-ro in the same boat with him," but the coldness with which the attempt was received caused the other members to put on their overcoats. It is not a name for the jester to juggle with, and the appointment is therefore looked upon with great dissatisfaction by the ever-increasing army of Great Britons who jest at all things, human and divine.

One thing is certain, and that is that a hearty support will be given to the new Commissioner by the friends of law and order, no matter what their political opinions may be. Mr. Monro has a most difficult task before him. He succeeds to office at a time when the East-end Terror is in full swing and the West-end Terror is due according to the almanac, and, unfortunately, he takes the command of a force which has become to a certain extent discontented and disorganised. It is an open secret that between the late First Commissioner and the present there were grave differences of opinion as to the internal management of the police force. The new rule will therefore be marked by a command of "Right about face," and that is in itself an experiment.

MR. MONRO.
The task that's before you's a big one, we know,
          Mr. Monro.
There's the square to defend from Burns, Graham, and Co.,
          Mr. Monro.
Strong signs of fresh mischief the Socialists show,
          Mr. Monro.
Over justice the Ripper continues to crow,
          Mr. Monro.
And the London detective is clumsy and slow,
          Mr. Monro.
Too much time upon drill the policemen bestow,
          Mr. Monro.
If you'd strengthen the force that has fallen so low,
          Mr. Monro.
And give us a little more quid for our quo,
          Mr. Monro.
Then his hat in the air will John Bull for you throw,
          Mr. Monro.
And we'll all be your friends, and you won't have a foe,
          Mr. Monro.
And a deep debt of gratitude London will owe,
          To Mr. Monro.

The Whitechapel murderer, having been arrested all over the metropolis and in several provincial towns, is now putting in an appearance in various foreign countries, and also in the United States of America. He has been identified abroad as a Russian with a religious mania, which takes the form of murdering Magdalens in order that their souls may go to heaven, and the latest New York advices to hand prove - or attempt to prove - that he is a butcher, whose mind is affected by the changes of the moon, and who has been much impressed by reading the book of Ezekiel, c. xxiii, v.25, 26, 33, 34, 46, 47, and 48. The chapter refers to the vicious lives of the sisters Aholah and Aholibah, and verso 25 is the key to the situation: "And I will set my jealousy against thee, and they shall deal furiously with thee: they shall take away thy nose and thine ears; and thy remnant shall fall by the sword." Verse 48 sums up the case: "Thus will I cause lewdness to cease out of the land, that all women may be taught not to do after your lewdness."

This theory, which for purposes of reference may be called "the Ezekiel theory," is probably as near the mark as any of the "guesses at truth" which have been so plentiful of late. A new murder is confidently anticipated by the Vigilance Committee for this (Saturday) night, and extraordinary precautions have been taken to prevent the man who has taken the Book of Ezekiel too literally walking off again.

It would be strange if the accession of Mr. Monro to power was to be signalised by such a universally popular achievement as the arrest of Jack the Ripper. From information which has reached me, I venture to prophesy that such will be the case.

The "Russian" theory of the atrocities is worth thinking-out. The Russians are a sensitive and excitable race, and mental exaltation is not only very common, but it usually borders on insanity. We all have seen how political fanaticism will drive a Nihilist to the commission of murder; but it is not so generally known that religious fervour drives some sects to the most horrible self-mutilation. The Russians are very apt to rush into extremes, and they seem to have an idea that social and eternal salvation can only be obtained by means most repugnant to civilised and well-balanced minds. It is therefore not impossible that the man Vassili, who, about sixteen years ago, murdered a number of women in Paris, and who is reported to have been released from a lunatic asylum last January, may again have thought it his duty to work out the eternal salvation of the wretched East-end women.

It is quite impossible to tell how many secret societies exist in Russia, but that the country swarms with them is an acknowledged fact. The societies are not all political, as the following example will show. Some years ago a great number of murders and robberies were committed in a small town, and all the efforts of the local police to discover the perpetrators were fruitless. At last the Emporer, the father of the present Czar, commanded that some members of his own police should make an investigation. The result was astounding. It was proved that the mayor of the town, the chief of the local police, and a number of the leading tradesmen of the place had all joined into a society with the especial object of committing these murders and robberies, and the society had existed for years! The plunder was paid into the common exchequer, and then divided in shares among the members, who felt almost surprised to hear that what they had been doing was wrong although they knew it to be unlawful.

Oct. 6, 1889.
I sent Albert Edward over the other day to interview the gentleman who has been taking my portrait to newspaper editors and to Dr. Forbes Winslow, and assuring them that it is like Jack the Ripper, and that is the sort of man the police have to look for. I am pleased to learn that the gentleman does not say that I am Jack - but only that he is very like me. The gentleman in question keeps a coffee-stall, and is certain that one night after committing a murder Jack came and refreshed himself at his establishment. His story is very plausible, and there may be something in it, but Ican't say that I feel flattered to learn that the notorious lady-killer is as like me as one Dromio was to the other.
"Me think it was Dagonet!" exclaimed the coffee-stall keeper to Albert Edward; "not likely. Why, Jack the Ripper had three hot pork sausages at my stall, and a cold meat pie. If I'd thought it was DAGONET by the likeness, I should have known it wasn't by the sausages." Certainly the sausages are strong circumstantial evidence in my favour. My digestion has saved my reputation.

Oct.13, 1889.
Poor Mr. Monro has come in for a good deal of abuse lately for leaving undone the things certain people think he ought to have done; but the latest complaint against him is certainly the oddest. The gentleman who recently took my portrait to newspaper editors as that of Jack the Ripper took it also to Scotland-yard, and requested the Chief Commissioner to have facsimiles of it at once struck off and posted all over London. Mr. Monro having failed to comply with this request, is accused of having failed in his duty.
The worthy fellow who has been at so much trouble to hunt up the Whitechapel fiend is, I have no doubt, actuated by the best of motives, but he must have a pretty large bee in his bonnet to imagine that his mild and amiable suggestion would be carried out. If my portrait were stuck about London as the exact counterpart of "Jack the Ripper" - what price me?

March 1, 1891.
The newspapers which, thanks to the outburst of public indignation, found it advisable to leave off trying to hang Sadler for the crimes of Jack the Ripper, without trial, and on the unsworn and inadmissible evidence of his wife, have fallen back upon mysterious hints as to the real Jack being a well-known man. It has been freely stated in more than one serious journal that the police know perfectly well who Jack is, and that they have been shadowing him for years, but have had great difficulty to keep up with him "owing to his frequent visits to the Continent."
When I read this startling piece of news, and in a grave and sober daily, I was, as the old ladies say, "quite taken aback. " Was it possible that - I really hardly like even now to put into cold print the thought that flashed across my mind. And yet why should I not? I can prove an alibi, and I want the fullest inquiry. You have guessed it now. The thought that came like a bolt from the blue and nearly stunned me was that I myself, moi-meme, moi qui vous parle, was the person suspected by the police of being Jack L'Eventreur!
Of course the idea was an absurd one, but it came to me in a very natural way. As a matter of fact, a year or two ago my portrait (the portrait outside the early cheap edition of "The Social Kaleidoscope") was taken to Scotland-yard by a man, and the police were informed that it was an exact likeness of the murderer. The way I got mixed up in the matter was this. An hour or

two after the double murder had been committed on the night of September 30, 1888, a man of strange and wild appearance stopped at a coffee-stall. The coffee-stall keeper (knowing nothing then of the night's tragedy) began to talk about the Whitechapel murder. "I dare say we shall soon hear of another," he said. "Very likely," replied the wild-looking stranger; "perhaps you may hear of two to-morrow morning." He finished his coffee, and as he put the cup down the stall-keeper noticed that his cuffs were blood-stained.

The next morning - or rather, later on that morning - the news of the double murder in Whitechapel fell upon the startled ears of the coffee-stall keeper. "Good Lord!" he exclaimed; "why, that chap last night knew it. He must have been Jack himself!"

Walking along he came to a bookseller's and newsagent's. He looked at the placards, and then his eye suddenly rested on a book in the newsagent's window. Outside that book was a portrait. "Christopher Columbus!" exclaimed the coffee-stall keeper; "why that's the very image of him!" The book was "The Social Kaleidoscope." The astonished stall-keeper bought it, and, later on, when telling his adventures to the police, he produced the book and showed the portrait. Not only was this portrait of me shown to the police, but it was taken by the purchaser to the editor of the New York Herald (London edition), and afterwards to Dr. Forbes Winslow.

The matter came to my knowledge through the courtesy of the Herald editor, and Dr. Forbes Winslow also communicated with me, and I investigated the facts. The coffee-stall keeper, who was interviewed, was perfectly candid and straightforward, and at once explained that he didn't for a moment mean to say that I was his blood-stained customer on the night of the murders. All he meant was that his customer's features were very like mine.

I had forgotten all about the affair until I saw that extraordinary statement in a daily paper this week. Then it all came back to me, and at once the thought suggested itself, "Goodness gracious! is it possible that the police ever had an idea that -" Then I said to myself, "Pshaw!" but that little reference to "his frequent visits to the Continent" set me cogitating again. Fancy if for years the police have been keeping an eye on me, believing that, after all, I am - "O, of course, it is too absurd." But who is this well-known man they do suspect? Who is it that takes frequent trips to the Continent? What if, after all, it should be Lord -- No, that is too ridiculous. Wait a moment. I remember now; it is hinted that he is "a religious enthusiast." I have it. they suspect Mr.--. Does he take trips to the Continent? Yes; you know he went to and to --, and to --. Everybody knows that. But, bless us and save us, it never can be the great Mr. --! It may be Mr. --. He is certainly very fierce on certain matters. But, there, he wouldn't really hurt a fly!

The more I think it over, the greater the fog into which I find myself wandering. Will the police, please, clear up the mystery? Name, gentlemen, please - name!

If accounts of the burial of the Whitechapel victim given in the newspapers be true, the affair was a public scandal. One can forgive the floral decorations, but O, the ginger-beer, the nuts, and the ballads! I for one cannot see where the humanity of making a public spectacle of the murdered woman's funeral comes in. Certainly, the moral lesson it teaches is not visible to the naked eye.

January 22, 1899.

There are bound to be various revelations concerning Jack the Ripper as the years go on. This time it is a vicar who heard his dying confession. I have no doubt a great many lunatics have said they were Jack the Ripper on their death-beds. It is a good exit, and when the dramatic instinct is strong in a man he always wants an exit line, especially when he isn't coming on in the little play of "Life" any more.

I don't want to interfere with this mild little Jack the Ripper boom which the newspapers are playing up in the absence of strawberries and butterflies and good exciting murders, but I don't quite see how the real Jack could have confessed, seeing that he committed suicide after the horrible mutilation of the woman in the house in Dorset-street, Spitalfields. The full details of that crime have never been published - they never could be. Jack, when he committed that crime, was in the last stage of the peculiar mania from which he suffered. He had become grotesque in his ideas as well as bloodthirsty. Almost immediately after this murder he drowned himself in the Thames. his name is perfectly well known to the police. If he hadn't committed suicide he would have been arrested.

February 16, 1902.
The charitable organisation known as the After Care Association is in every way worthy of public support. It takes care mentally deficient patients who are
Discharged from Lunatic Asylums
because they are no longer mad enough to be kept in there. That is to say, it provides supervision and attention for the large class of lunatics who are liable after their release from asylums to be driven mad again by the stress of daily life.
The question of the premature discharge of lunatics is a very serious one. I have been hammering away at it during the whole period of the REFEREE's existence. To this premature discharge are due many of the daily tragedies which startle the newspaper reader. A certain number of homicidal maniacs are let loose upon society every week, are allowed to return to their families, and remain with them until a fresh outburst of insanity once more compels their removal.
Frequently this outburst - or, rather, this recurrence - of mania means a murder - sometimes a massacre. The homicidal maniac who
Shocked the World as Jack the Ripper
had been once - I am not sure that it was not twice - in a lunatic asylum. At the time his dead body was found in the Thames, his friends, who were terrified at his disappearance from their midst, were endeavouring to have him found and placed under restraint again.

July 13, 1902.
The Lambeth horror has taken its place as a new chapter in the great volume of London's mysteries. The mutilated remains of
The Woman Deposited in Salamanca-place
in the early hours of the morning have not been identified. It is possible they never will be. In these matters there is a tendency, after a certain point of unsuccess is reached, to relax effort. The finding of a dead body under ordinary circumstances is quite a common feature of London's daily life. There is a certain Thames-side district photographer who is specially retained by the police authorities to photograph the unknown dead. Rarely a day passes without his having a subject for his camera, and frequently he is as busy as the staff of a West End studio on an evening of Court presentations.
Public attention has been attracted in the case of the Salamanca-place sensation by the fact that some portions of the remains had been boiled and roasted. This gave an extra gruesomeness to the ordinary
'Dead Body Found"
announcement which may be seen outside almost every police-station in the metropolis all the year round. If the authorities thought it worth while to spend money and time, they might eventually get at the identity of the woman by the same process of exhaustion which enabled them at last to know the real name and address of Jack the Ripper.
In that case they had reduced the only possible Jacks to seven, then by a further exhaustive inquiry to three, and were about to fit these three people's movements in with the dates of the various murders when the one and only genuine Jack saved further trouble by being found drowned in the Thames, into which he had flung himself, a raving lunatic, after the last and most appalling mutilation of the whole series.
But prior to this discovery the name of the man found drowned was bracketed with two others as
A Possible Jack
and the police were in search of him alive when they found him dead. In the case of this chopped-up and semi-cooked woman, the best clue to the murderer might be the establishment of the victim's identity.

March 29, 1903.

Severino Klosowski is occupying the cell in which the late Mr. Edgar Edwards spent his last days. Edwards, when he was awaiting trial, was very interested in the Chapman case. His remark to a warder, who had told him the latest evidence at the police-court, was "He is a hot 'un, ain't he?"

I was rather surprised to find high-class newspapers suggesting

Chapman as 'Jack the Ripper."

"Jack" was a homicidal maniac. Each crime that he committed was marked with greater ferocity during the progress of his insanity. How could a man in the mental condition of "Jack" have suddenly settled down into a cool, calculating poisoner?

"Jack the Ripper" committed suicide after his last murder - a murder so maniacal that it was accepted at once as the deed of a furious madman. It is perfectly well known at Scotland Yard who "Jack" was, and the reasons for the police conclusions were given in the report to the Home Office, which was considered by the authorities to be final and conclusive.

How the ex-Inspector can say "We never believed 'Jack' was dead or a lunatic" in face of the report made by the Commissioner of Police is a mystery to me. It is a curious coincidence, however, that for a long time a Russian Pole resident in Whitechapel was suspected at the Yard. But his name was not Klosowski! The genuine "Jack" was a doctor. His body was found in the Thames on December 31, 1888.

April 5, 1903.

But that several correspondents have forwarded me news cuttings, and that two or three newspapers have inserted letters questioning my statement, I should not have alluded to

The Ripper Mystery

again. It is argued that "Jack" could not have drowned himself in 1888, because there were murders in Whitechapel in 1891. The last of the Ripper series was the Miller's-court horror, which occurred on November 9, 1888. The East End murders of later years were not in the same 'handwriting.

No one who saw the victim of Miller's-court as she was found ever doubted that the deed was that of a man in the last stage of a terrible form of insanity. No complete description was ever given to the Press. The details were too foully, fiendishly awful. A little more than a month later the body of the man suspected by the chiefs at the Yard, and by his own friends, who were in communication with the Yard, was found in the Thames. The body had been in the water about a month.

I am betraying no confidence in making this statement, because it has been published by an official who had an opportunity of seeing the Home Office Report, Major Arthur Griffiths, one of Her Majesty's inspectors of prisons.

I have the photographs of several of the victims taken after their murder, in my collection of criminal curiosities, and

I Was at One Time Myself Accused

of being the guilty person. Dr. Forbes Winslow will remember the man who came to him with my portrait, and who also went to the police and said, "That is 'Jack the Ripper.'"

I told the story at the time and also how one night I was actually on the spot where a murder was committed a few hours later, having with me a black bag in which there was nothing but a long and murderous knife - a curiosity which the late Paul Meritt had given me, and which I had carried with me to the Pavilion Theatre in Whitechapel.

I have no time to argue with the gentlemen, some of them ex-officers of the detective force, who want to make out that the report to the Home Office was incorrect. But putting all other matters on one side, it is an absolute absurdity to argue that a cool, calculating poisoner like Klosowski could have lived with half a dozen women and put them quietly out of the way by a slow and calculated process after being in 1888 a man so maniacal in his homicidal fury that he committed the foul and fiendish horror of Miller's-court. A furious madman does not suddenly become a slow poisoner. "Jack the Ripper" was known, was identified, and is dead.

Let him rest.

July 31, 1904

The strange case of Mr. Adolf Beck has drawn attention to the peril of having a double. I have had two in my time - one who was useful to me, and one who might have put me in a very serious position. The useful double was a gentleman connected with the theatrical profession, who on two or three occasions took a first-night call for me because I had sought safety in flight. The objectionable double was the demented doctor who committed the terrible Jack the Ripper outrages.

Twice a portrait of me was shown as that of a man who had been seen on several occasions in the neighbourhood of the crime on the night of its committal.

A Man Who Had Seen 'Jack"

at a coffee-stall in the small hours on the night that two women were killed and had noticed that his shirt-cuff was blood-stained took my portrait with him afterwards to Dr. Forbes Winslow and said, "That is the man. On the night of the murders, long before they were discovered, I spoke to him. In conversation I said, 'I wonder if we shall hear of another Jack the Ripper murder?' 'You'll very likely hear of two to-morrow,' was the reply, and the man walked hurriedly away." It was as he was leaving that the blood-stained cuff was noticed. The portrait shown to Dr. Forbes Winslow as that of "Jack" was the one on the cover of the first edition of "The Social Kaleidoscope."

At another time one of the detectives engaged in the hunt for the miscreant was shown my portrait as that of a man who had been seen late at night in Whitechapel and was strongly suspected of being the Ripper. The real Ripper, to whom the crimes were only brought home after he had been found a month old corpse in the Thames, was undoubtedly rather like me. The danger of being the double of such a man was great. On one such occasion I quite accidentally ran a terrible risk. I had borrowed from Paul Meritt, the dramatist, a long Japanese knife of

A Particularly Murderous Character

for melodramatic purposes, and putting it in a black bag, I had gone to the Pavilion Theatre, Whitechapel, late at night. I often wonder what would have happened if someone had cried out, "That's the Ripper" and my black bag had been opened. I could, of course, have proved my innocence at the police-station. But should I ever have got there if a crowd had had the first handling of the man with a knife in a black bag who was declared to be "Jack"!

1906.

The series of diabolical crimes in the East End which appalled the world were committed by a homicidal maniac who led the ordinary life of a free citizen. He rode in tramcars and omnibuses. He travelled to Whitechapel by the underground railway, often late at night. Probably on several occasions he had but one fellow-passenger in the compartment with him, and that may have been a woman. Imagine what the feelings of those travellers would have been had they known that they were alone in the dark tunnels of the Underground with Jack the Ripper!

Some of us must have passed him in the street, sat with him perhaps at a cafe or a restaurant. He was a man of birth and education, and had sufficient means to keep himself without work. For a whole year at least he was a free man, exercising all the privileges of freedom. And yet he was a homicidal maniac of the most diabolical kind.

This horrible phase of insanity is not, fortunately, a common one. But there are maniacs of the Ripper type still at large. There have been several crimes of the Ripper character committed in low lodging houses during recent years, and the perpetrator has always succeeded in making his escape and in retaining his liberty.

But the bulk of the dangerous lunatics at large are not systematic assassins. They are only wrought to frenzy by a fancied grievance or the stress of circumstance.

Sept.22, 1907.
Who was Jack the Ripper?

The deeds of darkness of this miserable wretch, cursed with one of the most terrible forms of blood lust, are known over the world. During his short career of carnage he built up for himself immortal infamy.

I have, while travelling abroad, purchased in various languages pamphlets and booklets on Jack the Ripper, more or less of the catchpenny order, and I have seen them eagerly purchased at country fairs on the Continent by the gaping village folks.

A year after the last of the murders I was in a little town in the South of Italy on market day, and I bought of a man who carried a banner on which the crimes of Jack were gorily depicted, the last copy of the red covered penny dreadful he was selling. It was entitled -

JACK

Il Terrible

Squartatoro Di Donne

and gave detailed and lurid account in Italian of the crimes of the Whitechapel fiend.

Whenever during the last nineteen years a wholesale slaughterer of women has been brought to trial in this country the cry "Is he Jack the Ripper?" has been raised in the Press. Deeming, Neil Cream, and Chapman were all in their turn brought into the controversy without the slightest justification. Their methods were entirely different to Jack's, and their motives were not the same.

From Germany, France, Spain, the United States, and South America there have come stories from time to time of women slayers whose deeds have led the local Press to revive the murder mysteries of the East-end of London.

A good many murders with which he had absolutely nothing to do have in this country been popularly attributed to the Whitechapel monster.

I have seen six, seven, and eight East-end murders of women debited to the Ripper, but, as a matter of fact, his murders were five in all, and no more. The other murders of women committed about the same time were in a totally different "handwriting."

The crimes that brought him into public discussion were all committed in a limited area, and within a limited period. They were as follows:-

1. Mary Anne Nichols, forty-seven, her throat cut and body mutilated, in Buck's-row, Whitechapel, Aug.31, 1888.
2. Annie Chapman, forty-seven, her throat cut and body mutilated in Hanbury-street, Spitalfields, Sept. 8, 1888.
3. Elizabeth Stride, throat cut, in Berner-street, on Sept.30, 1888.
4. Catherine Eddowes, alias Conway, mutilated, in Mitre-square, Aldgate, also on Sept.30, 1888.
5. Marie Jeanette Kelly, fiendishly mutilated, in Miller's-court, Whitechapel, Nov. 9, 1888.

Most of the murders marked an advance in the disease from which the madman who committed them was suffering.

The mutilations in the last murder, that in Miller's-court, were so ghastly that the full details were never made public. It was impossible for any journal of general circulation to describe them fully.

The mutilations were in all the cases, except one in which probably the murderer was interrupted, ghastly and revolting, and in one case an internal organ had been removed in a manner which showed almost beyond the shadow of a doubt that the miscreant was a person of anatomical knowledge.

Maniacal as was the fury with which he hacked and ripped his unhappy victims, the instance in which he skillfully removed and carried away with him this internal organ must be borne in mind when discussing the identity of the monster.

Into the separate details of the murders which during the autumn of the year 1888 kept the public mind in a state of seething excitement, and caused a panic in the East-end and were undoubtedly the main cause of the resignation of the then Chief Commissioner of Police, it is not necessary to go.

The public indignation over this series of unparalleled atrocities vented itself upon the police authorities, and the Home Secretary by declining to offer a reward came in for a considerable amount of fierce criticism. But when all has been said the fact has to be admitted that the best efforts of the police were foiled not so much by the cunning of the murderer as by the conduct of the victims themselves. Being of the unfortunate class, they willingly accompanied the man who was to murder them into dark and hidden places where, at the hour of night selected by the fiend as the most favourable for his purpose, there was little chance of attention being attracted.

In no case except in the last, which was the only one that occurred inside a house, was the faintest cry heard.

In the last crime, the murder of Marie Kelly, in the house in Miller's-court, two women living in the court declared that between three and four in the morning they heard a cry of "Murder!" It roused them from their sleep, but it made no impression upon them, and they closed their eyes again.

Such a cry usually means nothing in such a neighbourhood. Some years ago I stood in a little room in a slum in the East of London. It was a room on the ground floor, and the window opened on to a back yard.

In this yard a woman had recently been murdered. The occupants of the room had heard her shriek and call out "Murder!" but they had taken no notice. I asked the woman living in the room why she had not got up and given an alarm, or, at least. looked out to see what was the matter. Her reply was very much to the point.

"If we got out of bed in this street, sir, every time we heard somebody yell 'Murder' we should be in and out of bed half the night."

The cry to ears accustomed to it means nothing more than a quarrel and a fight.

The cry of Marie Jeannette Kelly, the most terribly mutilated of all the Ripper's victims, did certainly ring out upon the night, but the other victims were killed before they had time to utter a sound.

They were killed, hacked, hewn, and mutilated in the dark byeways in and around Whitechapel, and left lying where they fell to greet the horrified eyes of the first person who should pass that way.

To realise the most remarkable feature of these maniacal deeds it must be borne in mind that the murderer, after cutting the throat of his victim and hacking the body about with maniacal fury, always, except in the last instance, in a dark place, left the scene of his butchery, and walked home through the public streets.

He had a home somewhere, he slept somewhere, ate somewhere, changed his linen somewhere, sent his linen to the wash somewhere, kept his clothes and lived his life somewhere, yet never during the series of murders did he arouse the suspicions of any person who communicated with the police.

The first murder was committed on Aug.31, and the last on Nov. 9 - the night of Lord Mayor's day - therefore, five times during three months did the Ripper rise from his orgy of blood, and walk through the streets of London to his home without by his appearance attracting the attention of one single witness who could be called upon to give evidence of any value.

One man only, a policeman, saw him leaving the place in which he had just accomplished a fiendish deed, but failed, owing to the darkness, to get a good view of him. A little later the policeman stumbled over the lifeless body of the victim.

One other man believed that he had seen the Ripper soon after the double murders of Sept. 30, and he may have done, but there was no absolute proof that he was correct in his surmise.

This man was a coffee-stall keeper. In the early hours of the date of these murders, between three and four in the morning, as far as I can remember, a man came to the stall and asked for a cup of coffee.

The customer stood drinking his coffee, and the stall-keeper said, thinking of the murder of Sept. 8, that the Ripper had been quiet for a bit. "But," he added, "I expect we shall hear of another murder before long."

"Yes," replied the customer, "you may hear of two before many hours are over."

He put down the cup, took some coppers out of his pocket, and stretched his hand across the stall to give them to the stall keeper. The sleeve of his coat was drawn up by the action and the shirt cuff came into view. The cuff of the shirt was stained with blood.

The man saw the coffee-stall keeper's eyes fixed on his blood-stained cuff, bade him a gruff "good-night" and walked rapidly away, quickly disappearing in the darkness.

That morning the coffee-stall keeper heard of the two murders, the one in Berner-street which was discovered about one in the morning, and the other in Mitre-square, which was not discovered until nearly two o'clock.

The man with the blood-stained cuffs had suggested between two and three in the morning that "two" murders might be heard of in a few hours.

The coffee-stall keeper gave his information to the police and to Dr. Forbes-Winslow; who at that time was writing letters on the subject of the Ripper murders in the Press and expressing a very strong opinion that they were the work of a homicidal maniac, who had a trained knowledge of surgery.

What was the man with the blood-stained cuff like? That was the question. The coffee-stall keeper described him from memory. A day or two later passing by a stationer's shop he saw exhibited in the window a sixpenny book entitled "The Social Kaleidoscope." On the cover was a portrait of the author.

"That is the living image of the man I saw," he exclaimed. He purchased the book and went off with it to Dr. Forbes-Winslow. "That is the man I saw, or his double," he exclaimed, handing over my little book to the astonished doctor, who knowing me fairly well, assured the coffee-stall keeper that it might be the double of the Ripper, but it certainly was not the fiend himself

I present the portrait as one put forward by a man who had every reason to believe that he had seen and conversed with Jack the Ripper, as the "double" of the Whitechapel Terror.

Various witnesses who had seen a man conversing with a woman who was soon afterwards found murdered said that he was a well-dressed man with a black moustache. Others described him as a man with a closely-trimmed beard.

The portrait on the cover of the first edition of "The Social Kaleidoscope," a book which twenty years ago was in most of the newsagents' and small booksellers' windows, was taken about 1879.

There are two theories with regard to the identity of the Ripper. One has everything in its favour, and is now generally accepted by the high authorities who had the details of the various investigations gathered together and systematically inquired into.

It is betraying no state secret to say that the official view arrived at after the exhaustive and systematic investigation of facts that never became public property is that the author of the atrocities was one of three men.

Let us take them separately.

The first man was a Polish Jew of curious habits and strange disposition, who was the sole occupant of certain premises in Whitechapel after night-fall. This man was in the district during the whole period covered by the Whitechapel murders, and soon after they ceased certain facts came to light which showed that it was quite possible that he might have been the Ripper. He had at one time been employed in a hospital in Poland. He was known to be a lunatic at the time of the murders, and some-time afterwards he betrayed such undoubted signs of homicidal mania that he was sent to a lunatic asylum.

The policeman who got a glimpse of Jack in Mitre Court said, when some time afterwards he saw the Pole, that he was the height and build of the man he had seen on the night of the murder.

The second man was a Russian doctor, a man of vile character, who had been in various prisons in his own country and ours. The Russian doctor who at the time of the murders was in Whitechapel, but in hiding as it afterwards transpired, was in the habit of carrying surgical knives about with him. He suffered from a dangerous form of insanity, and when inquiries were afterwards set on foot he was found to be in a criminal lunatic asylum abroad. He was a vile and terrible person, capable of any atrocity.

Both these men were capable of the Ripper crimes, but there is one thing that makes the case against each of them weak.

They were both alive long after the horrors had ceased, and though both were in an asylum, there had been a considerable time after the cessation of the Ripper crimes during which they were at liberty and passing about among their fellow men.

The third man was a doctor who lived in a suburb about six miles from Whitechapel, and who suffered from a horrible form of homicidal mania, a mania which leads the victim of it to look upon women of a certain class with frenzied hatred.

The doctor had been an inmate of a lunatic asylum for some time, and had been liberated and regained his complete freedom.

After the maniacal murder in Miller's-court the doctor disappeared from the place in which he had been living, and his disappearance caused inquiries to be made concerning him by his friends who had, there is reason to believe, their own suspicions about him, and these inquiries were made through the proper authorities.

A month after the last murder the body of the doctor was found in the Thames. There was everything about it to suggest that it had been in the river for nearly a month.

The horrible nature of the atrocity committed in Miller's-court pointed to the last stage of frenzied mania. Each murder had shown a marked increase in maniacal ferocity. The last was the culminating point. The probability is that immediately after committing this murderous deed the author of it committed suicide. There was nothing else left for him to do except to be found wandering, a shrieking, raving, fiend, fit only for the padded cell.

What is probable is that after the murder he made his way to the river, and in the dark hours of a November night or in the misty dawn he leapt in and was drowned.

From this time the Ripper murders ceased. There have been no more. Women have been barbarously and mysteriously murdered since, but never with the unmistakeable "handwriting" of the Ripper upon the deed.

The other theory in support of which I have some curious information, puts the crime down to a young American medical student who was in London during the whole time of the murders, and who, according to statements of certain highly-respectable people who knew him, made on two occasions an endeavour to obtain a certain internal organ, which for his purpose had to be removed from, as he put it, "'the almost living body."

Dr. Wynne Baxter, the coroner, in his summing up to the jury in the case of Annie Chapman, pointed out the significance of the fact that this internal organ had been removed.

But against this theory put forward by those who uphold it with remarkable details and some startling evidence in support of their contention, there is this one great fact. The American was alive and well and leading the life of an ordinary citizen long after the Ripper murders came to an end.

It would be impossible for the author of the Miller's-court horror to have lived a life of apparent sanity one single day after that maniacal deed. He was a raving madman them and a raving madman when he flung himself in the Thames.

The fact that I had the unpleasant experience of having my portrait pointed out to the authorities as the portrait of the Ripper, caused me to take a keen personal interest in the East-end horrors, and I have in my museum some curious documents and gruesome photographs connected with the crimes. Two of them are unprintable. The photograph of the scene in Miller's-court is not one to be looked upon except by those who have in the exercise of their calling to study all phases of human perversion.

But no one who saw that awful scene, or its reproduction in the photographic exhibits prepared for the coroner's jury, could possibly believe that the perpetrator of the horror could return to the quiet enjoyment of the rights of citizenship, or even change the methods of his consuming madness and become a Deeming, a Neil Cream, or a Chapman.

Feb.25, 1911.
JACK THE RIPPER
The crimes of Jack the Ripper are still debated and from time to time the discussion as to his identity is revived in the press. Two adventures befell me as a journalist in this case. For many nights during the hue and cry I was in the area to which the crimes were confined. It was therefore with mixed feelings that I discovered that my portrait had been taken to Dr. Forbes Winslow, who was writing a good deal on the case at the time, and given to him with the request that he would send it to the police as there was no doubt I was the guilty man. As a

matter of fact the features of the man who is now believed by the authorities to have been Jack, did bear a certain resemblance to mine.

Three years ago, when the discussions as to Jack's identity cropped up again in the Press, I wrote on the subject. Soon afterwards a lady called upon me late one night. She came to tell me that the Whitechapel fiend had lodged in her house. On the night of the double murder he came in at two in the morning. The next day her husband, going into the lodger's room after he had left it, saw a black bag, and on opening it discovered a long, sharp knife, and two bloodstained cuffs. The lodger was a medical man, an American. The next day he paid his rent, took his luggage, and left. Then the police were communicated with but nothing more was heard of the American doctor with the suspicious black bag. "But," said my lady visitor, "I have seen him again this week. He is now in practice in the north-west of London." She gave his name and address and the names of two people who were prepared to come forward and identify him as the lodger with the black bag, the knife, and the incriminating cuffs. The next day I took the information, for what it was worth, to the proper quarters. But the doctor was not disturbed in his practice. There was ample proof that the real author of the horrors had committed suicide in the last stage of his maniacal frenzy.

1917.

As a journalist I followed the Jack the Ripper crimes at close quarters. I had a personal interest in the matter, for my portrait, which appeared outside the cover of a sixpenny edition of my "Social Kaleidoscope," was taken to Scotland Yard by a coffee-stall keeper as the likeness of the assassin.

On the night of the double murder, or rather in the small hours of the morning, a man had drunk a cup of coffee at the stall. The stall-keeper noticed that he had blood on his shirt-cuffs. The coffee merchant said, looking at him keenly, "Jack the Ripper's about perhaps tonight." "Yes," replied the man, "he is pretty lively just now, isn't he? You may hear of two murders in the morning." Then he walked away.

At dawn the bodies of two women murdered by the Ripper were found.

Passing a newsvendor's shop that afternoon the coffee-stall keeper saw my likeness outside the book.

"That's the man!" he said, and bought the book. He took it first to Dr. Forbes Winslow, who was writing letters to the papers on the Ripper crimes at the time.

Forbes Winslow, who knew me, told him it was absurd, but the man went off with the book to the Yard, and Forbes Winslow wrote to me and told me of the interview and the coffee-stall keeper's "mistake."

But it was a pardonable mistake. The redoubtable Ripper was not unlike me as I was at that time.

He was undoubtedly a doctor who had been in a lunatic asylum and had developed homicidal mania of a special kind.

Each of his murders was more maniacal than its predecessors, and the last was worst of all. After committing that he drowned himself. His body was found in the Thames after it had been in the river for nearly a month.

Had he been found alive there would have been no mystery about Jack the Ripper. The man would have been arrested and tried. But you can't try a corpse for a crime, however strong the suspicion may be.

And the authorities could not say, "This dead man was Jack the Ripper." The dead cannot defend themselves.

But there were circumstances which left very little doubt in the official mind as to the Ripper's identity.

THE SALISBURY AND WINCHESTER JOURNAL AND GENERAL ADVERTISER
SATURDAY MAY 14 1887

Dorsetshire

WIMBORNE
POLICE COURT, Wednesday – (Before Mr. C. J. Parke and Captain Carr S. Glyn) – William Dymott, gardener and Charles Brewer, baker, Wimborne, were charged with breaking into the dwelling house of the Rev. J. H. Lonsdale, and stealing a despatch box, containing a gold ring and papers to the value of 9l., the property of the Rev. C. Druitt, and an old brass blunderbuss, a sword, and a dagger, of the value of 10s., the property of the Rev. John H. Lonsdale. Thomas Dymott, coachman, and Jane Dymott, domestic servant, were charged with receiving these goods knowing them to have been stolen. The case created great interest, and the Court was crowded. Mr. H. Bowen appeared for Thomas, Jane, and William Dymott, and Mr. W. H. Curtis represented Brewer. Sarah Frampton, widow, said that on April 4th she was acting as housekeeper for the Rev. J. H. Lonsdale, in East Borough, Wimborne. She went to bed at about 10 o'clock on the night of the 4th, having fastened the back part of the house. Mr. Lonsdale and the Rev. C. Druitt were in the sitting room on the ground floor in the front. The front door was closed. There were two swords and a gun hanging in the hall. Towards morning she was disturbed by a noise. She stuck a light and looked out of the window. It was then twenty minutes past four. She saw nothing, and went back to bed. When she went down the stairs about six o'clock, she noticed a match which had been struck lying on the mat. The hall door was open. She went in to Mr. Druitt's room at about twenty minutes to seven. She drew up the blind and found the window was wide open. The cloth on the table in the window was disarranged and twisted; and the flowers outside the window were trodden down. Shortly after this she went to the back door to take in the milk. The door was unbolted and unlatched. After that she saw Mr. Druitt and Mr. Lonsdale come downstairs and go out. After they had gone she missed the gun and swords in the hall. Mr. Druitt and Mr. Lonsdale returned at about ten minutes to nine, and she informed them of what had taken place. She identified a box and case that were in Mr. Druitt's room, but she could not identify the gun and the sword produced. Mr. Lonsdale's room was on the right-hand side going in at the front door, and Mr. Druitt's on the left. John Hy. Lonsdale said he occupied a house in East Borough, Wimborne. The Rev. Chas. Druitt was staying with him. The last witness was his house-keeper. He remembered being with Mr. Druitt on the evening of April 4th. He had a sword, a blunderbuss, and a Japanese dagger hanging on a rack in the hall. On the following morning he came down at about ten minutes to eight and noticed they were gone. Mr. Druitt came down in a few minutes after, and they both went out to the service at the Minster. On his return, in consequence of what the housekeeper said, he noticed outside of Mr. Druitt's sitting-room that a plant was crushed, as if someone had trodden on it. Mr. Druitt came in a few minutes after, and in consequence of what witness told him they examined his room and found that his despatch-box was gone. They at once gave information to the police. He was, about a fortnight ago, show the despatch-box, blunderbuss, and the sword now produced, and which he identified. The despatch-box was Mr. Druitt's property. He went to the house of the prisoner, Thomas Dymott, with Sergeant Long and P. C. Powell. They saw Thomas Dymott and Jane Dymott. He heard Sergeant Long ask them if they knew anything about the things. They both denied any knowledge of the articles. The hall door was not open when witness went to bed on Tuesday night. Charles Druitt, who was the next witness, said he remembered using his despatch-box on the evening in question, and about half-past nine locked up some

papers in it and removed it to a small table in the window. It was not in a case. The window was shut. Mr. Lonsdale afterwards joined him and they went to bed at about 11 o'clock. He next saw the box at the police station on Thursday, the 28th ult. On the morning of the same day he had been to the house of the prisoner, Thomas Dymott, and saw him and Jane Dymott. Sergt. Long said, "We want to know whether you can tell us anything about these things?" Thomas Dymott said, "I don't know anything about them." Jane Dymott made use of some form of oath, and asked him as a clergyman to bear witness she was ignorant and innocent of the whole affair. Thomas Dymott consented to his house being searched. Witness had to attend service at the church, and therefore left and returned in half an hour. A search was made but none of his property was discovered. When the box was shown to him at the police station he found that the lock had been tampered with, and would not turn with its proper key. The total value of the articles lost was about 9l. The female prisoner called upon him the same night that he was shown the things at the police station. She assured him that she was innocent of any complicity in the robbery. Sophia Snell, widow, Wimborne, said the prisoner, Thomas Dymott, lived next door to her. She remembered Wm. Dymott coming to her house on Tuesday morning, the 26th of April, with a bag which he asked her to let him put in her back house. He gave her the bag and she put it there. About half an hour afterwards she saw two policemen go into Dymott's house. She thought there must be something wrong, and she called Mrs. James a neighbor. They had a chat together, and Mrs. James went out and took the things out of the bag. There was a box (now produced), a gun, a bright dagger in the case, and a sword. Mrs. James brought the box into the house. Jane Dymott was sitting close to the table on which Mrs. James put the box. Mrs. James said, "It looks like the one that was stolen over in the Borough." She then took the box back and put it in the bag. Witness said to Jane Dymott that she must take it away. She said, "William will be back in half and hour when he will fetch it." In the afternoon Mrs. James came to see her, and the bag was still there. They had a talk together, and witness took the bag and carried it to Mrs. Dymott's door. The box and the other things were in the bag when she took it there. Jane Dymott opened the door, and witness said, "Jane, you must take this bag; I can keep it no longer." She took the bag, and shut the door. The same day Jane Dymott came to witness, and told her that she "must not say anything about it." At this time there was a knock on her door, and she did not make any answer. On Thursday, the 28th ult., William Dymott came to her home in the morning, and asked her to come in, as Jane wanted to speak to her. She went in. There was a box on the table and an old sword. A second sword produced by Sergeant Long was the one. William asked her to say that was the same box and sword that were in the bag. She said no, they were not a bit like them. Jane and William said, "if you will say it was it will keep us out of a row." She told them it was a story, and she would tell no stories to please anybody. Elizabeth James gave evidence corroborating the previous witness. Eliza Holloway, aunt to William Dymott, living at the almshouses, stated that William Dymott brought two parcels, wrapped in brown paper, and asked her to take charge of them. He said they were a few things he had bought. She took them, and placed them under her bed. Police-sergeant Long gave evidence as to visiting the residence of Mr. Lonsdale. He had some bills printed and circulated offering a reward respecting the robbery. On the 28th April information respecting it was brought to the station. Acting on that information he went to the prisoner's house, in company with Mr. Druitt and Mr. Lonsdale. He told Thomas Dymott that he had been informed that his son William had taken a bag into Mrs. Snell's on the previous Tuesday, containing things corresponding with those that had been stolen from Mr. Lonsdale's, and that it had been brought back again and been taken in by his daughter Jane. Both the father and the daughter denied all knowledge of the matter. He cautioned them both, and said that if they had the things in the house they had better say so. Thomas still denied all knowledge of the matter. At this point Mr. Bowen raised and objection to this evidence going on the depositions, as the officer had no right to make any suggestion of the kind. After some discussions, the Bench conceded the point, and the evidence was expunged. Sergt. Long proceeded to state that with the consent of the prisoner they searched the house and found nothing but the three bronze medals. He subsequently saw Wm. Dymott in custody at the police station. He heard him charged with committing a robbery at Mr. Lonsdale's house and cautioned. Prisoner said he did not know anything about the robbery, and that he had bought the box and paid for it, and also the sword and the blunderbuss. He bought them of a man in Wimborne and gave him 10s. for them; but he did not know who the man was. There was no ring or letters in the box. He added that if a constable would go with him he would show him where the things were. Mr. Batty, the superintendent, refused to let him go. Prisoner then intimated where the things might be found. Witness went with Constable New to Mrs. Holloway's house, where they found the despatch-box and the sword and blunderbuss done up in brown paper. Witness saw Thomas Dymott again, who admitted that he put the bag outside the door in a wheelbarrow, but he said he did not know what was in the bag. On Saturday last witness was in the police cell just as Jane Dymott was brought in. William Dymott said, "You will have to have in somebody else now, I cannot stand this any longer. I don't see why my father and sister should have to suffer when other people are at liberty." Witness asked him what he meant, and he again said, "You must get in somebody else," and he subsequently said, "You must get in Brewer." Mr. Curtis, at this point, objected to this evidence against Mr. Brewer, but the objection was not allowed. Sergeant Long, continuing, said that he had Brewer brought in, and the prisoner Dymott said, "You know I bought the things off you, Brewer; we struck a bargain in the square; we afterwards met at the Three Lions, and I paid you 10s." Brewer said he did not know anything about it.—At this point the Bench enquired whether the police could carry the case any further against Brewer. Sergeant Long said they could not.—The Chairman said that in that case they would ease Mr. Curtis's mind and discharge his client. Brewer was then discharged. – P. C. new stated that on the 28th April he apprehended William Dymott and charged him on suspicion with committing a burglary. P. C. Powell gave evidence of searching prisoner's house. On May 2nd he made a further search of prisoner's house, and found a gold ring in a case and a bunch of keys. On the 6th May he again searched the house, and found some coins, which were identified by Mr. Druitt. P. S. Long, recalled, said he apprehended Thomas Dymott on April 29th. Mr. Bowen then addressed the bench on behalf of the elder prisoner, Thomas Dymott, contending that there was no case against him to go to a jury. The Bench committed all the prisoners for trial at the next assizes, but the father and daughter were admitted to bail.

Further reading

Tom Cullen, 'Autumn of Terror' 1965

Colin Wilson & Robin Odell, 'Jack the Ripper: Summing Up and Verdict', 1987.

Paul Begg, 'Jack the Ripper: The Uncensored Facts', 1988

Donald Rumbelow, 'The Complete Jack the Ripper' 1988

Philip Sugden, 'The Complete history of Jack the Ripper' 1995.

Daniel Farson 'Jack the Ripper ' 1972

Stewart Evans & Paul Gainey 'Jack the Ripper the first American Serial Killer' 1995

Paul Begg, Martin Fido, & Keith Skinner 'The Jack the Ripper A to Z' 1991

Stewart Evans & Keith Skinner 'Letters from Hell' 2001

Martin Howells & Keith Skinner 'The Ripper Legacy' 1987

Leonard Matters, 'The Mystery of Jack the Ripper' 1928

Printed in Great Britain
by Amazon